JAMIE REDKNAPP

WITH TOM FORDYCE

Me, family and the making of a footballer

HEADLINE

First published in 2020
by HEADLINE PUBLISHING GROUP

1

Cataloguing in Publication Data is available from the British Library

Hardback ISBN 9781472271938
Trade paperback ISBN 9781472279378

Designed and typeset by EM&EN
Printed and bound in Great Britain by Clays Ltd, Elcograf S.p.A.

HEADLINE PUBLISHING GROUP
An Hachette UK Company
Carmelite House
50 Victoria Embankment
London EC4Y 0DZ

www.headline.co.uk
www.hachette.co.uk

For my wonderful sons Charley and Beau.
I hope this book will bring you enjoyment and
maybe teach you a little about your dad.
I'm so glad you're my boys.

And for my dad, my hero and my inspiration.
I'd never have made it as a footballer
if it hadn't been for you.
I'm very lucky to have you as my dad.

CONTENTS

1

THE BEGINNING

I open my eyes and step out of bed and there's always a football there. Four years old, a football on the floor of my little bedroom, another on the landing, walking past my brother Mark's bedroom. Bumping down the stairs and running through the hall into the kitchen and out into the back garden.

Palmerston Avenue in Christchurch does not stand out. Pale-brick terraced houses in neat rows, semi-detached if you're on the end like us. Identical white doors on every one, each house with a bay window downstairs and three small bedrooms up top. A couple of scrawny trees; stumpy bushes between the tight front gardens. Not many cars about because once you turn right out of our front door there's only Pelham Close, which is a cul-de-sac, and if you turn left and go out onto Russell Drive that's only another quiet residential street in a quiet residential part of a place no-one comes to unless they're going home.

More footballs lie about in the worn-out grass of the back garden. It's not big out here, about the same as an adult-sized goal laid out on its side. You sprint it and you're slowing down as soon as you've got started. There's a brick wall at

1

the back, which is ideal as a goal if I'm playing against my brother Mark and perfect to knock the ball against if it's me on my own, though a wooden shed in the corner stained dark with creosote mainly gets in the way. Not many flowers in the flowerbeds, because anything that sticks out or gets in the way is going to get trampled or squashed or lopped off.

Mum knows what happens when we get into games in the house. It's why she insists on us using only a sponge ball if we're inside, or at least she tries to. Too many smashed vases, too many ornaments teetering on the mantelpiece, me and Mark suddenly struck silent, staring at each other in frozen shock.

Out in the garden it's hard footballs – plastic ones from the garage, the ones that swerve everywhere no matter how you kick them, a couple of leather ones Dad's brought back that have gone a bit soft and heavy from having been left outside. There are perks of having a dad who plays professional football, and this is the first. There's nothing from his days at West Ham, and Bournemouth, being in Division Four, are hanging on to every decent ball they have, but there's a beauty from the North American Soccer League, where Dad spends a chunk of each year playing and coaching for the Seattle Sounders. It's made by Adidas, with the three stripes on one of the hexagonal white panels and red stars on a blue background on another and the words 'Official NASL' in between.

We can bomb down the alley that runs down the right-hand side of our house and get into the space by the garages out the back. More room out there for bigger games, a peeling metal door for one goal, the one opposite for another. No-one uses their garage for their cars; it's all boxes of old stuff and maybe some bikes and unwanted furniture, so you can muck about for ages and no-one will bother you.

But it's concrete out there, and concrete is not the same as grass, which feels just right under your feet, and perfect if you're sliding, and soft like the lounge carpet if you're tripped and falling. Concrete doesn't smell. Grass and mud do. As soon as I get in the garden and that wet damp earthy aroma is all around me, I feel calm and I feel safe. It's the same if me and Mark take a ball and run down Disraeli Road and along the cut-through that takes you onto the playing fields towards the sea. There's Stanpit Marsh out beyond, all grey and salty, and then the sandbanks and tides out across the water towards Mudeford, but the patchy grass is all I notice. Me and a ball on the grass, running with it, clipping it, flicking it up and keeping it up. Passing it to Mark, chasing him down, getting a foot in, running off with him coming after me.

You can do things with a ball that fascinate me. It only does what you want it to. A little nudge to set it up in front of you. Toe down and coming down hard on the underside to ping it. Foot on top to stop it, then studs scraping down to bring it spinning sharply back and roll it up onto your laces and get it up in the air.

Brothers are meant to compete. Mark loves his football too so he comes at me hard, but there's never any malice with Mark. He's three years older and he's different. He's normal. He plays football for an hour and then he gets bored and wanders off to do something else. He goes in when it starts raining and watches *Jim'll Fix It* on telly.

I don't. I play football for an hour and then keep playing. When it rains, I don't notice. When my mum invites other kids over who are also going to start at the same primary school, I ask them if they can go and play with Mark instead.

Mum doesn't mind. Football wasn't her thing when she was a girl growing up in Barking. When she first met my dad she knew about West Ham, because you couldn't grow up in east London and not, but she didn't know at the start that this Harry was the Redknapp who played on the wing for them. But she lets me get on with it. Two boys mean she can't worry like she did when there was only one. There's not time. She goes from man-to-man marking to zonal. They're in the garden, fine. They're by the garages. Look out for each other, yeah?

And Dad? He's happy that I'm happy with a ball. Dad's telling stories because that's what he does. He's not making the tea. He's not even making a cup of tea. Mum does that. Mum does everything important, the stuff a family needs – breakfast, lunch and tea, the getting up early, like her dad used to make her do, the tidying up, the packing when we go away. The organising, the listening.

Dad does the football and the stories. And there is always a story, about everything and anything.

The shout first, to me and my brother. Sitting out in the garden in a summer evening's sunshine, sitting on a ball. Socks pulled up. Always socks pulled up.

'Jamie! Marco! Look around you. This is class. Did I tell you where I grew up, Barchester Street, up in Poplar? Boys, it was a bombed street, half the street weren't there. The ends of the street was rubble. That was our playground when we was kids, just bomb sites, air-raid shelters, rubble, bricks. That's where we grew up and played.

'Boys, you know where Nan and Pop are? That was it, same neck of the woods. When they moved us to this estate off Burdett Road, new flats, 18 blocks of them around a school in the middle, we thought we'd made it. Nothing like this. A bit of grass round the back we called Wembley, out there every night until it got too dark. We'd wait for the call to come round – "Big game at Wembley, lads!" – and we'd all pile down. Boys, it was amazing!'

We know where he means because while football has taken the family from east London to the south coast, all the old connections are still there. Dad's mates are his West Ham mates. Mum's sister Pat is over that way, married to Frank Lampard, who's doing well at West Ham, winning the FA Cup just before I can remember. Dad's old pal and team-mate Bobby is over all the time, and even though I've never seen any of the games or read any of the programmes, I know what he did at the World Cup in 1966, because when other people are over and they clock him they do the same sort of shocked face that me and Mark do when Mum's vases hit the deck.

All those connections, holding the family tight to the East End, and none of them as important as Pop and Nan.

Nan is the first one you see when you go and stay in their council flat on Salmon Lane. Standing on the little balcony, two storeys up the dark-brown brick building, waving as we park up under the elm tree on the street outside. Always a pinny on, big glasses, same gingery hair as Dad but much more of it.

Nan is the cook. Nan works in the cake factory down the road and then cleans offices up in the City, but when we arrive she's the cook. The lift in the flats smells like someone couldn't get to their toilet in time, and so when you come out on her floor you get a noseful of Dettol too, and then the two smells mingle and fight.

In through her front door and a crackling sound from a cut of meat cooking away in the kitchen. Fresh mint from the little pot hanging on the top railing on the balcony. Radio Two on, if it's during the day, Jimmy Young her favourite show. Waiting for the pips so she can shush us for the news, *Coronation Street* on the small telly if we've come up in the evening after Dad's had a game.

Nan's mum had been the wild one. She was the one who used to collect all the bets from the others on their street and pass them on to the proper bookie, Cyril the Paper Boy, when he came round to collect them. She was the one responsible for getting Dad so into the horses, letting him pick one out of the paper as a nipper, rubbing his red hair for luck when she made her own selections.

So our Nan is the sensible one. She's got the discipline. She stays in that tiny kitchen and sorts everyone out. A big pot of tea with proper tea leaves, always bringing the bone china out for the adults, everything done right. In the bathroom, a flannel folded on the side and a big bar of white soap. Everything is spick and span. Everything is clean and precise. When she makes chips, she uses a metal cutter so that they come out crinkle-cut, all the same size.

I like how organised she is, closer in character to my mum than Dad. Dad, in the best possible way, is all over the gaff. You step out of line with Nan and she'll always start with the same thing, whether it's me or Mark or someone twice our age: 'Listen, boy . . .'

And so it's Pop who is the entertainment, just like his one and only son.

Pop is not a big man. Even as a kid I can tell that. But it's like he's got electricity crackling through him all the time. He buzzes around like a sparrow in spring. He can't keep still. He's on the sofa in the living room when you arrive and that's the last time you see him sitting still.

Every morning he walks the mile and a half north from Limehouse to Roman Road in Bow for pie and mash, up the towpath or along Burdett Road. Hair Brylcreemed back, a natural bounce in his step. He seems to know everyone. When people spot him they give him a shout. 'Alright, Harry?' In return he calls everyone John, unless they're tall, in which case they're Lofty. He's in his fifties but fit as a fiddle. Nan making all that food and Pop looking at her like she's mad.

'Violet, what do I want to eat all that food for? Cheese sandwich and a cuppa tea'll do me. Now Jamie, how's the football?'

He'd boxed and he still plays darts but football has always been Pop's first love. He'd played non-league and then gone off to the war and got himself stuck in a prisoner-of-war camp.

When he came back, he told us that a different team would ask him to join them every week, but he preferred messing about with his mates, couldn't settle down. Too much action to be had, too many schemes.

When he takes me out with a ball to Victoria Park or Mile End, I can see it in him still. He'll do skills on the walk there, juggling the ball, doing keepy-ups from left foot to right foot and back again, always flat-out fast, always killing himself laughing as he does it. There'll come a time, 20 years on, when he's doing the same to me when I'm in the England team, and my younger cousin Frank is all grown up and doing the business at West Ham just like his dad, and Pop will keep nicking the ball through Frank's legs, and Frank will get so annoyed that he'll say, 'Harry, you ever do that again, I'm going to have to boot you up in the air.'

Pop wants to play football and he wants to talk about it. When Dad gets his move into management, Pop will watch youth team matches and recommend him young players, and it will be Pop who notices a teenage Rio Ferdinand, wandering around a little lost in midfield, and Pop who tells Dad he's just spotted potentially the best central defender he's ever seen.

When Dad had been young, Pop had taken him to watch Arsenal, a couple of buses up across the city to Highbury, even though everyone else on the estate was West Ham. He loved players like Jimmy Bloomfield and Danny Clapton, tricky inside-forwards and wingers, the sort of footballers he fancied he could have been. He also loved seeing the big names like Stanley Matthews and Tom Finney, so if Preston were playing somewhere in town, it might be a few more buses for him and Dad, or a long trek west to see Stoke at Chelsea.

No-one from the East End goes to see Chelsea, but that's how much Pop loves his football, and those are the tales he tells us when we're over, and those are the tricks he shows us down the park. All dribbles and feints, teasing us with the ball never quite within our reach, drawing us in and then flicking it away. Magic tricks and sleight of foot.

Nan has her stories too. She's never been further afield than Bournemouth. She's certainly never been on a plane. But she is all yarns, sitting me and Mark down round the table and telling us about the war back home, the air raids, how when the sirens sounded you ran for a shelter and just hoped you were going in a different direction to the bombs. About legging it up towards Bethnal Green to safety and finding out later that the shelter the other way, the other 50/50 option, had got wiped out; about her school getting a direct hit and her seeing two rows of her classmates laid out neatly on the pavement the next morning.

There are yarns and there are strange pearls. 'Listen boy, never trust anyone without any lips.' I don't really know what that means, but you listen to Nan because she is a strong woman, and Pop, for all his jokes, does exactly what she tells him as soon as she does.

Pop has had it hard. Growing up as one of ten kids, not all of them making it through the early and dangerous years, time spent in a children's home, his big sisters looking after him afterwards. Working long days down the West India Docks on the Isle of Dogs with his brother George, sticking Dad down for a job there too when he was a lad before West Ham got involved and saved him from that preordained fate.

He's also enjoyed himself, as me and Mark find out in another of Dad's stories in the car on the long drive up.

'Boys, every Christmas Eve, all the dockers like Pop, they wouldn't come home right after they'd finished work, they'd go out on the booze with their mates. One time he's supposed to be bringing the chicken home – we didn't have turkeys, Marky, we had chicken. No-one had turkey.

'Anyway, there's no sign of my dad, so we'd have to go and find him round the pubs, looking with your Nan. There was about five or six pubs they'd use, and I'd have a look in one and come out again.

'"Can't see him in there, Mum."

'"Right, let's go round the Earl Of Ellesmere."

'That's where I found him, the Ellesmere. He'd been there with all the old dockers. They're all having a dance with the birds from the cake factory across the road. They've still got their turbans on – my mum always had a white turban, like a scarf, that's what they used to wear working with food.

'"He's in there, Mum!"

'"Is he now. Call him over . . ."

'I'm at the door with Dad, he's boozed up. As he comes out, my mum gets hold of him, bosh, and she boots him all the way home. Every time he stopped and argued, she'd kick him up the arse again. She might be quiet but she's chunky, your Nan. She kicked him up the bum all the way home. Brilliant.'

There is nowhere safer than Nan and Pop's, so that's where me and Mark are allowed to stay for weekends. Nan takes us to Stratford Market and feeds us massive cream cakes and toast cut like doorstops with butter falling off it, everything that is supposed to be bad for us. She dips her toast in her tea, so there's a layer of liquid butter bobbing along at the top of her cup.

It's fuel for the afternoon, when we stagger down the stairs at the flats to avoid the stinking lift, Nan standing on the balcony watching us go, and head to the little caged-in pitch off Salmon Lane. Pop comes with us and joins in. There are more streetwise kids, because we're from Christchurch and these lads are East End all the way. But everyone knows Pop and so there's no trouble. Just football, from the time we wake up, all through the long day. Talking and playing, playing and talking.

•

Sandra Redknapp: He was always the stubborn one, Jamie. He'd sleep better than Mark, who was always up to something, but everything with Jamie had to be exactly right. He wouldn't eat mashed potato. He wouldn't eat baked beans, like all the other kids did. If I did them eggs he would only eat the white. Mark would eat the yolk. That's how the two of them were.

All he wanted was bacon and chips, every single night. On his birthday I'd do all the classics – jelly-moulds the shape of animals, a crocodile made out of sliced cucumber pieces, cheese and pineapple stuck out of a big fat potato so it looked like a hedgehog. He'd push them around and then ask for bacon.

It was the women who brought the kids up in those days but it was always the threat of Harry that kept them in line. I couldn't smack them when they messed around. My heart wasn't in it, and they knew it. I might try to land a glancing one on the back of their legs when they ran off upstairs but I'd always end up hurting myself more, so I'd use words instead – 'Wait 'til your dad gets home . . .'

That was the promise and it sort of worked, when they were karate-chopping each other's legs, or when they smashed an ornament. I had these lovely Lladro porcelain figures, brought over from Spain. Everyone did, we all collected them in that bit of the 1970s. Harry's mum used to come down from the East End on the train to babysit so that Harry and I could go out for dinner. And nine times out of ten something would get broken. A beautiful ornament all in pieces, and the boys knowing what was coming their way.

Harry never really lost his temper, but he didn't have to. The expression and the words were enough. One night Jamie and Mark managed to smash the glass coffee table in the lounge. The wait for Harry to get home was the real punishment. And then the serious look and the calm, angry question: 'Jamie, what you done?'

2

THE CARAVAN

Bedtime stories are different on Palmerston Avenue. There aren't loads of children's books lying around. I get *Match* and *Shoot!* magazines delivered every week, with their posters and fact files and Q&As with top players (Favourite meal? Steak and chips. Favourite TV show? *Starsky & Hutch*. Best car? Ford Capri 2.8 Injection) and I read them in bed, but it's when Dad gets home that the real good stuff kicks in.

There is only one topic in Dad's stories: the Ellises. The Ellises are a family in east London. Loads of boys, all of them up to all sorts, proper terrorising everyone in the neighbourhood but in a sort of good way.

Dad tells me they are real, that he knew them growing up on the Burdett Estate. I believe him, but I also know that the real Ellis family are only the rough basis of the tales he tells me, because while the idea of seven boys being amazing at football makes total sense to me, the fact that they've just won the FA Cup Final with an overhead kick in the last minute does ring a few alarm bells.

I don't mind because the tales are all belters. The Ellis boys have nicked a load of stuff, but only to give it to the Home for East End Orphans for Christmas. The Ellises have taken a team-load of football boots off the posh boys who play in the Regent's Park League, but only because they've been playing in army boots and jeans and that's all that is stopping them from becoming champions of the whole of London.

In my mind, the Ellises are super-human. Dad will sit himself on the edge of my bed, the superstars on my *Match* and *Shoot!* posters looking down from the yellow-painted bedroom walls, and he'll start somewhere normal and end up somewhere fantastic.

'Dad, tell me what the Ellises have been up to.'

'Yeah, well, Johnny Ellis was bunking off school one day, and . . .'

'Johnny Ellis? I didn't know there was a Johnny Ellis.'

'Yeah, Johnny was the other brother.'

'Another one? Is Johnny older than the other seven?'

'Yeah, yeah, there's eight.'

I'm a little bit scared of the Ellises. They're doing stuff that if I tried I would get Mum's threat of Dad and then the face and voice from Dad that makes your guts go soft. They're slightly like the Krays in my mind, because that set of brothers also pop up in Dad's stories a fair amount, the Blind Beggar and Jack the Hat and all, as well as occasional guest appearances from Bobby Moore. But they do sound like the most amazing characters, and I would quite fancy hanging out with them. They're a bit older than my Dad, but they like him and look after him, so that's a good sign. They've never been less than nice to Dad or to Pop, when he appears in the stories, and this makes me feel better too.

I would definitely like them on my side. I'd love to play football with them, not least because Brian Ellis is an amazing finisher, if his match-winning goal in the Cup Final is anything to go by, and I could see myself slotting in quite nicely to that midfield, a lone Redknapp in a sea of Ellises.

I've got to have a happy ending. I don't like the dark, which is why I asked to have the walls of my bedroom that bright yellow colour, because it makes me think about sunlight and sunshine and being outside with my football, and I don't like darkness in stories or in films when we go to the cinema. I don't want to hear about someone getting hurt. Stuff gets in my head, ideas of something going wrong, or something bad happening to Mark or Pop or Nan, and it gets stuck in there.

It's the same when I start primary school, getting in the back of Mum's car with Mark like I'm used to but this time getting out at the gates with him. I never liked playschool, being left by Mum with a load of kids who I didn't know. There's something about other kids' birthday parties that upsets me too, all that noise and chaos, knowing that I can't eat the food because I don't know who else has touched it. And so now Mum is dropping me off at school, where there are more children and more noise and more things happening that I don't understand, it feels far worse. I cry in the car on the way there. I won't stop until Mum promises to come in before lunchtime and pick me up then, or unless she turns the car around and says I can just do the afternoon.

Dad never finds out any of this. He's busy with football. I just think, I'm different. I'm not like the other kids. I'm a weirdo.

I try to deal with it by keeping everything else neat and orderly. Making sure all the marbles I collect are in the right pots and the different colours aren't mixed up. Taking the little blue plastic Smurf figures I keep and lining them up on the set of drawers in my bedroom so they are in a sensible order – Grandpa Smurf first, then Papa, and Nanny, Brainy, Dreamy and Lazy. When you're in control, then the bad stuff is less likely to happen to you.

I don't go to Dad when I feel that way. I don't want to tell him if I'm feeling really scared. Dad is football and stories. Mum is the one I speak to about these things. Softer. The listener. The one who mends the broken figures and glues it all together.

•

Pop and Nan had owned their caravan on the Isle of Sheppey for years. It was the part of Dad's childhood that he looked forward to the most – going down to the bus-stop on Aberfeldy Street on a Friday night once Pop had finished in the docks at 6 pm, jumping on the Green Line bus and spending four hours on those plastic seats messing around and swapping tales. Out through the Medway towns, stopping at a halfway house for a cup of tea and a sandwich, probably because the driver had been slipped a few quid to make sure he pulled in at that particular establishment. On through Sittingbourne and Kemsley and across the marshes onto the island and Leysdown-on-Sea on the eastern side, to see all the same people they lived around in Poplar all lined up in their own tiny caravans. A circle of grass near the wash-block which became the football pitch, all the kids gathering there at the start of the day for games that changed in numbers per side as meals came and went but never really ended until the light had gone. All the light.

Fifteen years on, Leysdown hasn't really changed. It's still flat fields behind, cold sea breaking on a rocky beach, amusement arcades and fish and chip shops and wind. All that's different is that Pop and Nan have now got an orange second-hand VW Beetle, so the backs of our legs can stick to the seats of that rather than the bus, and the M2 has been built, so we can get there in time for the last knockings of Friday's big match rather than needing to wait for Saturday morning.

The Beetle makes a right racket. It smells too. It is nothing like the Love Bug, and driving in it to Sheppey is about as far from *Herbie Goes To Monte Carlo* as you can get. But we don't care. Our car, the one that Dad uses to drop us off in Poplar, is a lime-green Fiesta, so we're not fussy. We're also so excited about going to the caravan that we'd walk there if we had to.

The caravan has been upgraded from Dad's time. It is now plumbed in, so you don't need to nip over to the wash-block unless there's a queue for the bathroom. There's the caravan, the access road and then the grassy area, otherwise known as Wembley.

As soon as we arrive, all the other kids start knocking, looking for Pop. 'Harry, what time's the game?' All queuing up, five years of age, eight and nine-year-olds. 'Harry, can I play, I'm four now.'

The games start off as an intra-campsite thing. Then a couple of adventurous ones come over from the campsite across the road, and suddenly it's Us against Them, England v Rest of the World, all organised by Pop. The pitch is a right state. The ball bobbles as it comes to you. At peak times there are kids everywhere, chasing you from all angles. Kids who are twice the size of you, trying to muscle you off it, kids who are tiny and on you before you know it.

It's like being swarmed. All shouts and yells and flying feet going everywhere. The cage up in Poplar is an unforgiving place to play football because it's so cramped, but this is something else again. Your first touch has to be perfect or you won't get a second one. You need eyes in the back of your head to see where the next tackle is coming from and you need an almost supernatural peripheral vision to pick out a team-mate to pass to, because there are no bibs to denote teams, just a random mix of West Ham and Spurs and Millwall kits, sweaty t-shirts and tops off. You've got to be strong, putting your arms and elbows out to hold off the opposition right and left, sticking your backside out to buy yourself a fraction more room on the ball. And you need stamina, because it's summer time in the south of England and it won't get dark until 10 pm if the rain holds off and the wind doesn't make it too cold by then.

The new caravan is still not that big. The beds pull out. There's no telly. But it feels like we've turned up at a hotel and got the best spot in the resort, because the pitch is right there and 10 yards the other way is the ice-cream stall. Each afternoon Nan will send me across with the money for a raspberry Mivvi, pulling open one end of the red packet and blowing into it to free the lolly inside, a thin layer of sweet fruit ice that you can chip away with your teeth to get to the vanilla ice-cream underneath. You feel thirsty because the last drink you've had was a cream soda or lemonade that Nan has stirred a couple of teaspoons of extra sugar into to take the fizz out, because you've been running about so much you just need to get it down you fast.

In case our sugar levels are in any danger of dropping below red alert, Nan will give us a couple of hard-boiled lollies each when Pop takes us off down Shellness Road to go cockling when the tide is out. She's already had a sugar sandwich, brown sugar sprinkled on the buttered bread and folded over, so we're all on the same page here. Why wouldn't you want more sweetness?

The three of us – me, Pop and Mark – walk out onto the beach and past the last few lonely cafés towards the Swale Nature Reserve. There's an abandoned World War II pillbox down there, a grey concrete block with thin slits looking out over the low fields and the drainage ditches cut through them, mudflats beyond and ships coming round from the mouth of the Thames estuary towards the English Channel.

On a still afternoon it's the quietest place in the world. Just the sound of the dark green marsh grasses swaying and the odd bird zipping about, Pop digging away at the mud with the fork he's stashed in his pocket, me and Mark taking the cockles out of his hands and lobbing them in the bucket. At the caravan Nan has had a big pan of water boiling, and the cockles get chucked in with a bit of salt and eaten out of their shells as soon as they're done.

These are our summer weekends and for three weeks in August these are our summer holidays. It's what we always want to do. There is no sense of thinking, oh, not again, or of wanting anything more sophisticated. If it's the holidays, Mum might join us at the weekend. Dad will be training or going to pre-season friendlies or the opening matches of a new campaign. We see the same kids every year, grown slightly bigger, and we play the same matches, only harder.

•

Mark Redknapp: When I was six years old I looked at Jamie playing football and saw it. He was so good you couldn't miss it. There were no other kids doing what he could do with a ball.

When he connected with a football it just made the sweetest sound. It sounded different to when the rest of us kicked it. It was like standing next to a golfer on the range when he nails a drive with his one-wood, or a batsman when he clouts a fast bowler off the meat of the bat.

We were closer than any other brothers I knew, going out the back to the garages, going down the caravan. I never felt jealous of him, even when I realised he was beating me, and that he was going to keep beating me, at football and at the other sports we tried. I wasn't going to beat him at table-tennis, and it wouldn't be long until I couldn't beat him at snooker.

That was okay. I just felt proud of him, and I looked after him. He would do things better than me but I would do them first, and I could show him how it was done. I twigged early on that it was amazing to have a brother like him.

No-one needed to push him. The environment around him was perfect: a dad who knew more about football than anyone, a grandpa who was only a fraction behind. An elder brother to test himself against.

Dad spotted what I spotted, which is why he started taking Jamie everywhere with him from the age of six. He wasn't pushing him in the back garden. He wasn't taking him on in one-on-ones or dribbling, or giving him a list of things he needed to work on and a set of drills to get him there. He didn't have to push him because from the moment he could run at a ball, Jamie was pushing himself.

I would go out in the garden for 20 minutes. Jamie would be out there for two hours.

That was it. Dad already knew Jamie was going to be good. We all knew.

•

Dad's football is taking us places. That summer he gets the usual deal with the Seattle Sounders. He's still playing at the start, although he's begun coaching too, helping out Jimmy Gabriel, the old Everton and Southampton midfielder who's moved into management. You move to America when you're a kid and there's so much to take in that it's almost too much. If we want a pizza, Mum can phone someone up and they actually bring it to your house. I've barely got my head around what a pizza is, and they suddenly start appearing on our doorstep with a bloke on a motorbike and a slightly forced smile. This doesn't happen when we order a Chinese in Christchurch.

Then there are the Star Wars figures. I've started collecting them back in England, the main ones like Luke and Vader and Princess Leia and Chewy. In America, you can get figures that just don't exist back home. Lando Calrissian. Admiral Ackbar. You can get a Millennium Falcon but you can also get an Imperial Troop Transporter and a Land Speeder. You can even get a radio-controlled Jawa Sandcrawler.

It's comforting for me to focus on the football stuff. Dad is happy to have me around him all the time and I'm happy to be around him. And the team, and the training pitches, and the ground. The Memorial Stadium on 5th Avenue North isn't big by the standards of Division One in England, but it does have AstroTurf. When Dad sends me off with a football as he chats to his team-mates, I can't get over the bounce and the smooth roll you get on the artificial grass.

When the Sounders move to a new stadium, the Kingdome, it's even better. They get almost 60,000 fans in for the opening game against New York Cosmos, who have got Pele and Franz Beckenbauer playing for them. It's a huge concrete bowl, the roof stretching and arcing away overhead, keeping all that Pacific Coast rain at bay. It's like looking up at the underside of a vast grey parachute, the stands circling the pitch and cutting in right up close to the corners of the artificial pitch. The Seattle Seahawks play there during the NFL season, but when the Sounders are at home I've got the run of it.

We drive over in a car that makes the lime-green Fiesta look like a Corgi toy. No need for seatbelts, me sliding about the back seats as we go round corners, wearing my favourite top, a pale blue football shirt with a big '24' on the front and on the shoulder of each sleeve. Mark is staying back at the rented house with new friends that he's made. I'm not interested because I like being on my own, and I love watching Dad and the team train. It feels thrilling to be around actual football players, listening to what they say, hearing what Jimmy and Dad are telling them to do. Why would I want to be around kids of my own age when I can be here, where the real stuff is happening, where proper footballers can show me stuff I can't do yet but so wish I could?

One of the players always has a piece of pink bubble-gum in his mouth. I ask Mum to buy me the same. Another always does his laces up in a particular manner. I ask him why. He tells me it's because that way they never come undone in a match, so I insist Mum does my own boots up the same way, tight as tight, and then teaches me how to do it on my own. Socks

23

pulled all the way up as always because it looks better. It's neat. It's organised.

There is no kids' nursery at the ground. Dad just digs out a football and throws it my way, and that's just fine with me. It's too big and heavy for a kid of my age, but I'll dribble it around, up and down the sidelines, round the corner flag, round the bottles of Gatorade left out on the grass. I'm not going to be bored. I can't be lonely because I've got a ball.

The matches are always the best bits. I can sit in the dressing room beforehand and then go into the dugout or the best place in the stands once it gets to the serious stuff. The Sounders kit is white with a thin black pinstripe, black shorts and white socks, quite Fulham. There are proper talents wearing it: Mike England, defensive legend for Spurs and Wales, Alan Hudson, former midfielder with Chelsea and Stoke and Arsenal. Bobby Moore is there for one season, and George Best flies up from Los Angeles, where he's playing for the Aztecs. Geoff Hurst is always around.

They tower over me. Mike England is well over six feet, his thighs as big as I am, great woolly sideburns on him. Alan has a modish curly perm to go with his silver necklace. Dad's hair is hardly tame, grown long over the ears like a shaggy ginger helmet. Bobby and George just have a golden aura that's almost like the Ready Brek glow.

I'm star-struck, but at the same time it's all so normal. There have always been football players round our house. Geoff Hurst might have scored the goals that won England the

World Cup. To me, he's just Dad's mate. I'm Harry's son, so they always accept me in return.

Mostly. We have a home game against the Aztecs. We lose 5–4, and the goalkeeper has a nightmare. Almost every goal is his fault somehow. One goes through his legs, another squeezes under his arm. It's obvious, and I can't understand why everyone's not honest about it. If you want to get better, why wouldn't you acknowledge what you need to work on?

The next day I want to talk to the goalie. I can't find him anywhere. He's not in training. He's not working on his shot-stopping. I follow Dad inside and there he is, face down on the physio's treatment table. Hiding away, although I haven't worked that out yet.

I've got the bubble-gum in my mouth, so I know we're in this together. Chomp chomp, big bubble, pop.

'Gee, Cliff, you really blew it!'

It's not meant to be sympathy. It's meant to be analysis. It's meant to be slightly American, because he is, and that's how I feel now. But Dad's reaction tells me I may have got some of that slightly wrong.

'You what? Shut your mouth!'

I can't quite work it out. 'But he did, Dad!'

'Get out of it, clear off!'

I'm in on other jokes. Everyone says Dad hates heading the ball, that they've never seen him doing it. So they have a bet. His mate Smudger, Dave Smith, is over visiting us. He has to buy me and Mark a banana split if Dad heads the ball in that afternoon's match.

We can't take our eyes off the ball. Surely this is going to happen. Dad's going looking for it, coming in off his wing far more than usual, shouting for long crossfield passes that he might be able to get under, but they're giving him nothing. Plenty of balls to his feet, any number into space ahead of him, but not a sniff of anything above knee height.

We're starting to worry. The minutes are ticking away. Our banana splits are melting away. And then Dad does it – waits for the next pass fired in at his ankles, flicks it up with his toes, clips it straight up in the air and heads it back the other way. There's even time for him to look round at us and give us a wink before he jogs off.

These are the things that routinely happen with Dad. The NASL ball, the beautiful Adidas one with the red star on the blue hexagon, has made a deep impression on me and it makes a particular impression on him.

The Sounders are playing the Cosmos of Pele again. The greatest player who has ever lived takes on a long-range shot. My dad, unusually, throws himself in the way to try and stop it. When he gets home, two hours later, the imprint of those red stars is still visible on his thigh. Pele truly has left his mark.

But already things are changing. Dad gets a move from Seattle to Phoenix Fire in the American Soccer League, and although it all falls through when the owners run out of money, we're over there for a couple of months, long enough for me to start playing for a kids' team. The coach is a slightly weird guy. He's called Butch, which is fine, but he's come back from serving in Vietnam, and it's left him a little strange

26

round the edges. He also doesn't appear to know much about football, because suddenly it's all, 'Jamie, how do you take a throw-in?' and, 'Jamie, can you show us how to trap a ball?' A six-year-old boy showing a grown man how to play football. What's that all about?

These adventures are routine and the superstars normal but it is never, ever boring. When we are back in England, George Best will come to stay at our house. Bournemouth manager Don Megson has signed him on a short-term deal at a point in George's career when it is only about the short-term deal.

The football at Dean Court won't really work out for him. At one point he will go to the bathroom before a game and climb out the back window and run away. No-one knows where. Another time he will be seen bowling about trying to sell a canteen of cutlery because he doesn't have any legitimate currency.

George seems happiest when the two of us are out in the back garden, passing the ball off either foot. I'm showing off, trying to convince him that I'm a player, doing my keepy-ups. George is not as trim as some of the other footballers who come over, like Bobby or Geoff, and he's got a big black bushy beard. But he's always smiling and he's even quieter than I am, demonstrating little tricks with the ball and dips with his shoulder.

I know Dad's trying to help him out, partly because he hopes maybe he can rehabilitate him a little, partly because he loves him like he loves Bobby. There's also the test he offers: the bigger the character, the bigger the challenge for a man already thinking about the time he moves from player-coach to manager. I know too that Dad considers him the best player he's ever seen. Not all the old balance is there, and the willow-iness has long gone. But there's enough for me to watch and study and think about.

It's not just George. There are Bournemouth players over all the time, men without a fraction of his ability or fame, slog-gers who have spent a career being kicked around the lower leagues. I can see what they have too, how hard they train each day and how well they look after themselves, and I can see that in this sleepy south coast town, they are still treated differently. It's not the cars or the money that make me want to be a footballer. It's how they live their lives. It's how other people are around them, how they show them respect, how they stand back a pace and stare at them and hang on to what they're saying. Everything about my Dad's world is exciting, and I want every part of it.

There is normality in other parts of my life. Me and Mum walk over to Cuckoos café in Christchurch after school some-times for tea and scones. Afterwards, she'll let me get a quarter of pink foam shrimps or cola-cubes from the newsagents on the corner, shaken out into the metal weighing bowl from a tall plastic jar on the shelf and then slid into a white paper bag before being handed over.

Mum's life is structured around football but she isn't obsessed with it. Just as when she and her sister Pat used to go on holiday with Dad and Uncle Frank before us kids arrived, the two men would spend all day performing in front of them, doing keepy-uppies or bouncing the ball off their shoulders and heads, and the women could not have been less impressed. She had never watched Dad play when he was at West Ham because she was working with Pat in the hair-dressers in Barking, having much more fun. They might stick the commentary on the radio, but that was it.

Then there are the family outings. When Dad asks me and Mark if we fancy going up to London to watch a game in May 1980, it turns out to be the FA Cup Final between West Ham and Arsenal. Uncle Frank is playing at left-back for the Hammers.

We are in the best seats, right on halfway, and in replica claret and blue West Ham shirts, even though they play in their change kit of white that day. It's baking hot, a proper blue-sky Cup Final afternoon. I'm actually more excited to watch Alan Devonshire on the left side of midfield than Uncle Frank just behind him, who I see all the time anyway, but when Frank brings his winners' medal over to their house later, it feels like a strange kind of magic has taken place. My uncle has just won the greatest trophy there is, and I'm touching the actual medal. It's a weird mix of the routine and the extraordinary. These things are not happening to the other boys at school. My world is not the same.

•

Harry Redknapp: When I was a youngster at West Ham, wet behind the ears, I'd listen to all the senior pros talk-ing tactics and strategy when they piled into Cassettari's

Café, round the corner from Upton Park. There'd be Dave Sexton, Malcolm Allison, Frank O'Farrell and John Bond, getting rid of the dirty plates and mugs on the table and using the salt and pepper shakers and the red and brown sauce pots as players. I'd sit there and soak it all up, everything they said. It fascinated me.

That's what I saw Jamie doing in Seattle. Training with us men aged five and six, listening to the chat from Mike England and Bobby Moore and all the rest. He was around them all the time. You could see it soaking in.

I could see in him too that he was a natural footballer. You can train all you like, but I think you've either got it or you haven't. At six years old, Jamie could just get the ball and play. Move the ball, see the shape of the game, control the pace and movement of it. I looked at him with these adults and thought: you've got the talent, Jamie, to be around who you want.

I would have been absolutely fine if he wasn't into football. I never pushed him into it; I wasn't one of those parents who stood on the side shouting at them every week. If he played well, great. If he didn't, he'd learn.

But it was great to see him play. Football had been my whole life. I could see what he had, and I loved how much he loved what I did.

3

THE COMPETITION

Nan's generosity has never been in doubt. We've eaten so many sweets at the caravan and at the flats on Salmon Lane that our tongues look strange when they're tongue-coloured rather than green or bright orange. Her and Pop have absolutely no spare cash. There's no room for fripperies. But everything they can scrape together seems to get spent on me and Mark, which makes us very lucky and their present on our birthdays the one to look forward to most. It will often be football boots but the lack of surprise is never an issue. They're always good boots and all new boots smell and feel so great when you first take them out of the box. The studs are perfect, no scars in the plastic moulded studs and no scuffs on the black leather on the instep.

It's always straight on with socks and boots and straight into the garden to test them out. The grass by the time my birthday comes round in June is generally dust and worn away, so there's no need for studs at all, but they feel right and they look right. The birthday morning when I first get a pair of Patrick Super Keegans has an air of unreality about it. Mark has had a pair for two years, but they look even better on your own feet – polished back uppers with two thin lines of stitching down from the laces to the toes, two red diagonal bands running down from the ankle, Keegan's name picked out in gold lettering. If I was allowed to wear them in the house, I would. But I'm not.

Then comes the day with a present like no other. There's no birthdays or Christmas involved, which makes the big delivery truck pulling up in front of our drive all the more miraculous. Nan and Pop don't mind a little flutter here and there, not in Dad's league or his own nan's semi-professional way but the Football Pools each week and a go at 'Spot the Ball' in the newspaper. This time it's the Premium Bonds that have come in, and come in big.

And I mean big. Four hundred quid! That's a lot of money in a council flat in Poplar, but most of it has been spent elsewhere, on what's being carried out the back of this truck in big rectangular cardboard box.

You see a package that size and that heavy and you're sort of hoping it's a snooker table, but you don't want to think it in case it isn't. It can't be, because it's completely flat. There is nothing that could be the legs. And then you rip open the end of the box and see the green and the dark wood and the white netting of the pockets, and you genuinely think you might explode.

It goes upstairs in Mark's bedroom, resting on an old table that Mum gets out of the garage. Six feet by three feet, proper slate bed, two cues, six colours, ten reds. There is nowhere near enough room around the table to use the cue properly if the white ball is near the cushion, so you have to line up shots at a crazy diagonal angle, which means we develop a slightly warped bridging technique with the other hand. It will be the same when we get a table-tennis table and are so cramped for space that we have to play with our belly buttons pressed against the end of the table. Your reflexes have to be absolutely spot on. All hands, very little feet, whipping out the forehand smash if you're offered any sort of bounce and width to work with.

Snooker is on telly all the time and it's getting bigger. Half the players look like they drink all day and the other half look like they never eat. Bill Werbeniuk is enormous. Alex Higgins and Jimmy White are barely wider than their cues. They're the mavericks, but it's Steve Davis who I'm drawn to. He's gradually becoming the best player in the world. That's all I need. Why would you not like the most successful player more than the ones he keeps beating?

The competition with Mark grows. Mum tries to turf us out of the house early because she knows we're like puppies – we need to burn off a load of energy or we're going to inadvertently wreck the place – but now it's not just football in the garden and the playing field. It's snooker. It's running. It's borrowing Dad's pitching wedge and trying to dink golf balls into a bucket. Sometimes it boils over and there are fights, which Nan and Pop take to mean that we should be fighting more but better, and so bring down as a present on their next visit a pair of red boxing gloves each.

We wait until Mum and Dad go out for tea. They're not massively keen on this new development, but we are, and so are Nan and Pop. This is normal in the East End, and so is the rule that there are almost no rules. Punching the face is fine. So are endless rounds, where there is no bell unless you're down on the floor and crying, and so is using the whole of the lounge, sometimes even reversing into the hall if you've been forced to retreat by your opponent.

Mark, three years bigger and stronger, is comparatively gentle. He'll let me hit him and make a funny song and dance about it. It's Nan who is the relentless one. She can fight. She's tough. Even the grannies can box in the East End, so she stands there in her slippers coaching us.

'Away you go!'

Jab.

'That's it!'

Jab.

'Use your knuckles, Jamie.'

'Yeah, but . . . ow!'

'That's it! Knock 'im out!'

By the time Mum and Dad come back, it's like a bare-knuckle fight. Chairs overturned, stuff spilled on the floor, broken Lladro figurines all over the carpet.

Boxing gloves and naked aggression aren't the only things they bring down. Pop will always arrive with a cheese roll for us in one pocket and a load of Fox's Glacier Mints in the other. But they won't let us win anything we play them at, and neither will Dad.

He comes up to Mark's bedroom for a frame of snooker. Mum's voice follows him up the stairs.

'Harry, give it them this time, will you? Harry?'

He doesn't. It's the same when he gets back from training.

'Hey maestro, fancy coming down the golf course? Where's that pitching wedge?'

We'll go round the back way so we can jib on without paying, and we'll only get a couple of holes in before the green-keeper chases us off, but it's flat-out competition while we're there.

Dad has serious sporting talents. When he hits a football he has a way of doing it that is sweet as a nut. The ball barely wobbles in the air. All those years of getting crosses in from the wing, putting his foot straight through the ball rather than wrapping his instep around it and curling it with less pace. He beats me at golf and he beats me at snooker. He beats me at tennis and he out-skills me with a football in the back garden. It makes me both a bad loser, because I'm absolutely desperate to get one past him, and a very good one, because I get so much practice at it.

I couldn't be happier. This is why I'm not asking Mum to invite kids from my class over to play. I just want to be with my dad. It's much more fun hanging out with him. It's more interesting talking to adults, particularly now Dad has started helping Bobby Moore out as assistant manager at Oxford City in the Isthmian League. He drives up there every Tuesday and Thursday evening to take the training sessions, and if I'm lucky and Mum's looking the other way I can jump in the car with him. Football talk on the way up the A34, watching the players as they do their drills and six-a-sides, hanging out with Bobby afterwards.

The posters on my bedroom wall are now no longer just random stars cut out of *Match* and *Shoot!*. For the first time there is one team that has taken over. Not West Ham, despite Dad and Uncle Frank and Alan Devonshire and his big moustache and lengthening mullet, and not Bournemouth, despite the fact we can walk in at Dean Court every home game for free. It's not the Liverpool team who have just won the European Cup again, and it's not the dreamy Spurs team of Ossie Ardiles, Ricky Villa and Glenn Hoddle that will win two FA Cups in a row, although the way Hoddle strolls around the midfield knocking beautiful passes around has definitely got a grip on my affections.

Instead, it's Luton. Little Luton, 140-odd miles away up the M3 and North Circular and the M1, with its plastic pitch and small home support and history of winning almost nothing at all.

It's all because of Paul Church. The Churches live just across the other side of Palmerston Avenue, having moved down from Bedfordshire, and Paul and his dad go to every home game. When Bournemouth are away, because a Saturday without live football is a miserable prospect, I go with them.

It's a good team, that Luton outfit. David Pleat has brought them up from Division Two and they're playing lovely passing football. There's Brian Stein and Raddy Antic, Mal Donaghy and David Moss, but it's Ricky Hill who I absolutely fall in love with. He's so smooth and silky in midfield. He can pass, he can score, and he's always got time on the ball. I want to drift like he does, I want to run with the ball. He's a big strong guy, and in the white Adidas home shirt with the navy shoulders and 'Bedford Trucks' on the front in blue lettering he stands out in every game I see.

Ricky is a cool name, in a world where most England players seem to be called Trevor or Ray. So it's the Luton kit that I ask for that Christmas and it's posters of Ricky that now look down from my walls. Paul Church can't believe his luck. Not only has he made another convert on the south coast but now the six-hour round trip is serious hardcore Hatters chat rather than staring out of the window.

Seeing Ricky Hill in the flesh is the only way I am going to stay across his exploits. Luton are rarely on *Match of the Day* because the cameras are only at a couple of Division One games. It's the same with the overseas stars I read about in *Shoot!.* I know about Zico and Socrates but I have never seen them play until the 1982 World Cup rolls round.

I have very faint memories of the 1978 tournament, mainly of ticker-tape on the pitch and men with big hair. But 1982 is when I will get caught, hook, line and sinker. The games are on at a perfect time, the first one each day starting just after I've got in from school, the second one after tea and before a delayed bed-time.

Ricky has not made the England squad. He'll have to wait until Bobby Robson takes over from Dad's old gaffer Ron Greenwood, with this team dominated by Trevors, Rays and

Steves. Neither has Alan Devonshire, dropped from the initial squad of 40 for the finals.

England, somehow, make a sensational start. Twenty-six seconds into my first proper World Cup, they've scored, thanks to Bryan Robson. I can't quite believe how he has manoeuvred his body to get the volley down and bouncing past Ettori in the French goal, and I love how he is all action and running in midfield, Hoddle doing the silky stuff alongside. Trevor Brooking isn't fully fit but he still looks fantastic. I study the way he lets the ball run across his body before cutting back and leaving the defender floundering behind, and try it out later against Mark.

The white and blue Admiral kit is a cracker. The shorts are small and the shirts tight. The bulldog mascot works for me. The team's official World Cup song, 'This Time (We'll Get It Right)', gets to number two in the charts and onto *Top of the Pops*. It's all great, except the team that I get fascinated by is not England but Brazil.

I might be the only boy in the world whose two favourite teams are Luton and Brazil. That's fine. Zico's free-kicks and scissor-kicks. Socrates strolling about with his beard and nonchalant passing. Eder chipping Alan Rough on the run in the 4–1 win over Scotland, the way he strikes the ball. Falcao running about with his hair going everywhere and his eyes out on stalks.

These players seem almost mythical. I've read about them and I have imagined how amazing they're going to be when I finally see them in action, even the workmanlike ones no-one really talks about. I don't want to miss a single game, and there is no match I'm looking forward to more than Brazil against Italy.

Brazil look sensational in their pale golden shirts and pale blue shorts. It is so simple and almost perfect. But then there's Italy's, which is just as simple but maybe even more stirring yet, and there's Paolo Rossi, who has started scoring and now can't stop.

I don't move for the entire 90 minutes. The colours on the TV screen are almost impossibly bright, as if floodlights are shining down on the players as well as the mid-summer Spanish sun. The commentary is crackly and giant Italian Tricolore flags keep waving in front of the cameras, but I barely break my gaze.

Rossi puts Italy ahead with a header at the back post. Socrates drills the equaliser in at the near post after Zico's magic turn and pass, Rossi scores again. That's just the first 25 minutes. With respect to Bournemouth, to the Seattle Sounders and to Ricky Hill's Luton, this is the greatest game I've ever seen.

Falcao goes mad after his equaliser deep in the second half. And then something strange happens. I find myself wanting Rossi to score again. I find myself cheering Italian tackles as much as Brazilian flicks. When Rossi spins on the edge of the six-yard box and lashes in his third, I'm off the sofa and leaping around like Mark's chasing me with the gloves on. When he scores again in the final to beat West Germany, who have put England out, there are big back-page photos in Dad's newspaper of him and Marco Tardelli going even more bananas than Falcao. The headline reads, 'PASTA CARING!'

•

I practise striking a ball like Eder and caressing it like Zico. All these things seem obvious to me. Then there is the stuff that no-one could plan for and no-one could really want to.

Mum has a mate called Evelyn from our time in Seattle. Evelyn comes over to stay for a couple of months, probably to enjoy a little sunshine for a while. We're sitting on the sofa having a slightly awkward chat when she slips her socks off, grabs her right foot with her hands, pulls it up to her mouth and starts biting her toe-nails.

It is disgusting, but I'm an eight-year-old boy, so it's also absolutely fascinating. She's not just having a casual nibble. She's cutting her toe-nails with her teeth. She's biting with amazing precision, working her way carefully around each toe before moving on to the next.

I don't know if this is a Seattle thing, something I've missed while I've been at the Kingdome, but when I'm in bed that night I give it a go. It's not easy – you have to really pull on your foot, and it makes your hip feel quite stretched afterwards – but I love to work at something until it comes easily, even if the thing coming easily is my big toe to my mouth, and after a few weeks I can get my right foot over the back of my head. My left isn't quite as good but it's still at lip level without too much effort, so when I'm out in the garden and Mark over-hits a pass so the ball is coming past me at elbow height, I instinctively lift my foot and turn my heel and suddenly I'm cushioning the ball and bringing it down from out there as if it's the most natural thing in the world.

I can do it when the ball is dropping and I can do it when it's pinged at me at pace. Until this moment, I've never been great at killing the ball on my chest. Now I don't have to be. I've got a replacement technique that makes me stand out even more, all because of a filthy habit that I have borrowed and will keep utilising all the way into my late teens.

My obsessiveness is like the tide across the Mudeford sandbanks. It picks everything up and carries it along and won't let go.

Mum's dad comes to see us less than Pop – his wife Betty died when I was six months old, and he's sterner and more serious than Dad's side of the family – but he's a skilled carpenter, and one day arrives with a beautiful bird cage on a long wooden base that he's made in his workshop. It goes in the middle of the garden and it looks great. Mum loves it. Birds love to perch on it.

I ruin it. To me, it's a bird cage only in form. It's actually a target. It's Paolo Rossi lurking on the back post, it's Trevor Brooking breaking on from midfield. It's Ricky Hill in space and time down the right. And so I take my ball out, stand as far away as the garden will allow and pepper it.

Once I have started, I can't stop. If I hit the bird cage flush then I try to do it another way, curling it in with the instep of my right foot, and then hitting the other side of the ball to bend it in from left to right. I clip it hard and I chip it. I ping it and I keep going.

It could be freezing. It could be smashing it down with rain, blowing in on a maritime front off the English Channel. I could be sodden with sweat on a blistering south coast afternoon. None of it matters. I won't go inside until I have reached the number of direct hits that I have set myself in my head.

It could be five. It might be ten. None of them can be glancing blows. They all have to be straight flush. It doesn't matter what damage it might be doing to that beautiful hand-crafted cage, and it doesn't matter what else may be happening around me. Mum might be shouting out the kitchen window that our tea is on the table. She might leave it five minutes and then start shouting again, but she also knows that I'm not coming in, not yet. Dad is the same. He never gets the hump about it.

'Maestro, what you doing? Yer mum's been calling.'

'Thousand keepy-ups, Dad. No break.'

'Yeah? Right you are, Jamie.'

Any errors and I'm not going in. It's pure compulsion but it's also easy. Left-foot keepy-up, right-foot keepy-up. Bringing the ball down from all angles, flicking it up again. A certainty in my touch that will stay with me for the next 30 years. Flat footballs, sponge balls, balls that are pumped up too much and want to bounce off in every direction. Hour after hour, evening after afternoon after morning.

Why would I stop until I've got it right? The set needs

completing. The Star Wars figures need ordering. The socks have to be pulled up.

It's both disciplined and a form of madness, and it leaks out in other ways. When I'm feeling unsettled, if something is slightly off and I'm feeling in need of comfort, I sit on the sofa with a pair of football shorts, find the silky washing tag at the back and rub it between my fingers. It has to be the right type of shorts, and if I can't get the sort of feel I'm after I'll open a new pack of shorts until I find one that works. Once I find a good one, I can stay there for the rest of the day, looping it round my middle finger, playing with it between my index finger and thumb.

Mark knows I'm strange but he's also used to it. If I thrash him at snooker he might lose his temper and throw his cue at me like a spear, but he'll be over it a minute later. If he beats me, I want to play him again immediately to put it right. If he refuses, content to have chalked up a single win, it hangs over me for hours. I'm straight to the sofa and the label in the shorts. If Mum ticks me off about something, if I've thrown the black plastic triangle from the snooker table at Mark's head, I won't say sorry when she tells me to. I'm stubborn. I'll go up to my bedroom and refuse to come out.

It isn't, however, just me in the family. I can see echoes of it in the way Dad is with horses. He's compulsive with those bets. He can't relax until he's phoned his bookie and laid on some cash, and he twitches until he knows whether they've come through or let him down. You can't speak to him in that waiting time because he's in a different world. It's the same with me and the bird cage and the shorts. I'm physically there but I'm miles away from you.

It's similar too when my cousin Frank comes over with Frank senior and Pat and his sisters Natalie and Claire. He's almost exactly five years younger than me, so we're hardly playing against each other, not yet, but when he's got a football at his feet, he doesn't want to let it go either. He goes into the same trance. Right foot, left foot. Against the wall, against the wall, against the wall. He watches me trying to destroy the bird cage, and when I turn round five minutes later to change my angle, he's still watching.

I can tell we've got something in common, despite the years between us. He's small but he clearly loves football. He can practise like I practise.

'Right, Franko, we've got to hit it three times or we can't have dinner tonight. Ready?'

•

Frank Lampard: Because they lived in Bournemouth we'd go down there in school holidays, always in the summer holidays. Jamie would let me come along on his paper round, which made me feel part of something. Almost a big boy, making a few quid together.

There was the bird cage in the garden and the snooker table inside, which was a massive thing to me. The beach was down the road, so the set-up felt great. I had two sisters and suddenly I'm with two boys.

We'd play snooker for a while, but we'd play football

in the garden for hours. It would be me running around and Jamie dribbling with the ball, holding me off and me trying to get it off him in various ways. He'd let me have a little go at his ankles. Humouring me, giving me a chance.

My dad used to drive me on. He would do his sprints, his extra running, trying to get me quicker. Going down to Bournemouth could feel like a release because Jamie was obsessive in a different way. It was cooler with him than it was with my dad. It wasn't about running, it was about technique. It was looking after the ball, passing it.

I looked up to him and I would study him. Mark was that little bit older, Jamie the one closest to me in age. I couldn't believe how he could strike a ball so well. It looked so smooth, the way he could do keepy-ups with both feet, control it wherever it came to him. He always looked like he had a bit of time and elegance, as opposed to what I felt I had at that stage.

The biggest part of his game that impressed me was his long passing. Watching Jamie he had every pass. But as a young 'un, my game was always about trying to score goals, about getting up and down the pitch. I was a bit chubby so I worked loads on that. As I got a bit older and began moving up the ladder I realised that to play in centre-midfield, you can't not affect the game in other ways. I'd watch Jamie play. I watched him being able to hit right foot, left foot, hitting long balls. Those were the things I would definitely try and replicate in my game.

I knew I was never going to be that type of player. It was quite clear as we developed that we were slightly different. But those were the things that I would pick up on, try to add.

So when I think about coming to Bournemouth, I do think about playing in the garden. I also think about Aunty Sandra doing the dinner, and having her cup of tea, and that softness she had. Most weekends my dad would be pushing me hard, but my mum always managed to put her arm around me and make a bit of dinner or give me a nice soft word. Her sister was exactly the same. In terms of balance of what you need to be a footballer, you can't just be football, football and not have another little side to you. I think we were both lucky that we had that.

4

THE EDUCATION

Changes are happening on the sleepy south coast. Dad's old mate David Webb, an apprentice with him at West Ham in the early 1960s before going off to stardom at Chelsea and then player-manager at Bournemouth with Dad helping out as assistant, has had an argument with the club's new owners and left to be a salesman, at least until Torquay down the coast come calling. Dad applies for the full manager's role only for Don Megson, the old Sheffield Wednesday midfielder, to get the nod instead. Don had been working for the Portland Timbers in the NASL while we were in Seattle, another one of those strands of the everlasting football family tree that I'm beginning to understand stretches across the game with us somewhere near the middle. So he knows us and we know him and most of the links in between.

It doesn't go well for Don. Bournemouth start the 1983 season badly and sink into the relegation places. By October, Don's gone too. Maybe it's because Dad keeps applying, or maybe it's because there's no-one else who wants it. But this time he gets the job. For the first time, and at the age of 36, my dad is a full-time manager in the Football League.

It's good timing, because we've upgraded from Palmerston Avenue. Old Barn Road is three miles north-west, where Fairmile Road turns into Hurn Road just before the parade of shops on the right. The new house is bigger – detached, with a gravel drive and gables over the front room and built-in garage. Mark's bedroom is at the front, looking out at the retirement bungalows and fir trees across the road; mine is smaller, but at the back of the house, overlooking the two small goals that we can now fit in the garden.

Most importantly the garden is twice the size. When we have one-on-one matches, the ball can't disappear into the neighbours' on the left because the hedge is taller than me on Mark's shoulders, but the hedge on the other side is only half the size. This is bad news for Jack and Winifred next door, because it means there is no protection whatsoever for their greenhouse, and it's worse when they complain about all the smashed panels as now we don't want to be seen getting the ball back, so we kick a big hole in the hedge so we can sneak through at shin height and escape their gaze as they stare out suspiciously from their kitchen window. We become adept at a combination of the commando crawl and a T. J. Hooker-style roll to cover the final few yards to the ball in style. Ball boys at Dean Court don't know how good it can look.

We can all feel the heaviness of the pressure now on Dad's shoulders. When Bournemouth lose he has the hump and brings it home with him, like he did as a player but much more intense. He'll never take it out on us, though. There's no outward aggression. It's more a deadening of his usual character. He's in the house but not really present with us.

'Don't say anything tonight,' Mum will advise us. 'Keep your heads down. You want to watch *E.T.* again? Get the video out, then. Eh? Probably still in the machine from yesterday. There you go. Sound down a bit, Jamie, that's it.'

If it's a home game, Dad will be in by half six. If it's away, it could be any time. Mum will wait up for him, and when it's a decent win, so will we. A big win as a manager means the same thing as it did when he was playing: a Chinese takeaway, and plenty spare to stick in the fridge for the next day too. A bad loss and the muted mood will hang over into Sunday instead.

'You've got to be like that really, haven't you,' Mum will tell me and Mark. 'If you don't care, then it's not worth doing it, is it?'

There is still a certain amount of fear in the air from the year before, when Dad had taken over as caretaker boss for a couple of games between Dave getting the heave-ho and Don coming in. Bournemouth had been away at Lincoln, the pitch at Sincil Bank frozen on a snowy December afternoon. Lincoln were a decent side, so being only a goal down just before half-time had seemed okay, until a defender called Phil Brignull chipped his own keeper for a horror own-goal, and then Lincoln started running all round them, quite literally, because they had come out in the second half in AstroTurf boots, when Dad's lot were still slipping and sliding every-where in studs.

Mum often spent Saturdays hairdressing in the box room

to make a bit more money. She had put the radio on for the match commentary. Every time I'd gone in to see her I'd heard two things – the hairdryer on full blast, and another goal going in.

Three. Four. Five. A sixth while I was still standing there. I hadn't gone back in after the seventh, so the eighth and ninth goals came to light only when Mum came down after her client looking like she was going to be sick.

Dad had tried to put a brave face on it. When the bloke on the radio asked him how disappointed he was, he replied, 'Well, to be fair I thought the seventh one was offside.' The following week the supporters' association clubbed together to buy the team their own AstroTurf boots. The consensus was that the game should never have gone ahead in such ridiculous conditions.

But it was a club record defeat, and back on Old Barn Road it had felt like the end of the world. I was convinced it was Dad's managerial career over. Mum, always the one with the kind words, tried to reassure us. 'Well, it can only get better, boys . . .'

All I kept thinking was that I had to go to school on Monday, and that all I would hear all morning would be kids slagging off my dad. Then it was the logical next step: the owners are going to think, he's not the man for us.

It's a strange and unsettling feeling, worrying for your dad and not being able to do anything to help him. So now he has the job full-time I look for all the reasons why it's going to work: a 2–1 win over Oxford United in his first proper game in charge; how much he knows about the game, how good he is with people.

He is totally dedicated to it. When we drive anywhere he's talking tactics with me. 'I got a hole in centre-mid now Jamie, cos that lad Nigel Spackman's gone to Chelsea with John Hollins. Could be a top, top player, Nigel. I got John Beck in there Jamie, he'll scrap all day, but I need someone alongside him who can get it down and play, don't I?'

Already I feel a sense of protection towards Dad, an anger when I hear anyone at the ground or in the street saying he's not up to it. We keep it tight in this family. Nan and Pop, Mum and Dad, me and Mark. Dad is an only child, with a lot of only-child traits. He likes his independence but he also needs looking after, and that's what Mum does for him and what she does for us. He's earned his chance at Bournemouth but he's lucky he found Mum, almost 20 years back, at the Two Puddings pub in Stratford, where all sorts of stuff has gone on down the years, and lucky that he won her over with a second date at the Lion and Lamb in Brentwood. Mum is happy to do whatever works for the family, so Dad does whatever he wants to do. Which is football, all the time, all the conversations, all the connections.

You can't help but notice how many mates he seems to have. He gets on with almost everyone and almost everyone gets on with him. His mate Smudger – the one who came visiting out in Seattle and had that bet about the header – has the biggest house of anyone we know. He's got the same taste in music as my dad, US soul and R&B, and he's got a music system that can record singles and LPs onto C90 cassettes. So Dad will go off and record a mix-tape of Luther Vandross and George Benson, Anita Baker and Shalamar, and me and Mark will play on the arcade games that he's got in a special room in another part of the house. There's an actual Space Invaders, with the graphics of hairy yeti-like monsters on the sides, a joystick on the left and a big white Fire button on the right, and lines of aliens coming down the screen at you, and your spaceship scuttling along the bottom, hiding behind bunkers and firing up at the aliens with a laser cannon as they fire down at you. I can't quite believe that we're allowed to play it. I can't believe that Smudger has got it set up so that when the screen comes up with INSERT COIN <1 OR 2 PLAYER> you just hit play. No coins required.

It feels like the best house in the world. It's almost my favourite possible family outing: Dad looking relaxed and laughing away, Mum doing a little dance to Luther, me and Mark playing again and again. When we get home, we switch from Space Invaders to Subbuteo, which means Dad can get involved too.

I've got the Luton team in the orange kit. Mark's got West Ham. We iron the pitch before we play to get the surface absolutely dead flat, line up the players and battle for hours. Satisfaction is getting enough lift on a penalty to get it past the constantly moving goalkeeper. Disaster is accidentally kneeling on a player and thus inadvertently amputating him at the knees. You try to glue him back on to his base but after an injury as serious as that he's never quite the same player ever again. Happiness is saving up to get actual working floodlights for the four corners of the pitch and a two-tiered grandstand with green roof and brown terraces full of plastic supporters frozen in various poses of celebration and outrage. It's getting a big scoreboard and sticking goals past Mark as he gets angrier and angrier, always rearranging my players in the perfect 4–4–2 formation after each re-start, my lucky ones in centre-mid like me and Ricky Hill.

We save up because Mum and Dad don't dish out on anything unless we work for it. Mark has a paper round from Dewey's, the newsagents in the parade off Hurn Road and Marlow Drive, and I'm his back-up man. Most of the time that's a cushy number. I sit out the back of the shop, reading *Match* and *Shoot!*, eating an ice-cream or working my way through a quarter of pineapple cubes or sherbet pips, waiting for Mark to come back. I can eat an ice-cream before breakfast, at 9 am, whatever. I just tell the newsagent to take the cost off the Redknapp brothers' salary. But I have to learn all the rounds by heart, because when Mark can't do it, or he's running out of time to get it all done, I have the chance to step in and get myself a cut of the £3.70 bonanza he picks up.

Dad knows that I'm going to struggle lugging those broadsheets around the nicer houses spread around St Catherine's Hill, and he always tells me – come back and get me, we'll do it together. So when the newsagent looks at his watch and makes a face, I'm onto my BMX and flying down Old Barn Road like I'm Elliott and his brother and mates trying to get away from the cops in *E.T.* Dad spots me. 'Stick your bike in the back, we'll do it in my car.'

Most people don't mind their paper being a little late on a Sunday morning. Christchurch is a sleepy town on a Monday at 9 am, let alone on the day of rest. But there's one time we do get caught out, just as we think we've cracked it with our system of me doing one house and my dad doing the next, so pleased with ourselves that we're twice as fast as Mark on his usual solo mission.

Dad's kneeling down by a front door, trying to stuff a fat paper through a letterbox that's too small, when the door gets pulled back in front of him and a man is standing there in his slippers and dressing-gown, fury all over his face.

'Where on earth have you been? The paper's supposed to be here an hour ago!'

My dad stands up. 'Yeah sorry, they was late in at the shop.'

The bloke clocks Dad. Double-take. Disbelief.

'Harry Redknapp?'

Dad gives him the paper and a wink.

'Yeah, tough times at Bournemouth, they don't pay me enough.'

And off we go, onto the next road, laughing our heads off as soon as we're round the corner.

•

The E.T. infatuation has triggered its own related BMX obsession. I have a sweet Kuwahara bike, purple rather than the red and white one that Elliott has but still a thing of beauty. I still have the marbles, the Smurfs and the Star Wars figures but now I have neat rows of E.T. memorabilia too, sent over from the States by friends of Mum's from the Seattle days. I love all the Steven Spielberg films I have seen, and *Raiders of the Lost Ark* is a blinder, but nothing comes close to this. I can do the E.T. voice and I have a plastic E.T. finger that glows red at the tip. Dad has managed to get a pirate copy of the film on VHS, and I'll watch it every single afternoon when I get in from school.

None of the kids in my class have got it. Neither have any of them lived in the USA, so when they're amazed by the scene where Elliott's brother phones out for pizza delivery, I can play it cool. Yeah, done that, we used to do that for tea. But it feels like more than just a film to me. I know it so well, every line that Elliott says, all the little shocks, like when Drew Barrymore screams and E.T. screams back, or when the figure in the safety suit and breathing apparatus suddenly looms at the front door, that I almost feel like I'm in it. I look at Elliott with his floppy hair and all the time he spends on his own and I see me. I watch his noisier, more sociable big brother with his noisier mates and it's Mark. Elements of the landscape and culture are recognisable from Seattle and Phoenix, but it also hints at events and patterns I have no idea about, and I like that too.

And then one evening it all changes. I'm home from school, glad to be back, warm and safe at home. I'm counting through the familiar scenes, building up to the climax I know is coming. E.T. is out in the forest. The wind is blowing. There is a light in the sky as a spaceship approaches.

And then, suddenly, there are horses. And jockeys. And a load of shouting.

Dad has recorded the afternoon's racing from Wincanton over the top.

I am devastated. E.T. is about to go home and instead the commentator's screaming about how they're coming to the final furlong. I could kill him. I could kill Dad. I cry my eyes out, and no-one can say anything to make me feel better.

I hate going to school at the best of times. It's harder still the next morning, knowing that there's no hanging about with Elliott when I get home. There's nothing wrong with Christchurch Junior School in itself: the playground is big, with the outline of a goal painted in white on the dark brick, and there's a playing field out the back with an oval running track bleached into the grass around the perimeter. There are trees around the edge of the courtyard formed by the square of classrooms, and pale green corrugated roofs that stick out over the edge of the buildings so you can sit underneath in all weathers and drink your bottle of milk with its straw stuck through the silver foil lid.

My dad tells me I'm lucky to be there. He tells me horror stories about Susan Lawrence Primary in Poplar, and scarier stories still about Sir Humphrey Gilbert Secondary Modern, which he says was the worst school in the entire East End, more like a cross between a nuthouse and a remand centre than a place of education.

Of all the lessons I sit through, it's English that I dislike least. Maths never gets a hold of me, but I like listening to stories.

There's been enough practice with my family, and I also find I enjoy making up my own. There's usually a footballer in there. Sometimes there's an Ellis.

There are even cool teachers. Mr Walker might have *Planet of the Apes* sideburns and teach maths, but he is not a teacher who believes in giving everyone a go at football. He believes only in winning. Since this is exactly how I feel, we get on like a treat. He always picks the best players for our school team and he never takes them off, not even when we're 5–0 up. The more goals you score the more Maltesers he'll dish out afterwards. Football and sweets. It's as if Pop and Nan have had a quiet word.

The rest of it I hate. I get bullied. I don't want to be there anyway. There's always somewhere else I'd rather be. I want to be with my dad, whatever he's doing – training, talking, driving about, talking about training. I take my full Smurf collection into school to try to make friends, and someone nicks the lot of them. We go out into the playground for lunch and they're all on the bookcase. When we come back in at the bell, they've gone. I never see them again.

Salvation comes in an unexpected form. I'm in the car with Dad when he sparks up one of his stories.

'Jamie, while back, Pop rings me, tells me, "You know what Harry, I've seen one of the best lads I've seen, playing for London Schools."

'Now I went to school with his dad, proper lad, same estate as me. So I say, "What, he's got a boy?" "Yeah, proper player, left-footed, plays at the back. Different class. He can really play."

'Thing is, he's done something on the way to England school-boy trials. Messing about on the train. Throwing water out of the window at people on the platform. He's been at QPR, 14 years old, and he's done their centre-half Bob Hayes – proper centre-half, 6 ft 3 in, 14 stone – he's done him like a kipper. Gone over the top in training, nearly broke his leg. They've kicked him out, he's gone to West Ham, same thing's happened, now no-one wants to touch him because he's bad news.

'Now his dad's rung me up too. "Harry, will you take him? I gotta get him out of here."

'Jamie, I've heard about this left foot like a magic wand. He's got blond hair, baby face, bit tubby, face like an angel. He's still only 17, and he can do anything with a ball, so I've said yes. Come down to Bournemouth.

'I've put him in digs, he's run home. I've put him in different digs, he's run home again. So long story short, he's coming home to live with us.'

That is my introduction to Paul. Over the next few weeks, in front of Mum and Dad, he's a delight. At breakfast it's, 'Morning, Mrs Redknapp.' When my dad pops in it's, 'How are you today, H?'

The other stuff is just below the surface. When the adults have gone, he's smoking out of the back window. When we get on our BMXs and ride along the pavements to the golf course down by the river, a load more leaks out. Me and Mark and Paul, just a few of Dad's clubs shared between us, taking ages to complete each hole. A well-spoken bloke comes up to us on the next tee.

'Excuse me, you three, you're taking far too long. Do you mind moving on?'

Paul has an iron in his hands before I can move.

'Hurry up?' A twitch.

'Hurry up?' Incredulity.

'Shut your f***ing face now. Cos if you say one more thing to me, I'm wrapping this club round your f***ing face.'

I'm so shocked I don't know what to do. The well-spoken man is both shocked and openly terrified. As he stumbles backwards Paul tosses his ball down on the grass, swipes it down the fairway and marches off.

I don't know quite how it happens, but Paul finds out about a kid at school who bullied me. I'll come and sort it out for you, he tells me.

I never see him near the school gates. He certainly doesn't come in with me. But the next day, the bully arrives in class with a cake for me. He can't meet my eye. He never meets it again.

Paul is definitely a great footballer. His left foot is indeed lovely. When we go down to the park, he's all tricks and he can bang a casual pass into your feet from wherever he is. He's also the hardest kid I've ever met. He's old East End come to an East End family gone south-west and much softer.

Monday morning, eating breakfast before school, and Dad's on the phone out in the hall, talking to one of his confidants.

'It's this lad Paul. Every week we're playing, he's waiting 'til the ball is up the other end, and he's sparking people out. There's murders. The other team's always kicking off.

'Saturday night, there's a fight down the Palais in Boscombe.

Paul gets arrested by the police. I get called down the police station Sunday morning.

'He's crying his eyes out. "Please sir, I ain't done nothing. Please sir . . ." The officer goes, "Okay Paul, don't worry. I'll leave you with Mr Redknapp." And as he goes out, Paul's looked up at me, all tears suddenly gone, and winks. "F***ing hell, H, get me out of here, will you?"'

I like Paul. He's always incredibly nice to me. I'm also working out that he's not going to be staying with us forever. It's like lobbing a box of fireworks in the oven: it might stay quiet for a bit, but you know the explosions are coming. He also can't solve all my problems for me.

I get picked to run for the school at the town athletics championships, down at the track in King's Park, right next to Bournemouth's ground. The nerves start nudging me as soon as I wake up that morning, and they grow steadily throughout the day. By the time we get to the track, I'm all over the place. I want to run but I also want to run away.

I'm the favourite for the 100 metres. Everyone else from the school is confident, based more on what I can do with a football at my feet rather than how I run without one. Standing behind the start line with a red bib over my white England shirt, white shorts, trainers. Crouching down on imaginary blocks as I've seen Daley Thompson do on the telly. Feeling a spasm in my guts, feeling a spasm lower down the digestive system.

The gun goes and so too does my bum. Before I've taken a stride, I know something has gone terribly wrong. By five metres in I can feel something warm and sticky in the gusset of my pants. By 15 metres there's more of it. By 30 metres I'm slowing down, because I know it's going to start escaping the elastic and sliding down my leg if I stretch out any more.

The crowd can't understand why the hot pre-race tip is being overtaken. Mr Walker can't work out why his best all-round sportsman is falling apart in front of his eyes. I can't believe this is happening in front of all the cool kids in the entire town.

I come home last, thighs clamped together, knees tight. Straight through the finish line, straight past the main stand, gesturing frantically at Mum. Out into the car park, where her maternal instinct has kicked in and she's waiting with a stricken look on her face.

'Jamie?'

'Mum. Get me home. Now.'

Into the car, Dad behind the wheel, without a thought for the mess. Onto King's Park Drive and the A338 dual carriage-way without a thought for the speed limit.

Somehow, no-one else ever finds out. It's the greatest miracle I will ever be part of. My life could be ruined before I've reached double figures. Jamie Poo-Pants. Red-Arse. Shitknapp. But I escape, just as Paul finds himself deeper and deeper in a mess of his own making.

Dad, on the phone to the same mate a week later.

'It's Paul again. Yeah. He keeps wanting to go home. He's got himself a bird back there. He's said to me, "Harry, can I go back to Stepney? Me mum's having a baby."

'"Oh, is she?"'

'"Yeah, she's pregnant, she's having the baby this weekend. Can I go home? I wanna be there."'

'So I've said to him, "Okay, no problem Paul."'

'Off he goes. Comes back Sunday night, walks into the house. Sandra says to him, "Hello Paul, how's the baby?"'

'"The what?"'

'"The baby. You said your mum's having a baby."'

'"Oh, yeah. She had it. Dead."'

'We don't say nothing. Bit shocked, obviously. But we know his mum's coming down next weekend. So Friday comes around, and he says, "Sandra, H, when she gets here, don't mention the baby, will ya? She'll get terribly upset."'

'His mum comes round the house. Tight jeans. Full of beans. Sandra takes me aside. "Harry, last baby that woman had was 17 years ago. And he's standing in my kitchen."'

So Paul, eventually, leaves our lives as quickly as he has blown in. The best babysitter we will ever have is no more, but his legacy remains. No kid at school tries to bully me ever again. Even without Elliott, I am safe.

Dad's career also begins to look brighter. In January 1984, Bournemouth get an FA Cup third round draw against Manchester United.

It's a bit of a step up from Windsor and Eton in the second round. United are the Cup holders, having beaten Brighton the year before, and they'll win it the year after too, thanks to Norman Whiteside's curler against Everton. Their team includes Bryan Robson, the best player in Britain, and

Ray Wilkins, who's not far off. There's Arnold Muhren, Frank Stapleton and Whiteside. There's Ron Atkinson managing them in a beige suit and shades. They are second in the top flight. Bournemouth are 21st in Division Three.

Dad is in his element. He always finishes off training on a Friday with a southerners *v* northerners five-a-side. This time he does that as if everything is normal but then takes the players to La Lupa Italian restaurant in Charminster. Over a slap-up meal he promises them a £200 bonus and a holiday if they win. The owner gets into the spirit of things and offers goalkeeper Ian Leigh as much free pizza as he can eat if he keeps a clean sheet.

The tricks and treats keep coming. An overnight stay at the Roundhouse hotel that night, which never happens before home games, and a coach to take them to Dean Court, which never happens either. Dad leaves it five minutes before joining the players in the dressing room and tells them he's just spotted the Man United boys watching the horse-racing on the telly in the lounge. It's not true, but they don't know that. Then he reminds them about an interview Ron Atkinson has given, where he says the game is going to be a training exercise. 'We're winning this, lads. They don't fancy it. They don't know what we've got.'

I've never seen so many people inside the ground. I've never seen so many people outside the ground, trying to get in.

Bournemouth in red, United in white with 'Sharp Electronics' across the chest. For an hour, it's tight. It's massive fun. And then Gary Bailey drops a corner, and Milton Graham hooks it in and it's bedlam. And just as the choruses of 'We shall not, we shall not be moved,' start ringing out, Robson makes a mess of another clearance and Ian Thompson makes it two.

At the end, we're on the pitch. We sing all the way home and we dive about on the sofas when we get there, and of course we stay up late to watch *Match of the Day*. Jimmy Hill introduces the show from Craven Cottage, where he's been watching Fulham in a 0–0 stinker against Spurs, wearing a sheepskin coat with lapels so big you could play five-a-side on them.

'We start by toasting the happiest man in football tonight – Harry Redknapp, the manager of Bournemouth United, who this afternoon beat Cup favourites Manchester United 2–0.'

It cuts to Dad being interviewed on the pitch at Dean Court, wearing a navy old-school Adidas trackie top with three white stripes down each sleeve, surrounded by kids with red rosettes pinned on their parkas and waving cardboard versions of the FA Cup covered in kitchen foil to give them the authentic silvery look. I recognise the look in Dad's eye, the twitchiness he's inherited from Pop, the electricity crackling through him when he's pulled off a win and the adrenaline is still whacking through him.

'It's gotta be the greatest day of my life, and I'm sure the greatest day in the lives of all the players.'

Massive cheer from all around. 'It's a great afternoon for

everyone in Bournemouth, we're delighted. I've had a feeling all week, John, that we would win the game. I had a strong feeling we would beat Manchester United today.'

Little grin. 'The supporters were tremendous, but the players were the fellas who done it, not me. The game's about players, not managers.'

Nice one Dad, but don't undersell yourself. This is massive.

'It's about the fellas who get on the park and play. We keep seeing managers on TV, and the managers are becoming more famous than the players. The lads have done it today, so all credit to them.'

I'm so proud of him. Even though he's giving all the credit away, even though he has said on national television that winning was better than the day he got married to Mum or the June morning I arrived in the world, I'm fine with that. It's football. It's Dad.

The dream doesn't go much further. Middlesbrough win 2–0 against us at Ayresome Park in the next round. Bournemouth will finish the season 17th in the division, and Ian Leigh will never get his lifetime of pizza. The restaurant is taken over by a new proprietor, a certain Mr H Redknapp. 'What can I do?' Dad will say. 'Nipper's already 5 ft 10 in and 15 stone. He'll eat me out of business.'

Ron Atkinson says afterwards too that it was a nothing match. 'Two very good players made two very basic errors.' He doesn't see what happens at our house on Monday morning, where there are TV cameras filming us eating our cornflakes and reporters asking Dad what his secret is.

For once I'm happy to go to school. Kids want to talk to me. Kids want to say nice things about my family. This game is life-changing for everyone.

•

Harry: Even in the early days managing Bournemouth I'd always go to watch Jamie play every Saturday and Sunday morning. I'd never shout at him either, just let him play and enjoy it. Even when he came home I would never badger him about the game.

I would stand out the way, because one time Sandra was on the touchline and gave it a, 'Come on, Jamie, come on!', and he walked over to the touchline and went, 'If you say, "Come on Jamie" one more time, I am walking off. I'm not playing.'

You could still use a few old manager's tricks. When Jamie was 10, his team was short of a goalkeeper, so I stuck in a ringer. He was 14 and massive. The other manager couldn't believe his eyes. 'What, he's ten, is he?' 'Course he is Mick, would I lie to you?' And then I turned round, and the 'keeper's leaning against his post, smoking a fag.

Jamie had a good size for a footballer. He had my footballer legs and he had a bit of height and plenty of strength from Sandra's side of the family. Some kids are not built to play football. Jamie was athletic, he was quick enough.

He would also come down to the club with me

whenever he wanted. He could have the pitch to himself, have the run of all the facilities. Maybe not many other kids have that. But Jamie always loved it. Every week he played he always tried his absolute hardest. He wasn't one of those kids where you had to say, why didn't you run about or do this or that? It was like he was managing himself. I didn't have to tell him what to do. He knew.

5

THE OBSESSION

You can keep the real world at arm's length when you lose yourself in football and its simple weekly rhythms of matches and training and structured practice, but you can never push it completely away.

There is a little playing field just over the grass levee from the River Stour. It takes me and Mark about three minutes to bomb down there on our BMXs – right out of the house, another right turn where Old Barn Road meets River Way, then a sharp right-hander and onto Stour Way before it gets to the big caravan park tucked into the wide meander of the river itself.

It's not flashy, just a rectangle of grass with short, wind-blown trees on three sides and a red-brick toilet block on the other, with tight little semi-detached houses beyond. There are no swings and quite a lot of dog-dirt, but it's all we need. If there's enough daylight after school we'll be down here most afternoons. If it's half-term we're there morning and afternoon, pinging the ball to each other, bringing it down on our chests or turning and killing it as it drops over our heads.

When Pop has come to stay he'll come down with us and do his tricks and skills too, testing our touch by firing it at us suddenly or with pace at our wrong foot. Mark is turning into a lovely striker of the ball, with a right foot that can caress it or drive it flat. It's when I'm down there one afternoon on my own that the trouble leaches in.

I've taken my purple Kuwahara and a couple of Dad's short irons to hit a few balls about in the longer grass beyond the gravel car park. When I come back to the bike 20 minutes later, both the tyres are flat, which is weird, because they were fine on the way down, and I haven't gone over any broken glass or gone off-roading in the woods near the hawthorn trees.

I'm looking at the tyres and moaning to myself and getting ready to walk back when an older bloke strolls over from the direction of the river.

'Hello son, you had a puncture?'

'Yeah.'

'Two of them. That's bad luck.'

'Yeah.'

'The good news is, I can fix them for you.'

'Yeah?'

'I've got a pump in my caravan. You come back with me and I'll get them sorted.'

He's staring at me now. 'It's only over there. It won't take us a minute.'

Alarms going off in my head and a sick feeling rushing into my stomach. I grab the bike and run off like I've got a forest fire on my heels. I don't look back, even as the man is shouting at me to wait. I don't look back and I don't stop running until I get all the way home.

Dad's just got back from training. He's straight in the car and down to the playing field at a thousand miles an hour, golf club gripped in the hand that isn't holding the steering-wheel.

The bloke has gone. I give a description but no-one at the caravan park recognises him, and so some of the darkness remains.

On future visits, we smash balls against the wall of the toilet block and practise our control when the ball comes rebounding back, but we never go into the toilets themselves. In my head there are bad things and bad men lurking inside. I don't even want to go near the door, even though we've seen no-one go in and no sign of movement in the hour we've been there.

It helps to throw ourselves into the football. If we want a game we'll run up and over the levee and onto the soggy pitches that lie between the grassy mound and the rushes by the river. The goalmouths have bare indentations in the middle where the 'keeper has been standing and diving about. When it's been dry for a few weeks, the mud dries out and cracks and turns to dust. When it's wet, it's just a giant puddle.

Playing one-on-ones against each other we learn to clip our shots so that they don't land in water and die before the goal-line. Usually we'll commentate on ourselves too. I might be Glenn Hoddle or Enzo Francescoli, who I've read about in *Shoot!* but never actually seen in action because Uruguay games are not a regular feature on *Football Focus* or *On The*

Ball over on TVS. It works because Mark is a natural defender and I love to dribble. If I can get past him I can go past anyone my own age.

'Hoddle. Still Hoddle. Oh, what a strike!'

Mark can't always be there. He's got a job at Dad's mate Gordon's fish and chip shop, half a mile down Fairmile Road, peeling the spuds, coming home stinking from the deep-fat fryers. Dad will drive us up there to pick him up, then maybe get a film on VHS from the video shop two doors down the parade. We might see Andy and Stevie coming round the corner from Walcott Avenue. They're Mark's mates but I like hanging about with them while we wait for the fish and chip shop to close up. Stevie's an apprentice at Bournemouth. When Dad's not listening he tells me stories about the jokes they play down there, smearing Deep Heat inside each other's pants, carving up the blocks of yellow soap that are meant for the showers, taking the slices of cheese out of their mates' sandwiches and sticking the soap in instead.

Mark's in demand. He's wanted back out in Phoenix by a team called the Firebirds, who have spotted something emerging from the Redknapp genes. But the relentless competition he has thrown my way over 11 years is starting to pay off in other ways too, when I win the first trophy of my own budding footballing career.

'Player Most Likely To Succeed'. It's admittedly not the most glamorous of gongs. It comes with no guarantees, and only a modest plastic trophy. Most likely but you can't be sure, because you're only 11, and football is a fickle business. You can also read into 'succeed' exactly what you want. Is that in Sunday league football, or with England?

Still, you've got to start somewhere, and a week-long summer camp up in London with the Alan Mullery Soccer School is a lot more fun than any other school I've been at so far. There's no sign of Alan himself until the end of the week when the awards get dished out, although he has just taken over as QPR manager so he's a little preoccupied.

It sets me up for the season ahead. My earlier spell with Mudeford Youth (orange kit, a little bit Dundee United) has led to a move to Greenfields (navy-blue shirt with red and white stripe down the side). The pitch is on the same fields down on the inlet at Mudeford where we used to play when we lived on Palmerston Avenue, still whipped by the wind off Christchurch harbour in winter and soaked by the rain that comes in with it. You learn that the best way to stay warm is to be in constant motion, to demand the ball and be at the centre of everything that happens. You don't feel the cold when you're dipping a shoulder and then swerving past a midfielder the other way, or when you're hunting down that defender who's dallying on the ball and not looking up at who's coming in to clatter him.

It's just a field, with bumps and rogue tufts of grass, and posts that lean slightly askew from the southerly sea winds. There is a big scorched circle in the corner where they burn the grass clippings in summer and have the Guy on the bonfire in autumn, or where we make our own little fires sometimes and incinerate sausages that we've borrowed from Mum's fridge. There are crisp packets and faded Coke cans in the bushes and there is more dog-dirt, because where there is grass there is always dog-dirt.

It still feels like a special place. I run out there with my laces tied tight and my socks pulled up and I feel in control. I am in charge. There is calm amid the yells and elbows and whistles.

I never worry what our coach says about my performance, or what the opposition manager or parents might say. I just look at my dad to see what he thinks. He has three signals from the touchline: a nod for well done, a fist-clench for get stuck in, a stirring motion with his hand to work harder. Never a shout, never any criticism. He doesn't have to push because I'll always try hard, and that's all he wants.

I play a year above my actual age, sometimes two. In a Cup game, the other team's manager will try to stop the match on the basis that I'm too small. I can see Dad on the point of losing it by the side of the pitch. 'Too small? Have you seen the lad play?'

There's also a difference between height and strength. I'm taller than average for my age but I've also got a build. Mark's the same – big legs, solid backside. Pop might have brought the fun and the tricks but our strength has come from Mum's father, Bill. He's never kicked a ball in his life, but he's all muscle, and he's all discipline. When Mum was younger, he'd make her get up at 6 o'clock every morning to make breakfast, even if she'd had a night out. Now, when he drives down to see us, he gets up at 3 am, leaves Brentwood by 3.30 am and arrives at our front door when Mum is still getting up out of the old childhood habits.

He can be stern. His wife Betty had died when I was six months old. Everything has to be just right. He loves proper coffee at a time when people think Gold Blend is a bit fancy, getting bags of fresh beans, grinding them himself. He cooks better than any other man I know, partly because he's had to learn.

I find some of that structure and discipline coming through to me too. Dad is loose. He's all stories and the stories are all about scrapes and jokes. That's why his players like him. He can be intense too, losing his temper from nowhere, and easily distracted, and Mark is the same, which is why the two of them are the ones to have rows. I'll have fun before training sessions, but as soon as we begin I'm bang on it. I never mess about when there's work to be done, and neither do Mum and her dad. My dad can blow his top. He's up and down and a little bit manic. He tells me how I feel about things. Mum never does. She doesn't lose her temper and she never complains. Maybe it's all the years of hairdressing, of being a silent sounding-board for frustrations and hopes and any old nonsense, but I can talk to her when I'm upset and she will listen. She is calm. She is soft in the best possible way.

You can see so much of Mum in her sister Pat when we go up to stay at Uncle Frank's. Gidea Park is green and leafy like Christchurch. Their house is between the tennis club and Romford Golf Club. Their garden is also designed around foot-ball. There's a swimming pool too, but we barely ever go in it. You can go out through the TV room or the garage, over the cobbles by the patio and then onto the grass, and it's a beautiful surface. There's a putting-green in one corner and the rest of it is mowed and rolled to almost the same lovely smooth perfection. In our heads it's Wembley ready for the Cup Final. There is a little summer house and we pull the goals out of there and set them up, do one-twos, play non-stop games.

You can tell that Frank is intelligent. He feels like a surrogate little brother. He's so grown up and ahead of his time that it's never like being with a little kid.

Our dads coach us in contrasting ways. Mine doesn't say a lot. Frank senior can be ferocious. He's on his son all the time, telling him what he really thinks. But you could put me and Frank anywhere, and we'd still be desperate to succeed. It's not coincidence. It's not because our dads were footballers or that it's in our bloodline. Frank wants it more than anyone, and so do I.

●

Frank Lampard: Our dads grew up different to us. They had it really hard. We didn't. We were quite well brought-up. We had it nice and cushty. They had different ideas of how to develop us too. Straight after a game I'd get the run-down from my dad on how he thought I'd done. It was pretty harsh. Jamie had it another way.

They'd both come through what was a great academy of football in West Ham. They'd both reference Bobby Moore as a huge influence in terms of how they should act, how they trained, what it takes to be a professional. I think we probably got given those stories in slightly different ways. But the message at the heart of it was the same, and we both took it on board.

I was forever told that I had another load of steps ahead of me to go. I never thought that I'd made it at any stage, and I genuinely mean that. Both our dads had seen talented kids fail. We knew the rules. Unless you worked and did all the tough stuff and behaved well, it could come crashing down at any minute. So when we walked into a club at a young age, neither of us thought, 'I've made it.' You knew what the hierarchy had to be.

I never felt I lost that respect. I remember walking into Manchester City as a player at 36 and being as nervous as back in the day at school. People ask, why are you nervous, you've won 100 England caps, you've won the Champions League. And I'd think, there's David Silva there, I'd better be good. That's what our dads gave us.

Both Jamie and I were obsessive. We didn't let much get in our way. I definitely had it naturally, and then I would see Jamie do it and I'd get what it looked like in real life – the 100 keepy-ups, the hitting the bird cage, being able to do it this way or that way. Because I had two sisters, all those things at home would be done on my own. In those pre-teenage years, seeing somebody else doing that practice, the way he did it and the little tweaks he would put on it, certainly influenced my development.

You don't always want to hang around with a kid five years younger than you at that age. I never felt it was like that with us two. When it came to football, we were out in the back garden talking the same language. I was always asking questions. We were always very open. Jamie would talk about how many times he'd given the ball away, how many touches he'd had. We'd discuss players who were composed in a game, the ones who could pass like quarterbacks. All that sort of stuff was great from my point of view. I think I would have made it anyway, but it helped me so much along the way.

•

Football is my obsession but it's not only footballers that fascinate me. Ian Botham is everywhere on the telly, blowing Australian batsmen away, launching their bowlers into orbit. His bleached mullet has accelerated past that of Glenn Hoddle's and is close to matching Chris Waddle's. He's also turned up in Bournemouth, not for panto, although that will come later, but to come on as a sub up front for Scunthorpe United.

I can't get my head around how someone can play for England in one sport and also be a professional in a totally different one. I can believe he wants to say hello to my dad, because everyone does, but when he says hello to me too, it's like I'm shaking hands with Superman or Han Solo. I imagine myself being interviewed in *Match*. Favourite meal: bacon sandwich. Married: no. Most difficult opponent: Mark Redknapp. Sporting hero: Ian Botham.

The last answer could also be Daley Thompson. The Los

Angeles Olympics are on the telly every time I turn it on during the summer holidays, and Daley is the emperor of the LA Coliseum. I love watching Carl Lewis run, how elegant he is coming round the bend in the 200 metres, how perfectly upright he is in the last 50 of the 100 metres or accelerating down the runway in the long jump. But Daley has something else, the same arrogance but tempered by nonchalance and that look in his eye that says, hold on, we can have more fun here.

Lewis wins four golds across four relatively similar events. Daley wins one gold for being incredible at 10 totally contrasting challenges. Steve Ovett will describe the decathlon as nine Mickey Mouse events followed by a slow 1500 metres. I prefer Ron Pickering's mixture of excitement and disbelief as Daley dismantles the best that West Germany, the USSR and the USA can throw at him. He smashes the 400 metres. He soars in the pole vault. He pulls it out of the bag at the death in the discus. 'It's a better one, it's a better one, it's a better one, it's a better one! And the man comes good, and he's dancing in the circle!'

These are my heroes, the ones who I think deserve it, who have worked themselves into the ground in every training session, not the ones who fluke it or only do it once. It's why I want Steve Davis to beat Dennis Taylor when it comes down to the black in the final frame of the Embassy World Championships, and why Jimmy White's perpetual near-misses at the Crucible are not sob-stories to me but a fair reflection of the gifted but maverick player he is.

I like winners and I want winners to win. Dad picks me up from school one Friday not long after my 11th birthday, and the fuzzy medium-wave commentary on Radio Two is telling us how 17-year-old Boris Becker has beaten Anders Jarryd in four sets to make his first Wimbledon final. They can't quite believe that a wildcard in his first ever All England Championships has got to the final. They talk about it as a triumph. I'm excited – I love the way Becker plays, the dives at the net, the total commitment to getting any ball back – but it's only when he beats Kevin Curren in the final on Sunday afternoon that I put him on my pantheon with Hoddle and Beefy and Daley and The Nugget.

All the time I'm watching them play and what they do afterwards, analysing it and logging it. A couple of weeks later, Dad is playing in a midsummer charity football tournament. There are other retired players there, not least George Best – who is as smiley as ever and comes over to juggle the ball with me – as well as some proper television stars. I'm saying goodbye to George in the marquee – 'You're coming along Jamie, you're a player now' – when I spot the bloke who plays the posh holiday camp manager in *Hi-de-Hi!* on TV.

I like a bit of *Hi-de-Hi!* on a Saturday evening. I know this man is called Jeffrey Fairbrother in the show, but I also know that's not his real name, so when I go over with a pen and paper I ask for his autograph with a careful, 'Excuse me, mister.'

He looks at me like I've come out of a dog's backside.

'Can you sign this for me, please?'

He looks down his nose at me. 'What are you doing in here? This is a grown-ups area, young man. It's not for kids. So no, I won't sign that for you.'

He turns away. I feel as if he's just shrunk me to the height of an Ewok. I look at the back of his jacket, the back of his head, and there's a big gingery lump in my throat.

I want to disappear. I want to cry, but I'm too embarrassed. I want to go home.

I wander around for a bit, booting my ball ahead of me. Dad spots me. 'Alright, maestro?' I tell him what has just happened.

Dad's face goes red. His eyes start flicking about.

'Where the f*** is he?'

He's breathing hard. He's staring over my shoulder towards the marquee.

'I'm gonna knock him out. I'm gonna f***ing kill him.'

Jeffrey Fairbrother will never know how close he came to requiring an updated publicity photo. He has just left, with the sort of timing that probably got him the role on *Hi-de-Hi!* in the first place. But the humiliation stays with me, and it's a lesson too. If I become famous, I think to myself, I'll try my best to sign every autograph. All of them, whatever I'm doing, wherever I am. I will not be Jeffrey Fairbrother.

•

It's not only football that fascinates me. When we go on our first foreign holiday, to a place with tennis courts and a pool on the Algarve, there is a lot of football on the beach with Dad and

Mark. Dad still hasn't worked out that juggling the ball on his shoulders and knees while wearing Speedos does nothing for Mum. But there is tennis, too, and golf, and swimming races. There's always a football in the apartment and within stretching distance, don't get me wrong. The first thing Mark and I do when we arrive is try to find a sports shop so we can spend our holiday money on a new ball and possibly a Lacoste polo shirt each, although our heads are on English opening hours, so there's a lot of hanging around in the blazing heat outside shuttered shops at two in the afternoon and coming back at 7 pm when they finally open again post-siesta.

But the tennis is as competitive as any of the matches at the playing field off Stour Way. It's a sport of disputed line calls even when John McEnroe isn't involved. It turns out to be almost the ideal way to have a fight with your brother. Dad's the same as he is on the table-tennis table back in our garage in Christchurch, or the snooker table in Mark's bedroom. It's the only form of maths I like: adding up how many points I've nicked off Dad before he's beaten me, how many wins across all the different sports I've chalked up over my brother.

Which leads to its own rows and boot-offs.

'Marco, what's the score? Marco, Marco, what's the score?'

Brief pause, massive commotion. 'Argh, Mum, he's lobbed a snooker cue at me!'

So there's competition all year round. And it's paying off, because Dad gets a call from Peter Shreeves at Tottenham later that summer.

'We remember Jamie from when we came down to Bourne-mouth for pre-season training, would he like to come up and train with our youngsters?'

It's not a hard decision to make. And while the journey is a long one, two hours meandering up to Waterloo, we've got the perfect man to look after me when I arrive.

Pop. He's waiting for me on the platform, Glacier Mints in his pocket, grin on his face. Into the orange VW Beetle, all the way across town to Spurs' training ground in Mill Hill. He stays around to watch training – 'Hello, John!', 'Alright, mush?' – and then drives us back to Poplar where Nan has done a porter-house steak and triple-fried chips.

That's good in itself. What happens a week later is like some weird supercharged dream.

'You seem relaxed, would you fancy training with the first team for the session?'

'Yes.'

'Right. You're with Glenn.'

Just me and Glenn. On our own, in our own part of the pitch, both of us with a ball at our feet.

For a while I can only stare at him. Socks round his ankles, tiny blue shorts. Tanned limbs. Shirt untucked, boots with the tongue flapping back over the laces. Navy sweatbands around each wrist.

He knocks the ball to me, all casual touch and bouncing hair. I control it okay – come on, Jamie – and clip it back. He takes it on his left foot mid-air and then volleys it back first time. Left foot, right foot, chest, instep. It doesn't matter where I hit it, he just brings it down from wherever it is.

I start trying to copy him. A few flicks, controlling the ball myself from up high thanks to my patented nail-biting flexibility drill. All the time thinking, I'm 12 years old and I'm chipping balls to Glenn Hoddle.

He's really friendly too, even though all I'm thinking is, don't make him run for any of your passes, Jamie, get them all straight to him, don't make the greatest English midfielder of his time have to dig your pass out of a bush. He offers advice, tells me what he likes and what I need.

'Keep working on that left foot, Jamie. You need both. Practise working on bringing the ball down, doesn't matter where it's arriving, make it yours.'

When he runs, his heels do a strange click together. Back home in Christchurch I try the same thing. I get a pair of sweatbands. I can't go for the socks down, and I can't do the untucked shirt. It's too messy. But when a box of Spurs training kit arrives a week later, I've got the Hummel tracksuit, the Hummel shorts and the Hummel shirt with the chevrons chasing each other across the front. I've even got Hummel boots, with thick cream-coloured moulded studs.

Hummel will surpass themselves with the kit they make for Denmark a year later, the red and white shirt worn by Preben Elkjaer, Michael Laudrup, Morten Olsen, Allen Simonson and the rest of that dashing side that take the 1984 European Championships by storm. I'll love that kit and that team too. For now though, it's all about Glenn.

6

THE DARK ARTS

With the games I play comes a method of trying to deal with the turmoil and anxieties they can bring. I'm tight before a game. I'm tense. It matters to me, and I want to do it right. It's not just kids' football. It's my football.

The night before a match I will take everything out of my bag that I have carefully put in there that morning. Boots, polished so that they shimmer. Shinpads, wiped clean and with the Velcro strap fastened so it doesn't catch on anything else. Shorts, folded into quarters. Shirt, folded with the sleeves tucked back behind and the badge and sponsor showing. I take them out, check them, and put them carefully back in. The bag goes on my bedroom floor, just by the door. I want everything in place and everything controlled. Same tea that night, same breakfast in the morning. If Mum has cooked something else, if we're out of the right milk for my cereal, the apprehension takes hold and begins to grow.

Mum is a planner too. She can instinctively understand why I want to lay my kit out properly. Dad has always insisted that my boots are perfect. If they're dirty, he'll never do them.

He tells me they are the tools of my trade, and that it's up to me to look after them.

And so I enjoy cleaning them. Chipping the little dried rings of mud and grass off from around the studs with a knife, wiping the dirt off the upper with a damp cloth, working in the polish with a soft brush and then buffing and polishing with a stiffer one. I find the process and the ritual therapeutic. In a few years' time, I'll be in the cramped boot room at Dean Court, one of my duties as an apprentice to look after the boots of the first-team stars, making them shine as if they have spotlights lighting them up.

That's all before we even set off for the game. When we kick off, it's all about my first pass, my first touch. Just get my first pass away and keep it simple. Easy ball, give it, go for the return.

I don't know what I think is going to happen if I don't. I know it won't somehow take away my ability, or shrink time so that I no longer have 89 minutes in which to demonstrate all the things I can do. Sometimes there are unspoken fears that sit just below the surface. You look for them and they swim away or fade into the depths.

Mark takes me to a house party at one of his mate's. I'm the youngest one there by three years, but I've always preferred hanging out with his friends, and I know most of them pretty well. There's a few on the stolen cans of lager but that doesn't bother me. It's not in my world and holds no interest.

What no-one has told me is that someone has brought a

VHS tape of *The Exorcist*. I'm not ready for it and I'm not ready for what it does to me.

I am genuinely terrified. I want to get off the sofa and get out of the house, but I can't. I don't know why I'm watching it. I'm frozen, in this horrible new world where there's the devil and possession and stuff that you can't control and can't explain.

It ruins me that night and it ruins me for weeks to come. I can't get it out of my head. Now it's not enough that the walls of my bedroom are painted sunshine yellow. To get to sleep I have to have the light on too.

The first time I watch *Jaws,* that won't leave me either. For years, when I'm in the shallows off Boscombe beach or Alum Chine, I'll be convinced that a great white is slicing towards me from the deep, even when the only shark ever spotted off the coast of Dorset is a confused basking shark, and only then once a decade. Everyone of my age feels the same about *Jaws,* which makes it easier to joke about and push away. Memories of the things I've seen on *The Exorcist* will terrorise me for years. At one point, I'll genuinely think I need therapy. Telling myself that's it's only a film doesn't help, in the same way that if a child is scared of burglars there's no use telling them that no bad guys can get in, because they'll just imagine the burglar knows openings and routes that their parents don't.

When Dad is down at Dean Court I'll go with him, because there's nowhere I feel safer than with him. But it's an old, decrepit stadium, and when Dad has to work, and sends me off

from his small office on the corner of the main stand to enter-
tain myself for a couple of hours, the noises and fears chase me
down the corridors and dark passages.

Under the stands are cramped walkways. The brick foun-
dations and old wooden beams stick out at strange angles,
casting weird shadows from the occasional florescent light
or the floodlights burning up above. There are hidden nooks
and crannies and there is always the scuttling of rats as I run
through, ball at my feet.

To keep the fear from taking over, I set myself tasks. See if
you can dribble all the way through the stand without the ball
or an elbow touching a wall. If I can't, I have to go back to the
start. All the time the scrabbling of rats and the lights flick-
ering through. When I see the pies for matchdays delivered
with just a thin piece of Clingfilm stretched over them, I want
to run and tell all the fans who'll be buying them, 'There's rats
everywhere, they'll have been all over them . . .'

I hear other things. I dribble into the away dressing room
and it's full of apprentices, cleaning up and arguing and
whingeing. It falls silent as soon as they see me, because they
know I'm the manager's son, and some of the complaining
has been about what the gaffer is or isn't doing. I develop the
ability to fade conversations out, to ignore talk that I know isn't
meant for me. A ghost under the stands, alone with his ball,
keeping his head down.

When the stadium comes alive on the Saturday of a home
game, it's all so different. People everywhere, red scarves and
bobble-hats, all animated talk and shouts. The smell of fags

and beer on supporters' breath, the corridors bright with light and songs.

When the final whistle goes and they all drain out onto Thistlebarrow Road and Littledown Avenue and the suburban streets beyond, it's even better. Mark and I are allowed out on the pitch with the match ball, right into the home goal-mouth, nets still up. It's like sneaking onto the stage at a gig the moment the band has walked off. There are still the indentations of a thousand studs in the hard rolled mud, strips of white tape torn off the tops of socks at the final whistle. There are fag ends blowing about on the terraces and scrunched plastic cups. The floodlights illuminate it all for us because Dad has told John the groundsman to leave them on. We dart around the penalty box and try and replicate the best goal that Bournemouth have scored. John waits beyond the touchline with his fork and bucket, chuntering away, wanting us off the pitch so he can get off home too.

Dad is never awkward with us when the club's staff or players are around. Brian Clough might refer to his son Nigel as 'the number 9', but with us it's Mark and Jamie or Marky and Maestro. His present provides a footballing playground and his past offers a route into my future.

Everton have called him up about me. There are connections there through Jimmy Gabriel, Dad's old head coach in Seattle, now helping him out here in Bournemouth. In his playing days, Jimmy had been a midfield general in the Everton team that won the league and FA Cup in the 1960s. He had moved on from Goodison Park when Howard Kendall had emerged as a player, and now Kendall is back as a manager and building maybe the best team in Everton's history.

Dad is insistent that it's not the usual sort of try-out, that they're not testing me to see if I'm good enough.

'You don't go on trial when you're a good schoolboy player, Jamie. You're being wanted by clubs. You're going to look at them and make your mind up where you want to go. You wasn't going on trial with Tottenham, you ain't going on trial now.'

It certainly doesn't begin like a trial. Everton are playing down in London that weekend, so rather than Dad driving me from Bournemouth to Liverpool, or me getting two Inter-City trains for five hours, I get the train to Waterloo again to be picked up this time not by Pop in his orange Beetle but by the Everton team coach – with the Everton team on board.

It's quite something, walking up the steep steps of a luxury coach and seeing, as you say hello to the driver, the league leaders laid out in front of you: Kendall and his assistant Colin Harvey in the front two seats, then Andy Gray, Trevor Steven, and Graeme Sharp. Looking further down the aisle to see Peter Reid, Gary Stevens and Neville Southall.

I sit exactly where they tell me to sit. All around there is swearing, matey arguing and relatively detailed chat about girls and what specific ones might have done. I'm nervous but I'm not scared. I'm used to this. It's all familiar – maybe not the calibre of player, but the way players talk. And there might be half the England team here, but Bobby Moore treats me like a nephew and George Best tells me I'm a player.

I filter out what I'm not meant to hear, just as I do in the away dressing room at Dean Court. It's hard not to stare a little bit at Peter Reid, sitting down the back with Paul Bracewell and Kevin Sheedy, because I think he's a fabulous player. There's a physical side to him but he can do everything. But some of the players do talk to me – Adrian Heath, and Steven, and Gray. I know they've heard of my dad, even though he wasn't a super-star player and hasn't yet managed outside Division Three, but he's like a reference from an employer. Harry is one of us, this is Harry's boy, so he's one of us too.

Later, I will have interest from West Ham. But while they seem almost to take it for granted that I want to go there, with all the family connections, it never feels as comfortable close to the roots as it does on Merseyside. There's the Jimmy Gabriel thing. There's Everton's youth officer, Ray Minshull, an old Liverpool goalkeeper and a real gent. I've heard all the stories about Alan Ball and how good he was in midfield as a teenager and what he did alongside Bobby and Geoff Hurst in the World Cup Final, and there's the fact the club puts me up with Colin Harvey's mum and dad in Fazackerley. The Harveys are lovely people. They make me feel at home rather than 250 miles away from it. I get picked up by their son each morning and taken down to the training ground.

When I get home I send a thank-you card. In return the club sends me tracksuits, official club Umbro t-shirts. Ray sends me letters, typed out neatly on official Everton note-paper. The badge is top right – *Nil satis nisi optimum*, nothing but the best is good enough – and the club's name in blue and white print top right.

Dear Jamie,

Thank you so very much for your card and I am so pleased that the tracksuit was suitable for you.

As far as we are concerned Jamie, you can come to Bellefield any time you wish and we shall be delighted to look after you again.

Whenever you are available, please do give us a ring and I will make the necessary arrangements and you can stay with Mrs Harvey again if you so wish.

I shall be getting in touch with your dad in the near future regarding another visit for you Jamie and in the meantime – enjoy yourself.

I always seem to be looking for the Bournemouth results since you came up and I am pleased to see that they are still well in the hunt.

Cheerio for now, give my regards to your mum and dad and I look forward to seeing you again shortly.

Best wishes,

Ray Minshull, youth development officer

Everything about the club impresses me. Everything they do, they do right. It feels a very special football club, and my affection for it will stay with me for the rest of my life.

Jimmy Gabriel gives me something else too. He's a lovely man, Jimmy – battle-hardened, tough on the field, receding hair but a nice size for a player, stocky legs. He's also incredibly kind and gentle away from the pitch. Dad loves him for this, as an assistant, but he loves him too because he was such a good player. And Jimmy takes a shine to me, not because I'm the gaffer's son but because he can see something in me. You're going to be a player too, this is what you need to know if you're going to be a footballer. I'm going to add another string to your bow.

What he teaches me is how to go over the top of the ball. He teaches me how to hurt someone.

This isn't about being vindictive, and it definitely isn't about skill or finesse. It's about protecting yourself from what others will definitely try to do to you. There will be a moment a couple of years later, when I'm 16 and playing my first pre-season game for the Bournemouth first team, when a player in his early thirties tells me he's going to break my legs. That's how it will be. There will also be players on my side whose job it is to look after young midfielders. One will whisper in my ear, 'Don't worry, I'll get him . . .' Two minutes later, the one who's done me will be carried off on a stretcher.

I'm already very good with my hands. I've watched Gazza at Newcastle, and I know he's going to Spurs too. Gazza is brilliant at getting his arms up and his hands in people's faces, not to hurt them but because it disorientates an opponent if you stick your fingers in their face as they're coming in at you from the side. You're just keeping them away. You're giving yourself that yard so you can play. So as soon as anyone comes in at me, my first thought is, I'm going to put my fingers in your face, and you're staying at arm's length.

Jimmy had been a fine midfielder. He knows that my dad,

as a tricky right-winger, would never have had to worry about this. So as much as he's telling me how to bend the ball into the top corner, he's teaching me the intricacies of how to look after myself by going over the top of the ball.

This is how it works. There's two of you going for the same ball. As you come together, you turn your body slightly away from your opponent, with your studs up, and just catch the top of the ball and roll your foot over it and follow through hard onto their shin. I go in the garden and I work on my shooting technique. But I'm also rolling my foot over the ball.

It seems brutal but it will save me. It will save me when people are whispering in my ear that I'm Harry's son and so I'm going to get it. It will save me when there are rumours that I'm going to Liverpool and defenders who have spent a career fighting their way through the lower leagues don't like it. It will save me when I have long hair and have a nice pass and a face that looks anything but ready for all this. They won't realise that even though I haven't got the reputation for it, I can still do what needs to be done.

And I love it. I love learning about the dark arts because it's all football. If I want to be a footballer, I have no choice. This is what you have to do. It's self-preservation. Without the attitude you can't bring the artistry. It's a part of my game that will give me that extra edge.

This is my education. The formal stuff is now being taken care of at Twynham Comprehensive, two miles away down Fairmile Road, past the hospital and the chippie and right onto Sopers Lane.

I haven't become any keener on school than I was at Christchurch Primary, but again I've got lucky with the teachers. In place of the relentlessly competitive Malteser-dispensing Mr Walker are Mr Jackson and Mr Broadwell, both PE teachers, both who understand what I'm like as soon as I get there.

It's a big school, blue metal gates leading through the thick privet hedge into the car park and then the red-brick classrooms beyond. The playing fields are away over to the left, running up to Willow Drive and the roundabout beyond. The uniform is standard mid-eighties uncool: blue blazer with school badge on the pocket, blue tie with diagonal stripes, white shirt, dark grey trousers. No trainers unless doing PE, which I am most of the time.

Mr Broadwell is a strong man. He's good at hockey and he can throw the javelin an absolute mile. He loves a vest and flip-flops, and he'll push me at rugby and athletics.

Mr Jackson is a proper footballer. He's only 12 years older than us, a really nice creative midfielder, and when Fareham play Bournemouth in the FA Cup he's in their team and there are reporters down the school wanting to talk to the PE teacher who's trying to beat the dad of one of his pupils.

Both Mr Jackson and Mr Broadwell know I don't like school. There are other members of staff there who clearly think I'm a nuisance, who can't wait to get me out of the place. The maths teacher Mr Tykocki loses his temper in a flash. We have a cookery teacher called Miss Bonar, which is as hilarious to us as it is tiresome to her. She's really nice, always kind to me, and she understands that I'm a bit cheeky. She'll be the reason I end up attempting a GCSE in Home Economics. But she also takes no prisoners, and she knows my future is not in catering. I'm sent to the corner most weeks to make pineapple upside-down cake or apple crumble. An hour later the rest of the class have finished a full à la carte menu, and I'm emerging with a basic pudding thinking I'm Keith Floyd.

Mr Jackson and Mr Broadwell understand I want to play football. Unlike other teachers, they're okay with that. I never get told by them the old line that no-one ever makes it as a footballer. They believe in me. They just think I will. Jamie, do your school work and you'll be okay. Mr Jackson will put me in my place every now and then, but that's fine. He knows when to push me, when to pull me up on being cheeky.

We both love all sports and we have the same sense of humour. He's the cool teacher that all kids want but most don't have. When Dad is late in picking me up because he has stuff going on down at the stadium, I'll stay behind with Mr Jackson and we'll play badminton. Straightaway I can see how it's going to help me with football. I'm gangly, and this makes me sharp. I'm on my toes, darting forwards and back like I'm jockeying an opponent, going sideways and backpedalling and all of it explosive.

I'll spend hours playing with him, way after the final bell has gone.

'Mr Jackson, my dad's not here again. Fancy a game?'

'Jamie, I've got marking to do.'

'Just a quick one.'

'Oh, go on then.'

An hour and a half later and we're still at it. For me, it's like a World Cup Final. Both of us hate losing, so we fight for every point. His favourite tactic is to pretend to go long and then take all the pace off his shot and dink it just over the net, with me on my knees, sliding on the floor.

There is a time when I'm enjoying these games so much that I genuinely think I'm going to turn pro. I'm deluded – a half-decent player would clean me out – but I'm fascinated by the tactics, by how the shuttlecock goes faster than a tennis ball, at least for a bit, at how most people grip the racquet like they're holding a frying pan, rather than with their wrist closed so they can get a proper smash in. I ask for a racquet that Christmas and get a beauty, a Yonex with a white cover. With my Christmas money I accessorise that with a bigger cover that can take a couple of shuttlecocks and has a strap so you can casually sling it over your shoulder. Jamie Redknapp, international badminton superstar. In my head.

I don't have many mates. I'm weirder than I realise. I keep away from girls because none of them are interested in football.

There is someone who understands me. Alan Bungay plays right midfield to my centre-mid. He finds the pale blue school football shirts as scratchy as I do. He lives round the corner and is as happy spending every single break-time doing skills as I am.

We do a motor mechanics class together. He's actually

quite good. He's learning something. Me, slightly less so. There is a moped in the classroom for us to study, which gives me an idea. I tell Alan to keep chatting to the teacher to distract him. It's quite exhilarating, driving a moped round the school playing fields while everyone stares out of the window, although it's disappointing that Alan is no longer keeping his side of the bargain and distracting the teacher. I get away with it. I always seem to get away with it.

We become a good little team. When one of us spots a furious Mr Tykocki coming round the corner, we give it the same shout as on the pitch. 'Man on!' When there is trouble in a game because one of us has said something to make the other one laugh, there is always Andy Fagan to come to the rescue. He's tall, ginger and hard, although opposition players don't always understand that straightaway.

'Oi, ginger bollocks!'

'Mate, say that again and I'll knock you out.'

'Ginger bollocks!'

Sparked clean out, gone before his backside hit the floor.

Perhaps because of his bearing, Andy goes out with Joanne Lamont, the prettiest girl in our year. Debbie Waddington is also very highly thought of, but I'm not involved. I get asked out but I'm too shy, and anyway I'm not that bothered. What would we talk about?

Both me and Alan are also in the school basketball team. Mr Jackson picks it, so we're okay. He trusts us. We are playing away one evening, all packed into the school minibus, when Mr Jackson goes down the wrong street and starts making a three-point turn. I'm on the back seat with Alan, so he asks me to look out the back for him, guide him out.

'Not a problem, Mr Jackson.'

I look out the window. What's that over there? Is that a football pitch? I wonder who plays . . .

Crash. We're halfway across someone's drive. We're all the way through their concrete pillar.

'Mr Jackson? I think you'd better stop now . . .'

●

Alan Bungay: Jamie got away with that. Jamie got away with everything. I remember standing by the minibus, when it had been patched up, on the day we got our school reports. They had a note on them of how many times you'd been absent that year. Mine said one. Jamie's said 56.

So 56 days when he'd gone off to play football, and no-one seemed to mind.

Everything was a competition with Jamie. Badminton, basketball, crossbar challenge. We were doing well as a football team, and we played a side down in Exeter in one of the national Cups. After the game, an old boy came over. He said he was a scout from Exeter City, and would Jamie like to come for a trial? And Jamie looked at him and said, 'Nah, I'm alright mate, I'm probably going to sign for Tottenham, thanks.' And just walked off.

●

I don't want to be a footballer for the money. That hasn't entered my head. I want to be playing and I want to be answering the Q&As in *Match* and *Shoot!* I want to be on *A Question of Sport*, preferably on Ian Botham's team rather than Bill Beaumont's, because Bill might have won a Grand Slam with England but Beefy can do absolutely everything.

I have more of my answers ready for the football magazines. Favourite TV programme: *The A-Team*. Favourite item of clothing: Fila tracksuit. Mark is now so into his clothes that he's passing stuff on to me before he's worn it out. He's going quite football casual, so a pastel Best Company sweatshirt is the first thing I get my hands on. When we go up to east London, Pop will take us to Roman Road, so we'll see what knock-offs there are in the market, pop into a brilliant shop called Dice that does all the gear – Farah, Pringle, Stone Island.

Mark's ahead of the game. What he says goes with his mates. When he gets asked to do a bit of modelling, there is simultaneous huge respect and massive levels of piss-taking. He starts going up to Harold Hill, further out towards Essex way, to get rarer stuff. He does day-trips on the ferry from Poole to Cherbourg to pick up Adidas Challenger tracksuits, because French sports shops have them stocked in different colours to back home.

He starts messing around with his hair. First he gets it permed at the back, like late-period Kevin Keegan. He knows he's taking a risk because when he comes back into the house that morning he sort of creeps in, pleased with himself but also slightly bashful. Dad is on him straightaway.

'Mark, what you done with your hair?'

Looking around at the rest of us, Dad with a big grin.

'Look what Mark's done. He's had a Keegan!'

But he carries it off, Mark, he always carries it off. When he ditches the perm and grows it long instead, switching the vibe from footballer born in Scunthorpe to footballer playing for Roma or Fiorentina, it looks great. Most kids don't want to stand out. Most boys aren't ready for long hair and all the teasing it will bring, all the chat about you looking like a girl or being gay, all those stupid clichés. Mark styles it out.

These things – the clothes, the hair, the good times – do distract him. He's a good footballer but he doesn't have my obsessions. And he's fine with that. He enjoys those distractions. He's being true to himself. And he's still looking after me. It can't be easy for him, having a dad so well known, having a little brother being chased by Spurs and Everton. When I flip it round in my head and have Mark as the player everyone's talking about and me having to find other areas to shine, I can't handle it. I know there's no way I could be as nice to him as he is to me.

You watch your brother and you watch your mates and you learn all the time. You learn the most sometimes from getting things wrong. I'm out in Bournemouth with one of the apprentices at the club. He's only a year older than me, but he seems to know more about the world, not least because he's from Liverpool. He's a funny lad to hang around with; he can make you laugh, and he's always up to stuff, but he will push you too, find out what upsets you, see if he can rattle you and then pretend it was all a big joke and that you shouldn't really mind.

We're wandering round the shops, no money to spend, talking about the latest clothes Mark has bagged. I mention how much I like Swatch watches. A couple of kids at school have got them, and they look really cool. Good different more than weird different.

This lad winks at me. 'I'll get you one of them.'

I don't quite understand what he means. We've got about three quid between us. But then we're in a jeweller's shop, and he's asking the woman behind the counter to bring out the tray of Swatches. And as she's showing them to us, I suddenly realise: he's going to steal one. He's going to nick one, right in front of me.

I am not a hard kid. I might love watching Mike Tyson, mesmerised by VHS recordings of his latest first round knock-out victory on the sofa with Mum and Dad, making mental notes to discuss his style with Pop next time I'm up at his. But I'm not Mike Tyson. I've grown up in Christchurch, not Bedford-Stuyvesant. Tyson calls himself the Baddest Man on the Planet. I'm a goody-goody, pretty much. I also admire Nick Faldo and his Pringle-based wardrobe. I loved it when he won the Open at Muirfield in 1987 by parring every single hole in the final round.

I'm not rock and roll. Tyson was arrested 38 times before he turned 13. I've never been in any sort of trouble with the police. Until now.

I watch this kid do it. Point to another set of watches further down the counter. Wait until the woman looks that way. Reach out, grab a Swatch, stick it in his coat pocket and walk out.

Oh God. That's all I can think as we walk out. Up the road, his hand back in his pocket, holding out the Swatch to me. 'There you go.' And then another hand, this time with force, grabbing my shoulder, stopping me dead. Oh God.

'You! You're coming with us . . .'

I crumble, of course I do. I'm the easiest case ever for the store detective. I've got the watch in my hand and an expression on my face of panic and shame. They take my name and address. I have less natural fight in me than Tyson's little toe, and now all that's gone too.

All I can think is, this is the end. My dad's going to kill me. He's going to stop taking me down Dean Court. He's going to ground me. He's given me a chance and I've let him down.

I get home. I'm in bits. Mum spots it, of course she does, but she's already answered the phone to the police. She got there before Dad, and it's her now who takes me into the kitchen and sits me down. She's soft and lovely but she's also firm.

'Don't ever be involved with anything like that again. You understand?'

Me nodding. Can't speak.

'We won't tell your dad, but you need to promise me that. Okay?'

I promise. Dad never finds out, not that year, not when I'm 16, not when I'm a grown man. Mum keeps her word, and I keep mine.

And so the football moves on. You're not allowed to sign apprenticeship terms with a professional club until you are 14 years old. I love Everton, but it's a long way off. I'd have to go there by myself. West Ham are interested, but it still doesn't feel right. They never make me feel welcome like the other clubs do. They're asking Dad all the time if I'm going to sign with them, even though he tells them it's my decision and that he trusts me. So when Spurs academy manager John Moncur arrives at the house on the morning of my birthday, and Dad calls me downstairs from the frame of snooker I'm playing with Mark, I'm not shocked and I'm quite pleased. Tottenham have got a good group of schoolboys. I get on well with them. There's a young lad from the north-east called Shaun Murray who's a really good young player, a nice midfielder to play alongside. I like John Moncur. He makes you laugh, and he's got football in every inch of him. His son will play for Spurs and Swindon and then West Ham, for a long time, under Dad, and his grandsons will be professional players too. He sends me tracksuits, he sends me boots. It's not a hard decision for me to make.

It's only on the fringes that I'm aware of being steered away from other options. There is another club that is interested in me, and that has a good track record of developing youngsters. There are also rumours about one of the youth coaches there – nothing anyone can prove, nothing concrete, just rumours and whispers along football's bush telegraph. I'm barely aware of any of it, although those rumours will grow louder over the years.

There's just a sense of an immense grey cloud on the horizon. Don't go into the shadows. Stay with Tottenham. You can trust them. Boys are okay there.

•

Simon Jackson: As his PE teacher, I could see that Jamie enjoyed every sport we made him try. He played fly-half in the school rugby team in the lower age groups. He would have been a good player. He could kick and pass. Then he got to year nine when kids fill out, and it became less of a good idea putting the school football team's midfield maestro out there.

He found school football hard. He was used to playing balls in to players who could handle it in tight spaces and under pressure. Our full-backs couldn't. He played like he had wing mirrors on. He could see the whole game happening around him. It was all very subtle: when to play it first time, when to help it round the corner, how to spot a run. When some of his team-mates couldn't see the same things, he struggled to get his head round it. Schoolboy football at that point was smashing through three men and banging it forward. It was about getting the ball forward to a quick lad up front, not playing through midfield. That got him frustrated.

He wasn't cocky. He had a lovely sense of humour and was fun to be with. But he was bloody good to watch. He acquired physical skills very easily. He could take stuff on board having been in and around the game. Some guys get to the pro level because they're quick, others because they're really explosive. Jamie got there by being technically so good.

As kids get good at something, they want to do more and more of it. I can still see him now, keeping a Hacky Sack in the air with his feet for what seemed like forever. It was almost like he could catch with his feet.

7

THE PECKING ORDER

If you can play, you're in demand. Each year the Football Association selects 16 kids to go to their National School of Excellence at Lilleshall. Michael Owen, Sol Campbell and Jamie Carragher will all pass through the golden gates. It's a slightly strange set-up – a stately home that's 150 years old and looks a bit like a haunted house, with a drive that's a mile and a half long and a canteen with stone columns like a Roman temple dedicated to young gods – and it's in the middle of nowhere, unless you're actually from rural Staffordshire. The nearest actual town is Telford, and you get sent to a school in a little village nearby that isn't allowed to pick you for their first XI, which seems harsh.

Alf Ramsey's England might have stayed there before the 1966 World Cup, but Dad is not convinced it's a good idea for me. Two years away from home, having nothing to do once the working day is finished, missing my mum and dad and brother. I don't think I'll get in anyway. Not at this time. There are better players than me, or different players to me. I'm not quite what they're looking for. They want pure big and strong. There are kids with hairs under their arms and all over their legs. Dad looks at one of them, 5 ft 11 in, in his mid-teens, quick, powerful, bashing all the kids about.

'Hang about maestro, in another two or three years, where's he going to be? I've known a million England schoolboy internationals, down the years, none of them ever made it.'

When you make it to the last 20 kids in the selection process, you have to sign a form confirming that you'll go if you get in. Lilleshall don't make a fuss when I write a letter to politely say no to the next stage of selection. They will also turn down my cousin Frank and Steven Gerrard, so they clearly have riches. And England Schoolboys aren't particularly bothered either. I get picked for one game, against Northern Ireland at Carrow Road. We win 5–0. And I never get picked again. I don't even get a call. Not a letter, not a word to my dad.

It might be the only real rejection I face as a footballer, but it still makes me think: right, I'll show you. It also sharpens my mind on what I'll have to do to make it.

Now, when Dad's driving me to Twynham, we both edge towards the same outcome.

'You don't fancy school today, do you Jamie?'

'Not really, Dad.'

'You want to come training?'

'Yeah, I do, yeah.'

'Come on, then. Just don't tell your mum, yeah?'

So I've skipped school, and I'm in with the kids who don't need to be at school anymore because they're older than me. And one of the first apprentices I meet is a tough one called

Dave Morris, who I can tell when he looks at me that he wants to kick me up in the air.

Dave is different. His mum and dad aren't around. Dual heritage in a white kids' town, no-one to keep an eye on him or show him the way. He's got brothers, but they're all scrapping for themselves. No lifts to training, no nice detached house on Old Barn Road. Not for one second, when we're thrown together in five-a-sides or two-on-twos or one-on-ones, does he give a monkey's who I am, that I'm at Spurs and that my dad is the manager. It's about him and how far he can get himself. He only knows how to play one way. And that is to kick everything that moves.

Terry Shanahan, the youth coach for Bournemouth, spots this early on, and immediately decides this is exactly what I need. Terry pushes us, so whenever there's a one *v* one, it's me *v* Dave. And it's brutal. It's the closest I'll ever get to being in a boxing ring. Flat-out from the first whistle and it never relents – a small space, two small goals, each player trying to beat the other, to get past him with skill or strength, except when you get past him that's only the start, because they're chasing you back and getting a foot in, or an elbow, or sliding in and clattering you. If they score, you just start again. Never a moment with your foot on the ball, having a breather. Never standing there while someone else does the running, or relying on someone else to slide the ball home. It's all of you, all of the time.

The other lads stop what they're doing to watch. You don't want to be humiliated, so you can't stop. You arrive at tiredness and go straight through it. You've got lactic acid stiffening your legs. You want to crawl. You can't. You're now at a place that no-one in life gets to very often, because why would they? Beyond exhaustion, still fighting, still turning and going again.

Dave understands what his assets are. He's not going to dance past people with a swerve and a trick. Instead, he has a will to win that's almost scary. You can see it in his eyes: if you let me nail you, I am going to absolutely nail you.

I love it. I want him to kick lumps out of me, because that's exactly what's going to happen to me in matches. I have to work out how hard I can push him, because if I say something smart-arsed or go too far, he'll knock my head off. You know you're in trouble when he looks at you all serious and says, 'Leave it, mush.' That means I should clear off sharpish. There's me and there's Dean Giddings, who's from south-east London and a lovely midfielder, and because Dave is becoming like a bonus big brother to us, we'll sometimes be pulling faces and getting up to something behind his back, and he always spots it, and he always makes out he wants to kill us.

We don't argue or fight. We respect what we can do and we respect how much of ourselves we give to it. If you're Dave's mate, he's your mate and that's that. Being older than me, he also has a protective eye when we're up against others. He'll sit alongside me in midfield. If anyone on the other team kicks me, he's straight over. When Dave tackles you, you stay tackled.

Those battles forge us into a real tight-knit group. We're from backgrounds that couldn't be more different but we're aiming for the same thing and we've got the same determination to get there. When each training session is over, we head in contrasting directions: I get in a nice car with Dad and go home to my own bedroom and a big garden, a snooker table and table-tennis. Dave walks back across town to his digs on Knole Road, two to a small room, nothing to do but fall into trouble. Absolute carnage, all day long.

•

Dave Morris: We would go over to Jamie's house sometimes, just for a bit of escapism. To watch a big telly, to sit on a comfy sofa. But it was a double-edged sword because we had our actual boss sitting there with us. You wanted to hang out with your mates, Jamie and Mark, get away from Knole Road. But as soon as you started messing about, you'd spot Harry and get scared.

He could be fearsome at times, Harry. He could spot an atmosphere in a heartbeat. Let me tell you something as an outsider: those three Redknapp males are all the same. I spent a lot of time with all of them, and they can go from the nicest people in the world to just cutting you off at the ankles in a heartbeat. Peas in a pod. They'll come back to you, but in that moment, you've gone.

Jamie hated losing. I've never met anyone in my life who got that bad, so moody, so likely to get the hump. We'd be over at the house, and someone would beat him at snooker. We'd want to give him some shit, partly because it didn't happen very often and partly because that's what we all did. But we'd know what his reaction was going to be, and we'd know that if Harry heard it all going off then he'd come charging in too. You'd be edging closer and closer to the wall, waiting for hell to break loose.

But Jamie would get over it quickly. He never carried on, even if he never wanted to lose at anything. It wouldn't be a day-long paddy. And you could see him processing it. With his dad being who his dad is, you could see him getting used to keeping stuff to himself. He could box up how he was feeling and move on.

And that's why he could make it work at Liverpool, despite all the pressure of that record transfer fee and his age and the family name. He boxed it up and put it away. He could do the football obsession without obsessing about all the stuff that came with it.

•

So this is me at 15. Going up to London to train with Spurs on a couple of evenings, supposed to be at school the rest of the time, spending most of it instead training with the apprentices at Bournemouth, as if I'm one of them.

Of course, I shouldn't be there. I'm not old enough. I'm signed to schoolboy terms with Spurs, not Bournemouth. I should be at Twynham Comprehensive. But there's not much 'should' when your dad's the manager, when your favourite teacher's more like a mate, and when everyone knows you're going to end up there anyway.

When we play matches, I know that Dave will be there too. I know that I can throw myself about a bit, because he'll step in if it goes off. I'm not dirty. I won't take liberties. But if I get the hump, if I'm angry, I'll put the tackles in the way Jimmy Gabriel has shown me. I've got a side to me too. I'm also well aware of Dad's other side and how you don't want to end up on it. I see it in the eyes of the youth team, when they're in the dressing room and Terry Shanahan is talking and caning certain players for their attitude, and no-one's looking at him because Dad is in the corner watching it all and it's his temper they're really scared of. Everyone praying that it won't be them who he would pick to have a go at.

In time we will all realise that it will help us. Football managers are not going to dance around. If they think you've messed up, they'll tell you. They'll shout it at you. They'll scream. And you have to take it and not carry it over into the next day, or else you'll go under. It's survival of the fittest, and we all want to be among the ones who make it through.

There's no in-between with Dad. He can destroy someone with a few words or he can make them feel like they can walk on water. When he's happy he loves everyone. He'd adopt the world if he could. With me, it's the look he sends over. Nothing said, just a stare and gritted teeth. That's enough. Better liven up here, Jamie.

If I don't get an easy ride, Mark gets the toughest time by a long mile. Dad's on him all the time. Maybe it's the eldest son thing, maybe it's because him and Dad are even closer in character. Mark just soaks it up. He's turned into a really nice right-sided defender, but when he injures his ankle, no-one seems to believe it's as bad as he says. The physio can't find enough so Dad tells him to keep playing on it, even though Mark is telling anyone who will listen that there's something seriously up.

No-one wants to answer back. One lad tries something and the growl erupts and that lad gets it and so does Dave, just for standing near him. A kid called Sean Cope isn't doing enough in one game and Dad comes in at half-time and absolutely flips.

You all understand the pecking order at a football club. The manager defers to the chairman, at least in front of him. All the other adults defer to the manager, unless he's lost the dressing room, in which case the mutinies start small and silent and then develop into open warfare. The senior players – the ones over 30, the ones who have been at the club the longest or had the most impressive careers elsewhere – are the next most powerful. Then it's the playmakers, the most influential younger ones on the pitch.

Us lot? We're right down at the bottom. We're not even adults. We're dogsbodies. We're human training cones. We're cleaners. Some of the time we're invisible, at least until we do something that someone higher up the food chain decides is wrong, at which point everyone wants to know where we are.

There is no glamour. We train in King's Park, right next to the stadium. It's an actual park, used by members of the public. You spend the first 10 minutes of each session flicking the dogshit off what might work as a pitch, or trying to find a patch of grass that is actually grass rather than mud. Half of the time we use the bumpy old gravel pitch that on match days becomes a car park, and we slip and we slide and the ball bounces all over the place. There's the athletics track on one side and the cricket pitch across King's Park Drive beyond the trees, in front of the café, but you're only allowed on the outfield by the far fence, and only then if you're lucky.

One of my jobs is to clean the boots of Luther Blissett. Luther is a big name for Bournemouth, spearhead of Graham Taylor's Watford team that came up to the top flight and finished second behind Liverpool in Division One in 1983, getting to the Cup Final a year later to be beaten by Howard Kendall's Everton.

Luther has played for AC Milan. He's played for England, and he's scoring around a goal every two games for Dad, which makes him pretty much the most senior of all the senior players at the club. He can almost touch the top of the ladder, whereas I'm clinging to the bottom rung, which is why I'm cleaning his boots.

He has a pair of lovely soft Puma Kings, and he wants them perfect. He also likes them a little wet before games, so they're even softer, but trying to get the shine he wants out of them when they're not dry is almost impossible. I spend hours in the tiny boot room, cloth held in my right hand, left hand shoved inside the boot, my arm absolutely killing me. I'll take the boots to him in the home dressing room, and he'll look at them, toss them back and say, 'Get them shinier.'

There will come a time, in a few years, when I'm breaking

into the first team and playing just behind Luther, and I'll still be cleaning his boots. He'll still look at them and toss them back and tell me to get them shinier. I'll be nodding, thinking, we kick off in half an hour, maybe I need to get my own boots sorted.

I'll work out that he does it to relax me, to keep my mind off the actual match, because while he's hard on me he's always fair. And his movement up front is outstanding. I'm never going to be a target man but I can see all the little tricks he has, how he pulls off the biggest of the two centre-backs and onto the smaller one, how he times his runs so he doesn't overshoot the front post and have to angle his header or flick back across, how he'll start going near post and then switch back with the defender already committed and chasing the ball.

The pecking order all makes sense to me because you can't argue with the reputations of those ahead of you, and even if you did they'd quickly shove you back in your spot. Dad has signed Ian Bishop from Carlisle, and he's a beautiful midfielder to watch, all sweet passing and vision. He's a proper Scouser, lots of chat, likes his clothes, and although his hair isn't as long as it will get in his pomp under Dad at West Ham, it's on its way.

Bish can get the ball in midfield and hit a floating pass that will land on a daisy. He never looks like he's running. He glides round the pitch. It's almost as if Dad has bought him for me to watch every day. I'm in the house when he makes the first call one evening, and he fills me in before he dials Bish's number.

'This boy's quality, Jamie. Top player, cultured. We gotta get him in.'

So that's what I think, when I watch Bishop. He's here so I can learn from him. And he lets me knock a ball about with him after training, and I get an absolute lesson. He waits for me to charge at him, all enthusiastic like a puppy let loose in the park, then plays it round the corner, gets a one-two from one of the other lads and he's away. Next time I try to do the same to him. Sometimes it even works.

There's Shaun Brooks alongside him, once of Crystal Palace under Terry Venables, now another passing midfielder who in his head is playing for Roma rather than Redknapp senior. Then there's Tony Pulis.

Tony is not about the passing. After ten years of kicking people round the west of the country at Bristol Rovers and Newport County, he's been brought to Dean Court by Dad to stiffen up the spine of the team. And kick more people.

Tony isn't big. He's got a full head of black curly hair, and he's incredibly fit, but he has something else: a presence. The polite way he is described is no-nonsense. I'm terrified of him, because he will put in tackles that could end careers. There are legitimate tackles where you go in hard and accidentally do some damage. There are sneaky ones. Then there are Tony's specialities, the ones when he'll just wait and wait and wait until his target comes in for a tackle and then, in an explosion of limbs and studs and grass, make them wish they hadn't.

I see Tony put in tackles that are an arrestable offence. I see ones where he whispers to a team-mate, 'I'll get him,' and the next thing you know someone from the opposition is being carried off and no-one is quite sure, particularly the referee, how it has happened and when, only that it has.

Tony doesn't worry about possible retribution. His reputation is such that he doesn't have to. There are players like Bish and Shaun who have the ability to hit a 30-yard pass, and there is Tony's ability in knowing how to survive and knowing how to make sure that, if anyone's out to get him, he's going to get them first. It's just like Jimmy Gabriel has been showing me, but with infinitely more power and violence. Slow up the tackle when it's there, wait until it's a fraction too late, and go over the top side of the ball.

Tony is hard. Remarkably, he's not the hardest man at the club. That's Stuart Morgan, now Dad's chief scout and formerly a central defender, who even at the age of 40 looks like he could put a brick wall in hospital. Dad first met him as a player at West Ham, and again 10 years later at Bournemouth, and then had him back as an assistant a few years ago. Stuart's just back from managing Torquay, where his team avoided relegation from the Football League on the last day of one season with a goal scored in injury time, the injury in question being to the leg of his defender Jim McNichol when he was attacked by a police dog as he went to take a corner.

Maybe it's because even Dad doesn't have a story about a season being inadvertently saved by an angry German Shepherd called Bryn that he's got Stuart back on board. Maybe it's because Stuart has the same effect on the rest of us as Bryn. If Dave Morris is tough and Tony is intimidating,

Stuart is ruthless. If my dad were ever to find himself in a fight, Stuart's name would be the first one he would call. He wouldn't need to because Stuart would probably have instigated the fight, but still.

He's like a bodyguard for both of us, because I've spent so much time around him now that he considers me one of his gang too. There'll come a youth team game where I get clattered and the opposition manager shouts out there was nothing wrong with it, that I've dived. Stuart will set off from the other side of the pitch as he hears the accusation. He'll walk calmly along the touchline, past one corner flag, behind the goal, round past the other corner flag and all the way up to the manager. Who he'll then knock out with a single punch.

There is a phrase that all these men like to use. 'You have to earn the right, Jamie.' Earning the right means that for the first 20 minutes of any game you have to kick someone before they kick you. If you get the chance to do someone, you do it. After that, the game will settle down and you can play, but until then, you get stuck in.

Paul Miller arrives from Charlton just in case Bournemouth are lacking hard defenders. He's coming towards the end of a career that has seen him win the FA Cup twice with Spurs as well as the UEFA Cup, and he brings all the street-tough attitude my Dad expects from a kid brought up in Stepney. His nickname is Max, after Max Miller the comedian, but there's nothing funny about this Max. He goes over the top of the ball whenever there's so much as a sniff of it. He watches Deano training one day and shouts at him to do the same. Deano tells me afterwards that he couldn't, because he was sure he was going to break the other kid's leg. Max isn't bothered. I'm also not going to call him Max. Not when he's nearly 15 years older than me and likely to stand in my way when Dad lets me train with the first team. Not until he tells me I can.

Other kids look at the hair flopping down over my eyes and my touch and think I can't mix it. That just makes me love a tackle all the more. Lads we're coming up against now definitely know who my dad is. They know I've been to bigger clubs. So they try to kick me, and if someone tries to do me, I'm happy to do them. And if that doesn't work, there's Dave Morris.

'You f***ing touch him, I will have you!'

That's Dave on the pitch. By 'have you' he doesn't mean kick you. He means fight you. And we need him there because there is a Dave Morris on every team you face. It's like ice hockey. There is always a minder, a teenage Pulis, a Stuart Morgan in the making.

Our youth team plays Southampton's. Their coach is Dave Merrington, a Geordie who will help bring through Alan Shearer and Rod Wallace, among others. He's non-stop on the touchline, barking at his players, in their ears all the time about organisation and shape. At one point, I dip a shoulder and go past their main man in midfield. I like to dribble. I've got Gazza in my head. And the shout comes out from Merrington, loud and clear: 'Break his leg next time.'

Terry Shanahan goes mad. We're still kids. Merrington is a 45-year-old man. These games don't matter, not in the big scheme of things. But this is how it is. It's not just Southampton and it's not just Merrington. This is football in the late 1980s. This is the beautiful game.

When I hear the shout, I laugh. It actually gives me confidence. I'm winning here. I'm scaring them. It's my leg they want to break, I must be doing all the right things.

I always respect coaches, but this goes too far. I shout back at Merrington, tell him where to go. Then I think, I'll show you . . .

I know I'm never going to be a real hardman. But neither will I ever be scared of any kind of physical confrontation. I've got big legs. I've got a big backside. I can hold you off with my fingers up in your face. And I can mix it too. I can look after myself.

•

Ian Bishop: I was 24 coming up to 25 and at Carlisle. We'd finished second bottom of Division Four, and my contract had run out. Harry phoned me from nowhere, totally out of the blue, and I thought, I'll go down and speak to him.

He hid me away. He didn't really want me going back and signing for Carlisle, or it going to a tribunal and him having to pay. He wined and dined me for a little bit. 'Oh, don't go back, it'll be brilliant down here . . .' I spoke to my manager at Carlisle. But Harry had worked his charm. 'I've already promised Harry, I'm not going back on my word, more money or not.'

He was slotting me into something that was already prepared. It was like a jigsaw puzzle in his head. I knew he was saving me from the lower leagues. That season I spent with him at Bournemouth, it put me on the path to everything that happened afterwards. Harry had sold it to me straightaway. Very Harry.

Jamie was 15 when I first met him. I had three brothers, growing up in Liverpool, and we all played football. My brothers were all good footballers, but they always said I had this something else. I was always going to be a footballer. Jamie had the same thing. You could tell at that young age.

He was around us all the time. When he wasn't at school he was with the first team in the dressing rooms at the club. Always with the ball. He just wanted to hear and see football. For somebody so young, the things he would come out with and talk about – you could see what type of player he was going to be, even back then. He lived it and breathed it and sucked everything in.

8

THE BOYS

With that balance of menace and magic in his team, Dad is starting to take Bournemouth places. Getting them out of Division Three in 1987 has its practical issues, not least because the fixture list is doomsday for a club on the south coast; there are away trips to Middlesbrough, Darlington, Carlisle and Blackpool. The journeys to Bolton and Bury and Wigan seem almost easy in comparison. On those dark winter weekends, he leaves on the Friday lunchtime and gets back so deep into Sunday morning that no-one's interested in spring rolls and chow mein if the win's come in. But he's finding his blend, getting those players on his side, playing some nice football. Up to Division Two as champions, hanging on the following season in 17th place, starting to push on towards mid-table respectability as 1988 becomes 1989.

So more money comes into the club and players and management are rewarded. We move from Old Barn Road, with its hole still in the hedge where me and Mark burrowed through in search of lost balls, up to Ashley Heath, further out along the A31 towards Ringwood. It's a little further too from the bright lights in the middle of Bournemouth – there's a brass plaque on the post office proudly proclaiming that Ashley Heath high street is the smallest in Britain – but it's another notch up in comfort. The house is on a cul-de-sac and has its own gates, and the windows are leaded even though it's all dark red brick rather than Tudor beams, but the element that excites me most is the space – enough for a full-size snooker table now, in the room on the left as you come through the front door, and then, when you go through the wooden gate down the side, the garden, several times the size of the one back on Palmerston Avenue in Christchurch all those summers ago.

The snooker room is Dad's pride and joy. He buys the table from the tournament organisers after one of the big events at Bournemouth International Centre, which means Steve Davis and John Parrott may well have splayed their fingertips on this exact baize. When you walk down the three steps from the hall in the house you see the big rectangle of green, the brass light hanging low over it and a little bar in the corner. There are old photos of Dad playing football on the walls, photos of me and Mark in different kits, of me sitting on Bobby Moore's knee as a four-year-old. There is always music on, 80s soul if Dad's in charge, a little bit of hip-hop from me and Mark now the angry sounds of the US east coast and west coast have started arriving on England's quiet and sleepy south coast.

The garden, I can't quite believe. When we set Granddad's wooden birdcage up in the corner, there is now so much space that I'm clipping the ball almost from the edge of an imaginary penalty box to underneath the crossbar. There is a ridge around the outside by the fence that you can get someone to stand on, so you're chipping passes as if you're aiming at Luther Blissett coming thundering in at the back post. There's a camber too on the lawn so you're either passing it slightly uphill or slightly down, but it drains really well, so the surface is always nice. And there's no nonsense in between – the garden furniture is tucked away, the flowerbeds start and end at the perimeter and there are decent-sized trees round the edge to block any shots that go wildly off-target.

My room is at the front of the house, looking out back down the close. Mark is at the back on the left, Mum and Dad over the breakfast room where we'll sit down together for dinner. It feels so large to me. When we first move in I keep wandering around, listening to my voice echoing, kicking a ball against new walls and fresh unfamiliar angles. The size of the garden so intimidates Dad that he buys a sit-on lawn-mower. The initial emptiness of it all so intimidates Mark and I that we climb over the creosoted fences of houses up the road and borrow a load of pot plants and saplings in plastic terracotta-coloured tubs to fill it all out a bit. Dad must think Mum is getting into her gardening. Mum must think that this is very unusual from Dad, doing anything round the house, but maybe the sit-down lawnmower has convinced her that he's a changing man.

Next door on the left are Keith and Yvonne. I get a few nights of babysitting there when they're out for tea, which all makes a difference when you're saving up for records as well as trainers and tracksuits. The Moors Valley Country Park is just across Horton Road, with walking trails and bike tracks cut through the ferns and pines and a pitch and putt golf course, and our neighbours a bit further along will give me a few more quid if I take their Rottweiler out for walks there too, at least until I let it off the lead one morning and it bounds off into the trees and doesn't come back. Luckily for me, Rottweilers are intelligent dogs. Across the next two hours I can't find a trace of it, and I'm round the house almost in tears when the dog comes sprinting down the close and into their garden, having navigated at least one busy road, the park's lake, the adventure playground and possibly the miniature steam railway.

It's a great area to get some extra running in after training. I've got a nice loop that takes about 15 minutes, up Whitfield Park to St Ives Wood and then down Sandy Lane. Trees on all the streets, the soil sandy, not so far from the New Forest and its heaths and spinneys. No-one's telling me to do any more running. I'm not sure how many others in the youth team are sticking on some bonus endurance work, but I bet the ones messing about in the cramped house on Knole Road with Dave Morris aren't. When I'm a Liverpool player a few years later, living in digs near Anfield and living off teas cooked in the morning wrapped in Clingfilm and microwaved back to life at night, I'll do the same – work out a route around Stanley Park, pull on the trainers and get out there even when my legs are heavy and the rain's coming in sideways off the Irish Sea.

There is also Horton Road village green, which is even better for football than the new back garden. It's through a wooden gate off the main road, pine trees along all four sides to keep the wind off in winter or stormy autumn days, two white metal goals facing each other in the middle. Mark and I take our one-on-ones out here when we want to go ferocious, or when the birdcage starts listing too much in one direction from its repeated batterings. Deano and Dave come out at weekends. Pinging balls around, wearing out a muddy channel in the grass in the goalmouth and between the two sets of posts. There is a narrow strip of grass by the fence that for some reason is cut slightly shorter than the pitch itself, so that becomes a challenge too: we have to punch passes to each other without the ball ever going into the rough, or I have to run at Mark with the ball and beat him without stepping out of play.

It's just grass and trees and the noise of cars rumbling by. You wouldn't stop if you were passing. It's no better than council playing fields anywhere else I've been. There's nowhere to shelter if it starts to rain, nowhere to get a drink in summer. It's not busy enough for an ice-cream van to park up.

That's fine. To us it's Wembley, or the San Siro, or the Olympiastadion in Munich. Sometimes it's even Dean Court. It's a playground without swings or a slide, as much an extension of our house as the drive or the patio. It's anywhere we want it to be. It's ours.

Sometimes Horton Road village green becomes the Stadio Comunale in Turin. Dad has started taking us to an Italian on Charminster Road, on the corner before you get to Wimborne Road Cemetery. It's run by Lorenzo and his family, and has his name squiggled like a signature on the sign above the door. It's not flashy but it's real, and it has Serie A shirts on the walls, and scarfs and banners.

Lorenzo is a huge Juventus fan. So is his wife and their

three daughters. When we pile down there on a Saturday night, he tells me what it was like watching Michel Platini in the flesh. He has the Ariston jersey from 1985, and he gives me a team photo of that great side to stick on my new bedroom wall. I start obsessing about the team and about their Kappa shirts. We are in there when news comes through that Gaetano Scirea, the great Juve and Italy sweeper, has been killed in a car crash. He's only 36. I remember him at the 1982 World Cup, the persuasion alongside the violence of Claudio Gentile, so good he kept Franco Baresi out of the national team, and we're all shocked into unfamiliar silence.

The food is a big part of Lorenzo's. He's a fantastic chef. He'll welcome you in, little moustache twitching, and he always remembers what you had last time. Because we're in Bournemouth rather than Turin and because it'll still be a few years until Channel 4 start showing live Serie A matches on *Gazzetta Football Italia*, it seems incredibly glamorous. I'll love *Gazzetta* when it comes, from the way the '4' turns red, white and green, to the theme music, all the samples over the credits – 'Campionato!' 'Di Calcio!' 'GOAL LACCIO!' – and James Richardson sitting outside cafés with an espresso and pink newspapers. For now the fact that Lorenzo has VHS copies of last weekend's Juve games seems almost impossible. My usual experience of pasta is Alphabetti spaghetti. The penne all'arrabbiata he makes is as far from that as Christchurch is from Rome.

Word gets around. The Bournemouth first team start coming in for their pre-match meal of chicken and pasta or chicken in breadcrumbs. Shaun Brooks can't keep away. He wants to be Italian. He plays like some Italian midfielders, looking for the perfect pass, leaving the hatchet jobs for the lumps alongside him, and he's always dressed like an Italian anyway – baggy slacks, white shirts, waistcoats, sometimes a trench coat with a scarf.

Not everyone is impressed.

'Come on, Brooksie!'

'Aye aye, what the f***'s going on with that tie?'

I like it. I'm happy talking Italian football with him. I like the suits and I love the crazy notion that one day maybe I could play in Serie A too. Six years later it will nearly come to pass. Roma will make a bid for me when I'm at Liverpool. They'll be after a successor to Giuseppe Giannini, a midfielder so regal he's known as the Prince and who strolls around the middle of the pitch like it's part of his own private kingdom. I could do the same floppy long hair as him. I'll think how much the game over there might suit me, and I'll even make plans to bring Mark over with me like a south coast version of Gazza's Jimmy Five Bellies.

It will fall through because Liverpool don't want to let me go, but for now the fascination holds. Mark likes a Kappa top, right in the football casual sweet-spot. I'll start wearing boots made by Pantofola d'Oro, a hand-stitched thing of wonder so soft and supple that it translates as the Golden Slipper. You can see them on the feet of Roberto Mancini, of Jurgen Klinsmann and Ciro Ferrara. Tony Pulis does not wear Pantofola d'Oro. Dave Morris does not wear Pantofola d'Oro. But they're prepared to kick anyone who says anything about it, so that's all *molto buona*.

•

Dean Giddings: Jamie was in a Serie A shirt when we first met. It was the Napoli home one, the one they won the UEFA Cup in with Maradona and Alemao, Ciro Ferrara and Careca. Not many kids had that pale blue kit and not many of us could keep the ball up off the outside of our foot, like he was.

I got invited down to Bournemouth for a trial. There were 100 of us, all trying desperately to impress Terry Shanahan. On the second day he whittled it down to 24. By the end of the third day there were three of us, and we were allowed to stay.

Jamie was the first other lad to speak to me. It was all where are you from, and which players do you like. You could see what he had straightaway: a great touch, an elegance on the ball, always time to pick his pass. It could actually be annoying at times. You never saw him getting stuck in a tight corner getting his ankles nipped by defenders.

He would always be in on the laughs before training, but as soon as the football started he was deadly serious. He was getting the fundamentals right of how to be a footballer long before most of us – how you had to live off the pitch, how you had to prepare. He'd never drink alcohol, even when the rest of us were nipping away under age. He'd have one sip of Dave Morris' vodka orange to get the taste and then be on Diet Cokes for the rest of the night.

And he was always asking questions, Jamie. Always seeking to be better. He would speak to the senior pros, to the first team, and he would ask how they did things. We wouldn't have considered it. We weren't old enough. They were men, we were boys. But he had that quiet confidence from being around a football environment all his life. He didn't see himself as second best. He saw himself as a footballer, just like them.

•

I'm still going up to Spurs to train each week, and I enjoy it. But there are also things that make me wonder.

There are flash kids that I don't really want to be around. Some in the reserves, a few in the youth team. There are some great lads too, but there are others who have done nothing real yet. They haven't made the first team. If they do, they'll have to do more to establish themselves. I look around and see good players, but I see too that they're not knocking on the door. They're not being lined up for the next step.

Alarm bells sound. This is not me. I'm conscientious. I'm beyond that. I'm obsessive. I don't want to stop here. The clothes are nice, but they're nothing on their own.

It gradually takes hold of me. I'm at Tottenham, with four years of safety ahead of me if I want it: a two-year apprentice's contract when I'm 16, a two-year pro contract to follow at 18.

It's good money and it's four long years when most kids are hoping to cling on. The boys at Bournemouth would kill for it.

But there's something at Bournemouth I'm not getting at Spurs. A route through to the first team. Players who are pushing me. Mates that I love. As much as I want to make it as a professional footballer, I want Deano and Dave and the rest to make it through too.

It's the end of April over at the Highlin hotel, where loads of the apprentices have lodgings, when I first test the waters with my mate. The two of us walking into Boscombe to get a bit of food, a companionable silence between us. Then, out of the blue, I let it go.

'Deano, I'm thinking about not signing for Tottenham.'

'Really?'

'I don't want to be there. I'm going to get stuck. I'll be lost. I'll never make the first team.'

'So what you gonna do?'

'I want to stay here. I want to play for Bournemouth.'

You can almost see Deano working it out. First thing he thinks, because he's such a diamond, is that this is the best thing ever. The two of us will be together, playing together centre-mid, spending all our time together. Next thing: this will make us better as a youth team. It's only a day or two later that he'll wonder what it actually means for him, having another kid around who plays in exactly the same position.

Deano doesn't hold on to that thought too long. It's not the way he is. And his acceptance of the idea, the fact he can see it working, sets it in my mind.

We watch the Division One decider that May round at mine. Liverpool against Arsenal at Anfield, George Graham's Arsenal needing to win by two clear goals to steal the championship away from Kenny Dalglish's team. I want Arsenal to win, despite those Spurs connections, partly because it feels like a north *v* south thing, partly because I like that Arsenal midfield – Paul Davis, so upright and elegant, Paul Merson tearing about, David Rocastle with his balance and skills on the flanks. The last minute blows our minds and sends us leaping about the sofas, Michael Thomas doing his roly-poly and flipping about up there as he's swamped by his team-mates, us all doing the same on the carpet. But that sort of football, that sort of crowd, seems far more than 260 miles away.

The next morning I tell Dad where I want to be. And he goes mad.

'You what? You got to go Tottenham!'

I tell him it's not working.

'Not working? It's Tottenham, Jamie. You know how embarrassing this is for me? I got to go tell Terry Venables now. I got to tell him you don't want to go to his club.'

I tell him again that I'm not going. I've made up my mind. I want to stay at home.

'Tell Terry I'm homesick.'

'I get that Jamie, but you're a player. You can get it down and play. You got to push yourself.'

Then I try to explain.

'I can get in your team, Dad. I've trained with your team. I don't want to go and play in the youth team and get lost in the system. I want to play league football. I want to play for Bournemouth.'

So me and Dad drive up to White Hart Lane and go to see Terry in his office. It's the worst feeling in the world, like being called to the headmaster's office when you really like them and you've let them down. Terry's so nice even as we go in, all charm and grins and squeezing your arm as he shakes your hand.

He tells us he's signing 10 kids but it's me that he really wants. Dad sighs and says what he has to say. I say what I have to say. Dad helps me out. Terry, he wants to come and get into my team. He wants to play. He's not going to get that here.

We have to go to town on the homesick line too, which will make Terry raise an eyebrow when I head off to Liverpool before I've made it to my 18th birthday. But Terry still makes the deal work for him: Spurs will get a 25 per cent cut of a future transfer fee. And he won't hold it against me seven years on, when he's England manager at Euro '96 and looking for a young midfielder for his squad. Everyone is happy. Sort of.

We all know I'm leaving school. We all know that my 16th birthday will see me sign a YTS contract with Bournemouth, worth £29.50 a week in the first year, a massive leap to £35 in the second. Now there's just the formalities to be done: finishing off at a school that I've only intermittently attended, trying to get something out of the two GCSEs I'm actually taking, English Language and Home Economics.

I'm not expecting miracles, having missed 56 days on the official count and probably a fair few more that have slipped past the bean-counters. I am expecting the Home Economics exam when I turn up at school with the ingredients for a pineapple upside-down cake, which makes it even funnier for everyone else when it turns out to be the English Language exam instead.

A pineapple upside-down cake will go a long way but it won't solve a comprehension based on *An Inspector Calls*. I'm 5–0 down after the first three minutes, no chance of a draw let alone some kind of win. And I don't really deserve one, either, and no-one seems to mind. In my innocence, I'm not that bothered either. I was hardly here when I was supposed to be here. Now the exams have gone up in smoke and I'm allowed not to be here, why would I want to stick around?

When I turn 16 a few weeks later, it has sunk in a little deeper. Okay, football's still fun, but it's work now as well. I've given up on education, but I've given up on Tottenham too, with their kudos and money and four-year deal. I don't think of myself as naturally brave, and yet this is either massively ballsy or madness. There's no hiding place now. I know I'll get it from some – 'They're only signing him cos his dad's the manager' – and I know what others will be thinking. He's given it the big 'un, he'd better be able to back it up.

They're sort of right, the second lot. I have got to make this work now. I'm not a schoolboy anymore, not in the way Twynham see it, not in the way that football contracts are drawn up.

And I turn out to be sort of right. The young players from my group at Tottenham who make it as pro players have to leave in the end to get on. So now I've swapped one Terry,

a big-name player for Spurs and Chelsea, a man who's managed Barcelona and will manage England, for Terry Shanahan,
who has spent his playing career up front for Halifax and
Chesterfield and Millwall, and is now, in his late thirties,
looking after the youth team at Bournemouth.

They work you hard in the youth team. We are a diverse
bunch, that summer – local lads like me and Paul Mitchell,
Londoners like Deano, a Turkish lad, two boys from Northern
Ireland, one Catholic, one Protestant – but the one thing we
have in common is how much we have to do that has nothing
to do with a football.

Everyone has jobs. No-one is allowed home until the jobs
are done. For those in digs this sometimes means messing
around as much as possible, because staying at Dean Court
with your mates is preferable to lying on a single bed staring
at the ceiling, even when staying results in relentless manual
labour.

Our bosses are a strange, random group of men who seem
to have washed up at Bournemouth rather than been deliberately recruited for the roles they now have. There is John Kirk,
in his early sixties, who is both trainer and part-time physio.
He's been at the club since 1963, which is almost impossible for
us to get our heads around, and his attitude towards discipline
seems based around his experiences in the RAF during World
War II. Once a groundsman, a player for Poole in an era beyond
our understanding, his nickname is Captain, but his favourite
impersonation, rather than being Star Trek based, is of Tommy
Cooper. He also has a passable one of cricket commentator

John Arlott in his locker, but it's the Cooper impression that draws the plaudits. He's so into it that he actually has a fez that he keeps in his little office for whenever the occasion demands.

Then there is the old kitman, Ken Sullivan, who loves a bet almost as much as my dad. His nickname is Nimbus, after a famous old horse from his youth that won the Derby and the 2,000 Guineas, and not because he has its speed.

There's Percy, the maintenance man, who has a room in the bottom of the stand. Unfortunately for him, it has the lock on the outside, which is a temptation too far for Mark when he walks past. We're in the away dressing room, talking nonsense, when Percy's furious voice starts echoing down the corridors. 'Redknapp! I f***ing know it's you, Redknapp! Let me out! Let me out!' It's almost Mark's favourite pastime. If he sees the key in the lock and hears Percy inside, he can't help himself. Oh, go on, one more time . . .

The three of them make the rules. We try to break them. They dish out the jobs. We have to crack on.

In the summer, in the hot weeks before the new season begins, it's painting the crush barriers on the terraces at the South End. The ones by the exit are supposed to be yellow, to guide spectators out. All the other ones are in Bournemouth red. We are given large pots of paint and fat paintbrushes. Inevitably, the actual painting turns out to be a lot less fun than secretly flicking paint at someone working on the next barrier along. Secretly, for about 30 seconds, and then blatantly, and then open warfare. Captain Kirk wanders out of the tunnel to see his group of 15-year-old dogsbodies launching entire pots of paint over each other. We look like the Stone Roses at that photoshoot. The terraces look like their album cover. Captain is not into the Roses, John Squire or the whole Jackson Pollock vibe. This sort of thing did not happen in the RAF.

We love all three of the old boys, even if they could be three old blokes that walked in off the street and said, listen, I'll call myself the groundsman and you call yourself the physio and you can be the kitman.

Captain does not give in easily. His next task for us is to clean the floors of the corridors of the main stand. Not with brooms or mops and buckets, but on our hands and knees, holding clumps of wire wool. This sort of thing probably did happen in the RAF.

He keeps an eye on us throughout this time. All the way down the corridors, scraping, scratching, swearing. The floor is tiled. The dirt is in the gaps. The tiles are so old that they're the same colour as the dirt. You can scratch away all you like and it makes no difference. Captain will wait until you've done the whole length of corridor, bend down to have a look and shout, 'Do it again!' and we'll mutter stuff back that we hope he can't hear.

I work out that you can look like you're scraping without actually scraping. Get your head down and look diligent, and then start chatting as soon as Captain's tour of duty has taken him past you. You can sit up and kick back if you time it properly, although it drives Dave Morris mad, partly because he knows that the less I do the more he'll have to do, and partly because when he tries the same trick Captain always seems to swivel on his heel at the wrong moment and catch him trying to lob his wire wool at Deano.

We have to wash the toilets. I'm not an enthusiastic toilet-washer. We have to sweep underneath the wooden benches in the stands, and we're all given our own sections and Nimbus and Percy will check and compare efforts. I'm not winning. I never win. For once I can handle it.

The actual training, even the fitness drills where they push you so hard that there are lads chucking their guts up in any bush they can get to in time, can only come as a relief compared to putting your hand down a dirty 40-year-old loo. It is relentless in the best possible way. Find that spare patch of grass in King's Park, open up with a north v south game. The Catholic and Protestant sides of Northern Ireland come together for this one, and turn it into one of the fiercest sort-of-derbies I'll ever play in. And I'll play in Liverpool v Everton, Spurs v Arsenal and Southampton v Portsmouth. Not to mention England against Scotland.

The worst player is forced to don what we call the Yellow Jersey for the whole of the next week. It's only a yellow bib but carries with it great shame, because it goes to public vote, and none of us wants to be humiliated in front of the others. The bib never gets washed so it stinks, but so does all our kit, because you're only given one pair of shorts and socks and one top and one tracksuit, and if you're in digs like most of the boys your washing only gets done once a week.

The one-on-ones now have a new dimension. Those not involved now stand around the edge of the tiny pitch. You're allowed to use them as a wall, hitting them for a cheeky one-two pass. They might stitch you up, sending the ball back the other way, but that's the gamble you take. Then Terry will switch it up again, one goalkeeper, two players in the penalty box and not allowed outside it, both trying to score. Doesn't matter if you do – the game goes on to the death. For two minutes you're flat out, tackling, chasing, shooting, dribbling. It's pure nastiness. It's almost primeval. Survival of the fittest. Survival of the one who refuses to give in.

There is something called Doggies. Seven cones, set out in a line ahead of you, about five metres apart from each other. The whole team lined up on the goal line. Whistle from Terry, sprint to the first cone, turn as hard and sharp as you can, sprint back. Back to the goal line, turn, sprint to the second cone, turn and come back.

It's pure football fitness. You will do it until you almost can't run anymore, and then you'll still have to tear about in the practice match that follows and slide in to stop a goal. I can remember seeing Uncle Frank doing the same thing, and I've seen cousin Frank out in the back garden of their house in Gidea Park doing his sprints in running spikes every night, just like his dad used to do. Neither Frank was born fast. But my uncle made himself quick enough, and now my little cousin is doing the same. You either want to do it or you don't. If you can't handle Doggies, you can't handle being a footballer.

But it is horrific. It's so horrific that as soon as we see the cones coming out we start feeling sick. The only way it can get worse is if someone spots Dad wandering out of his office to keep an eye on things. Word flies down the line.

'Look out boys, Gaffer incoming!'

'J, it's your dad . . .'

Tony Pulis has started helping out with the coaching too. He's still playing in the first team, but he's worked out where he's going next in his career. Tony doesn't mess about. He's got a voice that could carry to the Isle of Purbeck and we all know what he can do in a tackle. That doesn't stop us giving him a new nickname as he sets up the Doggies, even though no-one would dream of calling him Tone the Cone to his face. But there's fear of an assistant coach, and there's wanting Dad's approval. There's wanting to impress him, to be the one who gets his occasional pearls of praise. Deano and Dave are in awe of him. Everyone is desperate to do well in front of him, not just because he's the gatekeeper to a pro contract and the first team beyond but because it's now unmistakeably his club.

He's buying and selling players but he's also redesigning the kit, once I talk him into changing it from bright red with a stripe of white across the shoulders or down the sides into AC Milan-style darker red and black vertical stripes with white shorts and socks. That's my obsession with Italian football kicking in again. I think, if the team looks stylish, aren't they more likely to play stylish football?

It's also a throwback to the early 1970s kit of Ted Mac-Dougall. Ted once scored nine goals for Bournemouth in a single game, albeit an FA Cup tie against Margate, so me and Dad are on safe ground, but it shows where he's aiming for, and even among us teenage lads in the youth team there's an unspoken agreement that he is the big boss, the one that everyone is now following and listening to.

The praise comes with a price. There's what we call Terror Tuesday, which begins with three lots of Doggies in eight minutes. That's almost no recovery. Then it's a balls-out 400 metres race around the gravel pitch. We'll play a nine *v* nine match where you're only allowed to tackle your opposite number, which means all these individual battles break out all over the pitch, like nine boxing bouts in the same ring. You can't let your man go because otherwise he can head straight for goal, everyone else having to back out of his way, and you can't make a lazy run or stop for a breather in case the other team break and your man is free and in space.

If you're mugged off, if someone makes you look daft, it's humiliating. We're all on show, all the time, as much to ourselves as to Terry Shanahan. I work out that you can wait for your man to get too close to you too quickly and then just toe it past them, all their momentum now a weapon against them. You can play little balls round the corner under even the most intense pressure. Every moment we're being set puzzles and tests, and we either solve them or we sink.

The ultimate embarrassment is being nutmegged. You get a bigger cheer for sticking the ball through someone's legs than you do scoring a goal. The most gruelling test is the extra run we have to do each week in pre-season. Terry will stick us in the minibus. He'll drive us up to St Catherine's Hill, across the River Stour and past the turning to our old house on Old

Barn Road. It will be up the steep paths that lead to the top, trails through the pine trees and wet grass, slogging away, and when we get back to the bottom Terry and the minibus will have cleared off back to Dean Court and we'll be running all the way back too.

Other times Terry won't tell us where we're going. He'll just set off, all of us shouting in the back, arguing and whingeing and dreading it, and we'll notice the houses speeding past, the signposts changing, and know we're in for a monster. Six miles from safety, booted out of the van, off you go boys, last one back does extras.

I'm okay. I don't love long-distance running, but I'll be in the middle of the front pack. Dave Morris hates long-distance. He'll come in 20 minutes after the first man, insisting he just took a wrong turn, that he was leading the way until we got to Seafield Gardens in Southbourne.

It's horrendous. And it binds us together. There are always hugs afterwards, and we mean them, young fighters who have just gone 12 rounds and know everyone around them has done the same. You feel so fit. Your legs thicken and new curves appear halfway up your calves and above your knees. Any puppy fat you had left just drops away until you look down one morning and there's a hardness about your stomach that's never been there before.

There is a joy going in every day, sitting in the passenger seat of Dad's car, jumping out as soon as he parks up in front of the main stand. I can't wait to find Deano and Dave, to nick a ball and start taking them on, to clatter into the empty away dressing room and wait for the others to come in, all jokes and rolled-up socks lobbed at each other, someone banging out a new hip-hop track on their Walkman, passing the headphones round, learning little runs through the lyrics. Whistling samples from De La Soul, shouting out NWA.

In the summer afternoons, we're down Boscombe beach with our tops off, doing what my dad and Uncle Frank used to do in front of Mum and Auntie Pat, doing keepy-ups in front of girls who couldn't care less. One-touch games in the sand, two-touch games, all of them involving a football, none of them involving touching girls.

I'll practise anywhere. The South Stand at Dean Court has a full-size goal painted on the brick wall at the back. It's been there since the days when Ted MacDougall was banging them in. It's probably been there since Ron Eyre was the main man up front and the club was still called Bournemouth and Boscombe AFC. Each part of the goal has a different number painted on it, in a different colour. One is bottom right, just inside the post. Two is up by the stanchion.

Ten numbers, ten targets. When I'm waiting for Dad to finish up at the end of a day I'll take a ball and position myself on the edge of an imaginary penalty box, which means standing in the car park, first-team players driving past on their way home, and try to hit every number in sequence. One to 10, then 10 to one, then every number three times in a row.

I put myself under pressure. All the numbers in under 90 seconds, sprinting to get the rebound, killing it, dribbling it back to the starting spot, clipping it again. Going further out, powering them from distance. Moving the starting spot out wider, to where the corner of the box would be, so now I'm curling them, bending them first one way then the other. I can't leave until I've hit each sequence I want. Darkness falling, all the players long gone, the noise of commuter cars escaping up the A338. The warmth from the day faded away, the cold sea breezes coming across King's Park. You don't notice when there's a target. You just keep going until you've made it.

We're all obsessed with how to hit a ball properly. At least us creative midfielders are. Deano's got a lovely touch, although he's not a natural when it comes to mixing it, and we'll go opposite each other and fire passes at each other, searching for the perfect feel, listening for the sound that tells you that you've just hit one bang on.

Deano and me talk about the Ping. He's got it in the bag. As a right-footer, it's when you plant your left foot alongside the ball, lean out to the side, get your left arm up high. Your striking foot is almost at right angles.

You can enjoy someone else's Ping as much as your own. It's a thing of beauty when it comes off a treat. We shout at each other when we're working on it – 'Hold the finish, Deano!'

Dad can do it really well. He'll do a demo in training, and it's still effortless. Mum has told me that he was a nutcase at my age, that he had all that talent but enjoyed himself too much, kept getting himself in trouble. That's where the ability comes from. My attitude comes from Mum, but I'm so lucky to have Dad's touch. He's a beautiful striker of a ball. He can cross it on the run better than any of his 25-year-old wingers, and it's all about his posture. When I watch him I almost slow it down in my mind. What's he doing that gives him that strike? Okay, let's try it – get your left hand up in the air, the right balance, get your left foot alongside the ball and then time it. It's all in the timing.

There is nothing he hates more than seeing one of his players out wide who crosses the ball behind the goal. He can't get his head round it.

'How the f*** have you kicked that over there?'

Anger rising, everyone trying to look the other way.

'No wonder you're in the f***ing reserves!'

Heads down. Dad picking up a ball, striding out to the touchline.

'Eh? Eh? This is what I want you to do, yeah?'

Bang. Crosses it right on to the head of the striker on the penalty spot.

'You got it now, have you?'

You need the natural ability but you need the work doing too. Shaun Brooks can strike it. Ian Bishop can strike it. Some players strike a ball and some players slap a ball. There is a difference. I can hear it down on the golf course too. That bloke slaps his drives, that one strikes them. I'll see it in a few years with David Beckham. I'll see it with Patrik Berger. The first time I pass the ball to Steven Gerrard in training with Liverpool, he will turn and hit a pass, and it won't be the strike that stops me dead. It will be the noise.

And the best strikes you hit are the ones where you don't even try. When it comes out to me and I hit it smooth, when

I don't try to whack it, it flies. It's not about power. When you try to hit it hard, you scuff it: you don't get the strike on it. The ones where you don't care and just let the ball go, they're the best strikes. Always.

We all become obsessed with our boots. It's the boots that make your touch pay off. It's the boots that give you the confidence. Bad boots make you think about them all the time. Good boots, you forget about. It's just you and the ball.

Everyone has their own favourites. Deano likes the Puma Super Kings worn by Maradona, black with the white logo sweeping down the side, the top of the tongue white and sticking up from the knot on the laces. Others go for the Adidas Stratos SL, quite low-cut at the back, a high heel cup, or the Adidas Profi, which is an absolute beauty – three white stripes down the side, the flap of the tongue sitting properly over the laces, big white Adidas trefoil, the cross-stitching in the leather arcing over the toes. You can even get them in dark blue, which feels both sacrilegious and magical.

The club gives us each two pairs of boots at the start of every season, one pair with screw-in studs, the other mouldeds. They are rubbish. The leather is poor, and it goes rock-hard the first time it gets wet. They last about a month. We have absolutely no interest in wearing them, so we trade them in at the sports shop and pay extra for the ones we actually want.

The boot room at Dean Court is next to the home dressing room. So after home games we wait in there for the first team to finish up, then slouch in to sweep the dressing room clean of all the ripped tie-ups and chewing-gum wrappers and empty cans of Coke. We find the boots of the player each of us is looking after, mud all over them, whitewash from the touchlines and halfway line and penalty box, and we get to work. Dave does Shaun Teale's. Deano has Sean O'Driscoll's Pumas.

A kind senior player will be strict in the standards he hands down but generous with his tips when you do a good job or it's Christmas. During September and October, we're operating at 50 per cent. Come late November, we're stepping it up. December, you're polishing for your life. But Deano gets nothing. And the boots are glimmering. I don't think Deano's forgiven him to this day.

I've got Luther's Pumas. When I put my left hand inside to keep the boot still as I polish them, they feel long and soft. He's the main man so he gets all the top gear, and these boots are kangaroo leather, which means they might as well be made from space dust. Polishing kangaroo leather is not easy. By the time I get one boot perfect my right arm is almost hanging off, but his tips are only slightly better than O'Driscoll's.

It's tiny in the boot room at the best of times. There is a bench on one side where you can stand to get proper downward force with your polishing, and the sloped roof on the other side where the angle of the stand above us bites in. The boots are hung up on hooks, studs facing out. With us all piling in, it feels like a cupboard, but it's also the centre of our universe. We're still the outsiders, the kids no-one wants to see around unless they're doing something for them. This is the only place where no-one bothers us, because no-one else wants to be in here. It's our den.

But it's not always safe. There is a tradition that has been passed from apprentice to apprentice down the years, and it's vicious. Your birthday might be a good day at home, but it's not a good day at the club. You keep it quiet and pray that no-one finds out, because you've seen what happens when they do.

There will be no warning. Then they grab you, all the other lads, and they drag you into the boot room, except this time the lights are off. Some of them hold you down and others strip off all your clothes. Then the same brushes you use to clean the dry mud off the studs of boots are scratched all over your legs and arse and back. The wire wool that you've been using to clean the tiles in the corridors of the stands is rubbed on your face and neck.

They get Deep Heat and spray it on your balls. They rub it into all those new cuts and deep grazes until you're screaming. Someone's nicked the big tubs of Vaseline from the dressing room, and that gets rubbed in your hair and your eyes.

Why do we let it happen? It's hard to work it out. It just happens. No-one sits down and decides we should carry on with it. No-one questions why we're doing it in the first place. And the strange thing is, as much as you dread your own special day, fear it so much, you can't wait for the next lad's birthday. You don't have a choice. You know someone's getting it, and that someone isn't you that day, so you shut up. It becomes hilarious. It becomes the most fantastic joke. Sometimes you can't get involved, but only because you're laughing so much. You can't make the connection between the kid on the floor that everyone's shoeing and the feeling you had in your stomach when you opened your presents at home and knew you would be in the car on the way to training at any moment.

I'm lucky. My birthday is in June, so most of the lads have gone home at the end of the season. They try to remember the summer lads, but you can fall through the cracks.

But not everyone is lucky, and it stops in the end only because it goes too far. Dave Morris gets grabbed because everyone knows when his birthday is. One of the lads is trying to hold Dave down as everyone goes mental, and he gets him in a choke-hold round the Gregory – his neck, or his Gregory Peck as we say in east London – to stop him moving.

Only he holds on too tight. Dave can't breathe. Nobody knows because all the lights are off. People hear the choking noise and it just makes them laugh more.

Then the smell comes and everyone suddenly gets it. Dave is half-dead. He's dying. There is shit coming out. This is real. This is bad.

It doesn't happen again after that. That changes things, forever. Dave comes back round, but the tradition is gone. The pain will stay on the rough pitches and the dogshitty grass of King's Park. The decision to suffer will be yours and no-one else's.

9

THE YOUTH TEAM

Tony Pulis: I ended up at Bournemouth at the time Jamie was coming through, mainly because of his dad. In every sense. I had the chance to leave the south coast for Huddersfield Town at the end of one season. They had a good team, with Iwan Roberts playing up front, and Eoin Hand the manager, getting in better players than me. Harry was building a really good team too. Ian Bishop and Shaun Brooks, lovely players. But I wasn't sure. I was knocking on. I kept going in to him and telling him I was going to leave. He kept saying to me, 'I don't want you to go, you're really important to me.'

Eoin rang me up. 'Tony, listen, I think I've got the team to get promoted here, it would be great if you came up.' And he offered me a £5,000 signing-on fee, which was enormous then. I spoke to my wife Debbie. She was sold on it.

I went back to see H. He said, 'Do us a favour, play in the reserves on Wednesday, Jimmy Gabriel is taking a team, we'll get it done.' Okay. So we drove over to Swansea and played, and Eoin met me after the game, and we organised everything. It was sorted out: the money, the contract, my role. I was pleased. I was getting an uplift and he was really going to look after me. Harry was good as gold. 'Yeah, I've spoken to Eoin, everything's alright. Come and see me tomorrow morning and it's done.'

I went into the office at Dean Court nice and early on the Thursday morning. 'Where's Harry?' No-one had seen him. 'Where's Brian?' No-one's seen the managing director either. I got changed and went out to train, thinking Harry might be there. No-one except Jimmy Gabriel and the players. I got back into the changing rooms. Still no Harry.

I began desperately trying to get hold of Eoin on a landline somewhere. He hadn't been able to track down Harry either. The transfer deadline was 5 pm. And Harry was nowhere to be found. A man whose life was spent at the football ground was nowhere near the football ground on the most important day of all.

It's 4 pm . . . 4.30 pm . . . No-one. No deal, no move.

The next morning I was waiting for H in the car park at 8 am. He had a new contract for me in his hand. 'Tone, I don't want you to go. Have this, stick around, it'll be good.'

That was Harry, and he was right. It was fun. The team was brilliant to play in. And there was Jamie training with us, first as a kid bunking off school, then a 15-year-old doing extras, then with the youth team.

You could see it in him then, in the way he looked

around, in where he had come from, in where he was going. I was from the docks in Newport. Big family, eight of us living in a three-bedroomed terraced house. I was the oldest boy so I had to look after the others. My father passed away when he was 64 and I was only 16.

It taught me a lot. People can bring good and bad things on themselves. Some can deal with negativity, others can't. Some people have that skill but then haven't got the ambition. It's not that they're not strong enough, or not mentally set to do it, but they don't want to push themselves all the way. There are so many people who go through life saying they could have done this or that, and they never could have done, because they didn't have that resilience or the dedication to it.

Then you see certain people – and there were about three or four during my coaching career – that you look at and think: he's going to get the maximum out of himself, because he's got what it takes. There are some you look at and think, irrespective of what happens, they're going to be successful. Jamie was one of them.

You can't teach it. It's either in you or it isn't. Not a sense of fear about the challenges coming your way, but a belief. 'This is where I belong.' Jamie was always going to be okay. He was always doing more than he had to. He was one of the very few where you're kicking them back inside after training. The rest you are pushing. With the elite you are thinking, don't leave too much on the training ground. You're going to be okay.

Jamie was talented, streetwise, enthusiastic. He was clever in picking the company he kept. It was so interesting to see this young boy manoeuvre his way around the senior players within the dressing room with such ease and confidence. Everybody who is anybody will tell you that once training starts at a professional football club, there is no hiding place, irrespective of age or ability. If you are not up to it you will soon be told, and told in very uncompromising ways. Jamie trained with total commitment. Add that to his ability and any misgivings the other lads might have held about him were washed away.

Because top sportspeople discover their own talent. Top players, realising what they have, strive relentlessly to fulfil it. Lots of players are talented, but not all are filled with that inner spirit and desire to squeeze out every drop of talent they possess. Jamie knew his destiny and used all of those qualities to achieve it.

•

As the season begins, the youth team has started taking on a recognisable look. Dave, Deano and me in a midfield three, Keith Rowland – who'll go on to follow Dad to West Ham – slotting in too, all sweet left foot. Andy Case up front, silky player. There's Justin Spires, a smooth left-back who seems to have a tan all year round. He spends a lot of time over at our house watching Fab 5 Freddy and Dr Dre on *Yo! MTV Raps*, which is not a channel that sits naturally with Dad. Justin's viewing habits have helped him develop the sort of hip-hop moves that most kids in the wider Ringwood area do not possess. He can jump through his own legs, which seems to work a treat with the girls who the rest of us are only occasionally managing to impress. He also spends hours looking at himself in the mirror as he practises his moves, and it's paying off. We dream of matching his dancefloor skills.

There's Eamonn Ferris, a big Catholic lad from Northern Ireland, who plays up front. He's always arguing with people, loves a dispute, but he'll run through walls for you, and he's never shy about putting a foot in when others are trying to bully him off the pitch, and so everyone likes him.

There's Neil Masters from just outside Belfast, a big lump already at six-foot tall. His parents send him over food parcels, as if you can't get food in one of the most comfortable parts of England, and it's not bags of fruit or cereal or tins of veg they're rushing out to him but boxes of chocolate bars. He's a seriously good player. He's chunky for a left-sided defender but fast and with a cross he can stick exactly where he wants. He'll get in the first team as he gets older and then get a move to Wolves that could have gone up to £600,000, at a time when £600,000 buys you a lot of talent. But he can't stay fit with us and he won't stay fit for them. He'll play a stretch of two or three games and then be out for the same again. Then there's Scott Mean, really good footballer, my dad's sort of player – good physique, great technique. Girls seem to think he's the best-looking boy in Bournemouth. There's Lee Bradford, big centre-back, his old man a builder, his house a whopper up in Ringwood where you can have some serious parties.

So it's evenings at the digs where Dave and most of the rest are staying, the Highlin hotel, which start off with one-touch games in the big dining room with the ten tables pushed against the walls, and then develop into hip-hop nights, NWA on someone's CD player, all of us nodding along to 'Express Yourself' and 'Gangsta Gangsta' like we can relate to what Ice Cube and Dre are going through over there in South Central. It shouldn't work but it does, precisely because it sounds so different and dangerous. There are no AK47s in Boscombe that we're aware of. If there are, no-one refers to them as gats. It starts to influence the clothes we wear and the things we say to each other. You've never seen a boy grow up until you've seen Philip McCauley, our rapid little right-winger. He arrives from the Irish sticks in bad stonewash jeans, listening to bad pop and old folk music, pale as a bedsheet, going bright red as soon as there's any hint of sun. He goes home two months later wearing an LA Raiders baseball caps and spitting rhymes about the LAPD like he's Eazy-E.

There are no other hotels in the area where the guests are sitting out on the front lawn singing about dirty arsed ho's and correctional facilities, but to call the Highlin a hotel in the first place is stretchy. It's a B&B where there are no en-suites and only one shower room, so everyone queues up with their towel over their arm each morning in polite British fashion, partly to make up for all the rude British stuff that has been going on the night before. A creaking 1930s house painted white and with rooms subdivided and squeezed in everywhere, out the back, down the side, wedged in under the eaves on the second floor. Two or three single beds in each, a sink in each corner which ends up being used for more than the owners would ideally want. Sometimes I stay over if Dad's at an away game and Mum's on a night out. There's always a spare bed. Sometimes there are guests there who aren't 16-year-old youth team players, and you can see on their faces that this is not a holiday booking they are going to repeat.

Deano is turning into a natty dresser. He favours Fila, but like all of us he enjoys hanging out at a shop called John Anthony, by the bus stop on Gervis Place in the smart part of town near the Arcade. It's not a big place but it's a step up when the lads are on YTS wages of £27 a week in the first year and £35 in the second. There are Italian brands that Shaun Brooks is all over with his first-team wages. There's plenty of Stone Island and Paul Smith, some CP Company stuff, alongside brands that we understand are not for us like Emporio Armani and Hugo Boss.

Mark, just turned 19, is still leading the way. Dave Morris, like on Terry Shanahan's long runs, is trailing at the back. When I get free sportswear, I can bung stuff his way. Other times he'll come over to the house with an empty bag, tell Mark he hasn't got a top for that night and leave with a top and a suit and a few more long-term loans. It's all fine because he's our minder on the pitch. We stick together, all of the time.

Because we are still only pretending to live the dream. When we're done at training we all have to pile into the communal bath, mud and grass bobbing about, the water soon filthy. There is only one bar of soap, which turns that from something meant to clean you into something that's more likely to infect you. Someone will always nick your towel because someone will always forget theirs. There is only one toilet, and so you pee where you can when you want. It's not La Masia in Barcelona. It's barely better than just going home dirty.

We are still the outcasts. At the corner of the ground is the supporters' club. The bloke who runs it hates us walking in. As far as I can tell, he hates pretty much everything. I am fascinated by the hygiene standards. He dishes out ham sandwiches in white bread that look like they'll kill you fast, unless you're unlucky and they kill you slow. All I ever buy off him is a can of Coke. Even then, when he gives me my change, I stick it straight in the fruit machines or the jukebox rather than my pocket. Because there is no NWA on the AFC Bournemouth Supporters' Club jukebox, I settle for Stevie Wonder and 'Superstition'. The bloke who runs it hates that too.

The better option for lunch is the Queen's Park pavilion café, away across the gravel car park. You can get a voucher off the club to get food there, but you have to get there sharpish or it's all gone. A good day brings gammon and chips. A brilliant day brings apple pie for pudding too. Word will come back from the first lads out of the communal bath and towelled off and over the road – 'Boys! Pie's up!' – and if you get there and it's all gone it's total devastation.

For the first time, we're noticing that Bournemouth is a sleepy kind of town. For so long it has seemed so big. In summer, the beaches are full and the promenades crowded and something is going on every night. The sun shines and we live our lives outside. But we start wondering what else there is out there, in a modest sort of way. Maybe slightly more cool clothes shops. Venues that play hip-hop rather than Stock, Aitken and Waterman and will also let in lads who aren't old enough to be let in.

You start looking around and wondering how many people actually get out of Bournemouth. People come here to retire. They come here when their lives are coming to an end. We're just starting out.

On Saturday morning I go back into Dean Court looking for Dad, and I walk out on the pitch and see John the grounds-man going slowly up and down with his mower, going only slightly faster than the grass is growing. It's like an ancient living nursery rhyme. One man went to mow. I jog up the steps of the main stand and there are cushions on the wooden benches. Cushions in a football ground.

I can't imagine Bournemouth in Division One. I can't see anything changing that much. When you live in Bournemouth you don't want things to change. That's the whole point. And I run outside quickly to shake off the creeping sleepiness, and I see the lads chasing balls round the gravel car park like puppies after crisp packets in the wind, and I get a great waft of relief. We are the triers. We are the doers. We're the generation who might get out, because we care.

And when the tedium takes hold we make our own fun. There's a match going on at the ground for 20 minutes before anyone realises that there is a vast shadow stretching across the pitch from one of the floodlights. It's almost bike-shaped, a spindly black triangle where there should be yellow light and green grass. You look up into the dark evening sky and see why. One of the lads' bikes is up there. Someone has gone to the effort of nicking it, hoisting it on their shoulders like a cyclo-cross rider and climbing all the way up the metal frame before wedging it over the top corner. That someone, going by the look of delight on his face and the way Ashley's chasing him down the corridors trying to give him a dead arm, is my brother Mark.

The club holds soccer schools for local boys in the summer holidays. The lads are aged between nine and 14, so us youth team boys are sent to look after them, organise the training sessions. They're meant to be with us for a week, but three days in we've reverted to running all-day five-a-side matches. There is one gobby kid who won't shut up. Whingeing about this, banging on about that. Messing about, booting balls away, kicking over cones. I wait until a stray pass comes my way, line him up and hit the sweetest half-volley straight into his napper.

Summer is the sweetest time. Piling down the beach, squeezing as many of us as we can into Neil Masters' car, Deano getting lodged in the boot because he's the smallest. He can't see a thing in there but he can chat if we shout, bang on the roof to tell us he's still alive.

Training our arses off all morning, filling up on apple pie, swimming in the sea. Someone with a ghetto blaster for a town without ghettos, now a couple of girls bothering to hang

159

around with us too. There's the twins Sam and Nina. Nina even digs the Jungle Brothers, who are at the funkier end of the hip-hop spectrum, samples from the sort of '70s soul tunes that my dad listens to but laid under words he would never use in front of my mum. All of us singing, *'Because I got it like that . . .'* and Nina wiggling to the little wobbly organ riff and eyebrows going up.

I briefly have a girlfriend. Her name is Louise Russell, and I meet her because her brother James is mates with Mark. She's a really nice girl, but I have absolutely no idea what I'm doing. I'm so serious about my football that there's not much else I'm interested in doing. Everyone likes Louise. It's not true to say that I'm not ready for a serious relationship. It's more that I'm in one already with football, and every week the romance throws up something new and exciting.

The senior players are the gatekeepers to proper football and they are the men who can get us into places that proper footballers get into. Luther Blissett will sit down in the dressing room at Dean Court and tell you stories about life in Milan, which have slightly more traction than his ones about living in Watford. Closer to home, he tells us about a club called Madisons, up some stairs above Miss Selfridge in the Square in the middle of town, and it sounds amazing. It also sounds terrible – neon sign with the name going up diagonally, disco balls and dirty mirrors inside, an absolute stench of sweat and booze and fags – but that is exactly what we want.

When we work out that the bouncers will accept a fake driving licence as ID, we think we've cracked it. We get them printed out and I spend the whole of the afternoon practising my answer for when I'm quizzed at the door, my new date of birth, my fake address. And I'm so flustered when the moment comes that I get everything right except the year, which I get wrong by getting right. I'm not meant to say 1973, which is the truth. I'm meant to say 1971.

Luckily, these bouncers either forget quickly or think we all look the same. When we get in a week later, older and wiser, it's like we're running out at Wembley. We can't believe it. An actual nightclub, with hip-hop upstairs and house downstairs, fine to be wearing jeans and trainers, decks in the corner where big names like Andy Weatherall and Carl Cox play on the techno nights, girls in the sort of tops and skirts they didn't wear round the Square during the day and definitely hadn't picked up from Miss Selfridge. We've done it. We've cracked it.

There will be other places we find out about. Kevin's House if you're bang into your proper 120 bpm dance music. Glasshoppers, a tiny, dark basement where the hip-hop beats bounce off the walls and you jump around like you're trying to tunnel out through the floor. Of course I'm too young, but the same rules work in these places as on the pitch. Dave Morris is older and much harder and he can handle it all, so he looks after me when we're in the queue and it gets lairy, or when we're on the dancefloor and someone lobs out an elbow or you nudge their pint or they become convinced that you're looking at their girlfriend or worse still their girlfriend is looking at you. It happens to Scott Mean one night – never his fault, just some tanked-up loon, but he gets glassed, and you can't forget something like that when you see it. It makes me start thinking of nightclubs like a football pitch: you need to understand that trouble can come from every direction. I start positioning myself with my back to the wall or somewhere where I can see everything in front of me. You never want to be surprised.

Dave's a minder on the move, and it all happens because I can play football. Not because of who my dad is, but because the respect and the bonds come through what you can do with a ball at your feet. And it works the other way too. I'm comfortable with my elders and wisers. I know that if I couldn't play it would be hard, maybe impossible. All the kids in our youth team have busted their balls to be here, and it's created the bonds between us but also a barrier around us to those on the outside. If you don't feel like we do about football, you're not coming in. If you can't do what we can do, there is no place for you.

I love the atmosphere around us and I never feel uncomfortable with it. It's an arm round the shoulder and boot up the arse at the same time. You try to stitch each other up with the little stuff, but when it's serious you all step in to help each other. Dave calls me a pretty boy. He says I'm a baller not a brawler. He'll also protect me from anything. He says I'm good enough to be here. That's all that matters.

It's still a small town to be growing up fast in. We come out of Madisons one night just after midnight, me, Dave and Deano, and the other two are staggering. There's no match coming up so we think we're okay, and I'm kipping over at the Highlin so there's no problem with Mum and Dad. At least there isn't until we wander across the road, all shouts and arms round the shoulders, and we hear a shout from a car waiting for us at the crossing and look over and realise with a lurch of the guts that it's Mum and Dad.

There's no way we could have guessed that they would fancy a late Chinese. There's no justice in the fact that they're coming back through town this way at the exact time we're between the two pavements. There's no way that Dad isn't going to go ballistic.

I get off slightly easier, only because it's obvious I'm not drinking. But it's a marginal thing. The temper is in full effect, the explosion of anger, the shouting, the arms. When we get into training the next morning, Terry Shanahan has been told. We're banned from going out, all of us. No more alcohol on Saturdays after games. Grassed up by your own dad, and none of us can complain about it, because it all comes from a good place. It's to make us better players. It's to give us a greater chance of making it. And making it is exactly what we want to do, because we understand that while we're nothing yet, we're also privileged in ways that others are not.

There is a trip for the first team to the west coast of North America, all Dad's old connections coming into play. He takes a couple of us youth-teamers for the experience. There are matches in Seattle, Portland, Vancouver, Victoria Island.

There are British navy vessels stationed in Vancouver. As guests from the motherland we are invited on board, and there are cans of beer everywhere. There are the posh ones going straight in as officers, and there are the lads from the same backgrounds as us who are in the ranks and stuck there. You can tell how much they dislike it. You can see the discipline and how it's enforced and how they push against it. Naval officers make Terry Shanahan look like a kindly old grandmother. Conditions on board make the Highlin look like the *QE2*. Meanwhile, Neil Masters is piling into the beers, and Dave is getting slaughtered, and it's sort of fun but also very weird, and when we leave we're all boisterous cheers and thanks but we're also a bit quiet, because we've seen the other side. We're footloose and free, not like those lads. We can go out when we want once Terry has relented a little. Football and beaches and clubs and messing about. A long way from three months at sea and a couple of brutal nights out on the other side of the world where no-one really welcomes you at all.

What's the hardest thing we have to go through? An afternoon at college in Southampton as part of the YTS scheme that most of the youth team is on. It's one day a week, and it is so boring to us that we walk out of the classroom and immediately forget everything we've been told. There's nothing that any of us think will help us afterwards, even the ones who are wondering if they're quite going to cut it with the seniors in a few years' time, and it's a massive pain to get there, half an hour on the train and a trudge either end.

I've got no interest in it. It's not playing football, so there is no way I can see the point of it. Deano tells Terry he would rather run round the gravel pitch all day or do his horrible six-mile epics, and Terry sort of agrees but there's nothing he can do about it. The only fun part is the race to Dave Morris's car each time. There's only room for half the team, even with Deano in his usual spot in the boot, so whichever five gets there first get the lift and the rest have to march on to the station. And that goes wrong too. Flying down the stairs at the college, not right at the front but safely tucked in the lead group, I trip on the final step and go over on my ankle.

I make a right mess of it. I can't play for weeks. Dad goes mad – you've done what, messing about on the stairs? – and I'm not sure if it's ever quite right again. Years down the line, I'll end up breaking that ankle a couple of times, and each time I'll think back to the stairs at a college I didn't want to be at, doing a course I didn't want to do, and it will stay with me. Lucky but unlucky, protected from the real world but still finding scrapes and shocks in our strange little bubble.

And it is still little. The youth team plays in the South East Counties League, Division Two. Division One is for the big boys – Tottenham, Arsenal, Chelsea, West Ham. Division Two can also be for the big boys, but only their own small boys. Spurs and Southampton have enough kids to run two youth teams, and the younger ones play in our division.

So we start away at Bristol City on Saturday 19 August 1989, my first official competitive match for the proper AFC Bournemouth youth team. Keith Rowland is left-back, Dave Morris is five, Deano six, Andy Case wearing the number nine. I'm number eight, centre-midfield, and we do okay, a 2–2 draw. We win away at Colchester, and I score a goal. We thrash Bristol Rovers 5–1, and Deano scores.

We lose 4–0 to Chelsea's big lads in the Cup. We ship six

to Spurs and a load of the lads I might have grown up with had I made a different choice. I don't regret it because there is nothing like scrapping with your best mates on your side for 90 minutes. Me, Dave and Deano together in midfield, knowing exactly where each of us wants the ball, knowing exactly where each will be when we have the ball at our feet and a man coming at us and a pass for us to find.

I score twice against Tottenham's younger lads, the ones actually my age. By early October, there's another goal against Aldershot, and I feel part of something bigger than me. Things are moving. We are on the way up, even if I'm still not old enough to drive a car or buy a drink, even if the next steps are Oxford United away and Northampton Town at home.

Opportunities open up, and it all seems natural. Terry Shanahan needs bodies in the reserves. He needs young legs as well as midweek games for senior players coming back from injury or trying to fight their way back into the first team. So some of us get the call-up. Home to Swansea, and I'm starting centre-mid alongside Peter Shearer, who is six years older than me and was playing league football for Birmingham when I was in the third year at Twynham Comprehensive. Denny Mundee's in defence, a bloke who can't stop talking and who'll end up playing every position except goalkeeper for the first team. Deano's on the bench. We sit next to each other in the dressing room.

I get picked again against Bristol City, still only two months after my 16th birthday, and this time I've got Shaun Brooks alongside me too, pure wannabe Italian style and so comfy on the ball. Torquay away, Deano getting a start now, Matty Holmes coming into midfield. By December Dave is getting a look-in, and by January I'm playing with my brother too. Bigger names from the first team dropping down, Paul Miller and Sean O'Driscoll, striker Trevor Aylott. Trevor is 33 years old. He scored goals for Chelsea, for Crystal Palace, for Millwall. He's from Bermondsey. He can handle himself. If your pass isn't exactly where you want it, he'll let you know. But I'm okay with that, because that's what he should do. It's what we're all doing. This is my normal. This is my world.

We're all wondering now. Who will be the first to travel with the first team to a game as a player, maybe named on the bench in a League Cup match? They're struggling a bit in Division Two, and there are injuries, so Dad is going to have to give someone a go. He doesn't have many other options.

It's one of those nights at the Highlin where we decide how we'll find out. We're all there, and someone mentions an Ouija board, and then everyone's pretending to be up for it. I'm trying to say nothing, because ever since *The Exorcist* the idea of deliberately doing anything that involves ghosts or dead people or the devil makes me go cold with horror, but I can't say no, not when everyone is shouting and laughing. So we all sit round one of the dining tables, fingers on the upturned glass, all us youth players around the board, and we ask the question – who is going to make a footballer? – and we wait.

Nothing for a moment. Then the glass starts to wobble, and edge, and then slide.

Straight to me.

I don't know whether to be sick or cheer. Everyone else is ooh-ing and yeah-ing, and then the glass starts sliding again. This time it stops at Keith Rowland.

It frightens the life out of me. The glass is moving, I can see it. We're all a bit freaked, even the ones who are laughing it off. We're strong boys now, some done with growing, others starting to look like men rather than lads. But we're still boys inside, even the hard ones. We don't have all the answers.

As for the ones who the glass doesn't come to, the ones who are already starting to think that they're not going to break in, the players who Terry hasn't called up to the reserves, there's a different sort of haunting going on. There's a glimpse into a different future, where they're ex-footballers, where they're another name on that endless list of nearly made its, of park players who will talk in the pub about how they were on a professional team's books, but injury and bad luck and others got in the way.

Everyone will struggle with the aftermath, one way or another.

•

Dave Morris: I still think about some of the things Jamie used to do. They're etched in my mind. On that trip to America, in one of the games, one of us played a ball into him in midfield, and he put one leg behind the other and hit a 40-yard pass out to a team-mate on the wing. He was just a cut above the rest, is the bottom line.

↑ Nice to see me working on my left foot early on. Footballer's legs already in development, nappy possibly ready for a change.

↗ Beautiful kit, beautiful image. There's no better way to celebrate your uncle winning the FA Cup for West Ham than posing in matching sweatbands with your big brother.

→ Look at the face. Look at the boots. That's how it feels to get a pair of Super Keegans from Nan and Pop for your birthday.

↓ Mike England actually played for Wales, and finished in Seattle with Dad. Confused? Don't be. He was a great player and lovely man. I'm the one clutching the red trackie top; the knee-high sock was a big part of late '70s life on the US west coast.

↑ I loved the plastic trophies with the gold-coloured players on them. The Adidas boot and knee-length sock hadn't lost their appeal either.

↑ Not many kids can name Brazil and Luton as their two favourite teams. I wanted to be Ricky Hill slightly more than I wanted to be Zico. I was a bit weird.

↓ There would come a time in Ayia Napa when all young footballers were wearing vest tops. I like to think I was just 25 years ahead of the game. Still in knee-high socks, btw.

↓ There is no better feeling for a boy than being on a football pitch, in football kit, with a football manager who's also your dad and your hero. Fact.

↑ We had a decent team at Twynham Comprehensive. There wasn't a single natural fibre in that kit, but as captain you got to hold the match ball and wear trainers for the big photo rather than boots.

→ I stayed out in that back garden for hours. Football practice was never a chore, always a joy. It was just what I wanted to do. All the time . . .

↑ It's only looking back that I realise my mum and dad were the epitome of late 1970s glamour. In defence of Dad, everyone loved a beige/brown combo at the time.

↓ My brother Mark was modelling at an age when I could still barely talk to girls. Hence his confidence in the denim shirt/knitted waistcoat combo. I'm so lucky to have had the dad and brother I have.

→ You go to a club aged 14 and it could be intimidating. Instead, Everton were brilliant. Ray Minshull looked after me so well. He genuinely cared.

↓ You probably shouldn't be ready to play first-team pro football at 16 years old. But it felt natural. Everything that had happened to me in my life to that point made it make sense.

↘ We both knew this would probably be my last game for the Cherries. I'd learned the sweet stuff and the darks too. Ian Bishop for the first, definitely Tony Pulis for the second.

Everton

EVERTON FOOTBALL CLUB COMPANY LIMITED
GOODISON PARK, LIVERPOOL L4 4EL.

January 14th. 1987.

Dear Jamie,

Thank you so very much for your card and I am so pleased that the tracksuit was suitable for you.

As far as we are concerned Jamie, you can come to Bellefield any time you wish and we shall be delighted to look after you again.

Whenever you are available, please do give us a ring and I will make the necessary arrangements and you can stay with Mrs. Harvey again if you so wish.

I shall be getting in touch with your Dad in the near future regarding another visit for you Jamie and in the meantime - enjoy yourself.

I always seem to be looking for the Bournemouth results since you came up and I am pleased to see that they are still well in the hunt.

Cheerio for now, give my regards to your Mum and Dad and I look forward to seeing you again shortly.

Best Wishes,

Ray Minshull

YOUTH DEVELOPMENT OFFICER.

Mirrorpix/Reach Licensing

TEAM SHEET

To be handed to Opponents

Date 19th Jan 1991

LIVERPOOL
versus
WIMBLEDON

Referee:- MR. H.W. KING.

Goalkeeper BRUCE GROBBELAAR
2 GARY ABLETT
3 DAVE BURROWS
4 STEVE NICOL (CAPT)
5 STEVE STAUNTON
6 GARY GILLESPIE
7 JIMMY CARTER
8 IAN MOLBY
9 IAN RUSH
10 JOHN BARNES
11 STEVE McMAHON

Nominated Substitutes:
12 RONNY ROSENTHAL
14 JAMIE REDKNAPP

We are playing in the following colours:
Shirts RED
Shorts RED
Stockings RED
Goalkeepers Shirt GREEN
Signed
Official responsible for the Team.
LIVERPOOL F.C.

↑ Signing for Kenny Dalglish is not like signing for any other manager. He looked after me like a son, literally — I used to stay at his house and have breakfast with his daughters.

← I'd been at Liverpool for two days. I thought I was at the game to watch from a nice seat in the stand. And then this went up on the wall.

↗↗ Lovely kit, hard yards. When you're in Liverpool reserves, every other player views you as the problem. You're the one in their way. And if you've got long hair . . .

→ Full debut, away at Auxerre, noise that I'll never forget. This was the most space I had all night. By a long way.

↑ If you're going to score your first ever goal for Liverpool, you might as well make it a blockbuster. It takes power, technique and precision to smash one home from two yards out.

← You didn't need a Christmas fancy dress party to have fun with Don Hutchison. You could be sitting on the sofa in your old kit. I always loved loons. Don was king of them.

Except where indicated, all photos courtesy of the author and his family.

Dean Giddings: There were moments when you just knew. Jamie's second game for the youth team was at Colchester. Alan Ball was their assistant manager at the time, to Jock Wallace. He watched Jamie score twice. As we walked off, Alan came over to Terry Shanahan and told him, 'You've got a player there. He's head and shoulders above everyone else on that pitch.'

Then there was a youth team game at Spurs midway through that 1989–90 season. It was a tight game, nothing in it. Jamie picked the ball up in the centre circle, beat his man, accelerated forward and stuck one in the top corner from 30 yards. The ball almost stayed still in the air, he hit it that well. A perfect trajectory, no deviation. You see that at 16 and it's different. He was one of us, but he was out on his own too.

10

THE CONTRACT

Dad has not built this Bournemouth team to protect his son. He's built it to stay in Division Two, to continue to beat the odds that say a club of this size shouldn't be in the same league as teams like Leeds and West Ham and Newcastle and Leicester, to maybe even think about a pop at the play-offs should they get on a real run. But for a young kid looking up, dreaming of the next step, there are examples of the sweet science – Shaun Brooks, Ian Bishop – and there are the football bouncers, Paul Miller and Tony Pulis, and it's Tony who is now forming a bond with Dad as assistant coach and occasional player that works for them and works for me.

Tony can't believe how good Dad's footballing memory is. They play a little game when they're having a cup of tea in the office after training. Tony names a lower league player. Dad reels off their clubs, what their attributes are, where you can hurt them if you come up against them. Tony is 10 years younger than Dad, and he can't work out how he can remember the name of everyone he's ever met. Dad walks into a room and it's 'Alright, Steve,' and 'Wotcha, Dave,' and Tony's shaking hands and shaking his head too.

The two of them drive up to London after training to watch another game or do some scouting. Dad's behind the wheel, Tony has got the *Rothmans Football Yearbook* out. It goes like this.

'Tone, pick a player, any player in the league.'

'Right. Mark Venus.'

'Wolves. Defender. Started Hartlepool, gone to Leicester. Decent left-back, only about 22, ain't he?'

'Yeah. Correct, H. Gary Bennett.'

'Do me a favour. Big lump, centre-half. Man City as a kid, then Cardiff, been at Sunderland ages. Good player for them. His brother's the winger, Dave, won the Cup with Cov in '87.'

For the second round he has to get within 50 games of their total league appearances. He rattles them off. Then the phone rings, a big brick of a carphone Dad's had installed. It's his bookie, and the next part of the journey begins.

'Ali? Ali? What's going in the first? You what? Okay. What's going in the second?'

An hour of bets going on. Over to Millwall for an afternoon kick-off reserve game in the Football Combination, up against George Graham's Arsenal, a few decent youngsters to watch and maybe think about bringing in. Over to Chelsea for their reserves kicking off at 7 pm, bad mood on the way because the bets from earlier haven't come in, back on the phone to Ali to lump on for that night's dogs at Walthamstow.

Tony is different to Dad but they're mates, and he's different to me as a player but a brilliant example. He's so fit for a

32-year-old. The first team squad are training over at Salisbury, and I'm with them to bolster the numbers and get some extra work in. Tony takes me aside and starts talking.

'Jamie, you can play. No doubt. You've got to run too, though. I'll take you out afters, we'll do some.'

Then it's the food. Tony has read a book with a foreword by Martina Navratilova called *Eat to Win: The Sports Nutrition Bible*. The yellow and purple front cover is dog-eared and dirty because he's gone through it so often. At the back are 27 pages of menus, and Tony has had his wife Debbie sack off the usual Pulis household teas and start cooking these dishes for him – unthinkable ingredients like rice and celery and brazil nuts. There's not a bacon sarnie or a chip to be seen.

It tells you what to eat for energy before a game and what to eat to recover afterwards. Which lunch you should have before a long run and which dessert will hit the spot but not slow you down. That's what Tony gives me, the stuff I wouldn't think about because my head is all about clipping passes and spinning to find space and dropping my left shoulder to switch the ball onto my right foot. And so when 1989 comes to an end and I'm playing well in the reserves and comfortable among the big lads, it's Tony who's telling me that I could be playing in the first team soon, and whispering in my ear that I'll be fine, that I'm ready, and that him and Maxie Miller and the rest will make sure that I'm looked after if I do get the chance.

It comes far sooner than I think: January 1990, away at Hull. Sixteen years and seven months old. Named as one of the subs, shivering in my tracksuit and padded coat as we get off the coach at Boothferry Park.

Tony sits me down in the dressing room. There are a lot of stories going round about Hull's striker, Billy Whitehurst. That he's the hardest man in football, that his elbows are attracted to opponent's noses and that his studs like dishing out their own particular massages. Six-foot tall, former bricklayer, shoulders on him like one of the outhouses he used to help build. There are rumours he had two bare-knuckle fights when he was at Oxford United – not messabouts on the pitch, but proper organised brutality in a barn or car park somewhere. Apparently, he won the first one with an early knockdown but the second one dragged on a bit, and although he won again, because Billy always wins, his face was so mangled he had to tell his manager he'd been in a car crash.

I've never been a brawler. My brother is doing modelling. Bournemouth has plenty of bingo nights but is yet to host its first bare-knuckle night.

I've seen Billy getting off the bus. One of his thighs weighs as much as I do. Then Tony decides to tell a tale about when Bournemouth came up against Billy when he was playing for Reading. It's not great for a 16-year-old's pre-match nerves.

'We were about fifth or sixth from the bottom, boys, and Reading were about third from top. We had this little Irish lad in the squad, great lad, he was big mates with Billy. Before the game, us all in suits off the coach, Billy comes bounding over to the little Irish full-back and they give each other a cuddle and he goes, "Which of these boys don't you like? Just give me a name, give me a number and I'll munch 'em."'

The story gets worse, although Tony's telling it with enormous relish. 'That was the day when Mick Tait played midfield and I honestly don't think the ball got touched for 90 minutes. It was just war. Broken someone's leg, then he's done me, and I come in at half-time. We wore all red that night, which was handy cos when I've taken my sock down it's mostly blood. I need about nine stitches down my shin, but what they did then, they wouldn't stitch you up, they just put the pad down there, wrapped it round and you went out again.'

Boothferry Park in the middle of January can already feel like travelling back in time – grey terraces everywhere you look, old tin roofs painted amber and black sloping up and down over the few covered areas, spindly floodlights in the corner. Wind coming in off the North Sea, only a brave 4,000 or so in there. And now the ghosts of Tony's past are coming back to the frozen present, because Billy is there in front of me on the pitch, and he's absolutely fuming – an angry man when he's at home on the sofa, a man with steam coming out of his ears and nose and wherever else when his team is 4–0 down at home and the opposition manager is about to send on his 16-year-old son.

I'm mesmerised by him. It's like watching a kettle boil. Every goal that goes in, the more lunatic he looks.

Dad keeps his final tactical advice punchy. 'You're going on maestro, just avoid that maniac Whitehurst.'

I run out. Luther's there, and Kevin Bond, and Maxie and Matty Holmes. Come on Jamie, this is it.

The ball gets played into my feet. I take a touch, and then I almost stop, because I can hear these noises coming up behind me, like a monster snorting, like an old steam train charging up a hill. I can see our left-back Paul Morrell out on the wing, big lad, been at the club ages, and my brain says, give it to Paul. Now.

So I do. But maybe it's the occasion, or maybe it's the state of the pitch, or the wind, but I sell him a bit short. The pass is going to his feet but not quite getting there, so he goes to receive it and knock it up the line, and as he does so there's a smack and a cry and he's flying through the air and Billy Whitehurst is standing over him, snorting.

Paul's up in a shot. No-one kicks big, experienced left-backs around. He's up and pushing at the amber and black chest in front of him and then he looks up at the face above it and, oh shit, it's Billy.

Billy just lifts him up. Handful of shirt, skin, chest hair, whatever. Lifts him up, pulls back his wrecking-ball fist and it all goes off. Shaun Teale piling in, Peter Shearer piling in, all the Hull boys, the crowd yelling and screaming and the referee blowing his whistle in pointless panic. And me in the centre circle, 16 years old, one pass into my professional career thinking, 'F***, I've started a riot.'

What I don't know, what none of us do, is that it will be the high point of our season. We pick up a few draws but then the defeats start piling up, 3–0 away at Newcastle, 1–0 at

Oxford, 1–0 at Sunderland. You can see the tension at home on Dad's face, on Mum as she tries to steer the family around it. No games of snooker in the evening, just lots of phone calls. A quietness over breakfast or in the car on the way to training.

By the time I come off the bench for my next taste of the real stuff, away at Oldham, we're sliding down the table, and we're up against a team going the other way. There are players everywhere you look who are being watched by scouts from Division One's big boys, players who are only a few months from career-changing moves – Dennis Irwin at left-back, Earl Barrett and Paul Warhurst in the middle of the defence, Mike Milligan knocking it about in midfield, Rick Holden cantering down the wing. It's been 37 games since they lost at home in the league. They've already beaten Arsenal and Everton on their way to the final of the Littlewoods Cup, and they're lining up an FA Cup semi-final against Manchester United.

And it is a sobering experience. It's 3–0 by the time I come on for Matty Holmes with 25 minutes to go, and there's nothing I can do about it. The ball bouncing everywhere on their rock-hard plastic pitch, Joe Royle bellowing at them in his blue coat on the touchline, Neil Redfearn and Roger Palmer coming at me hard, Ian Marshall winning everything in the air, his curly mullet bouncing all over the shop.

They're comfortably the best side I've ever played against. And so even as I'm worrying how bad this is for the family, I try to tell myself that it's an experience that other 16-year-olds aren't having. The kids in the Spurs youth team aren't doing this, even if the drive home takes five hours and we're now as close to the relegation zone as the middle of the table. When Oldham repeatedly peg United back in their semi the next month, I'm watching at home on TV, and as they push Bryan Robson and Paul Ince and Mark Hughes all the way, I'm thinking, I played against players who have terrified some of the best in the country. Two degrees of footballing separation, a long way off but in sight now, in sight.

Oldham on the up, Bournemouth listing badly. Injuries keep dragging us down. Shaun Teale is out for the season, and the goals keep going in. One point from four games. Dad there in the house with us in the early morning and the mild spring evenings but not a part of it all, replaying games in his head, standing out in the garden with his hands jammed in his pockets. I get used to Tony Pulis knocking on the door in his tracksuit. Blossoms on the trees in King's Park and on my running loop around Ashley Heath and Moors Valley, only a little light filtering through.

On the same midweek April night that Oldham and United are meeting for their replay, we're up in London to play West Ham. I've heard whispers from some of the senior players that maybe I need to be starting, that we need to try something new, that sticking with what got us here is going to keep us right in it. Shaun Brooks has been ill with a virus too, so when we get on the coach outside Dean Court I'm not sure if he'll be on it. Walking down the aisle, looking left and right, no sign of him. Okay, we're a creative central midfielder down. Sitting on the back row, counting the players on board, fitting them into different formations to see if there's a gap. What else could Dad do here? Who else could slot in?

Out of town and onto the M27. Following the signs for the M3 and London, and only then does Dad come down the aisle and give me a little pat on the shoulder.

'You're starting tonight, mate.'

And there it is. My full debut, against his old club, against Uncle Frank's old club, against a team I've taken an increasing shine to in the last few seasons with all those family connections and Ian Bishop there now, too.

I have long hair because Bish has long hair. His is flowing out behind him, and mine's got so long at the front that it's hanging over my eyes. This isn't the time for not being able to see the ball, your first game against West Ham. So I borrow some scissors from the physio's medical bag and I sit there on the coach frantically snipping away at the fringe.

It looks horrendous, but there's no time for worrying about it, because we're only an hour or so from east London, and because I want this, too. It's opening a present on your birthday. It's chatting to the best-looking girl in Madisons. And it's Upton Park, under the lights, 20,000 in, the South Bank terrace rammed. Men and boys swaying under the old iron roof and up against the pale blue metal pillars, scarves and banners tied to the crash barriers.

It goes fast. Warming up on the rolled pitch, groundsmen stamping on divots and digging in forks, tannoy crackling with team news. Clattering down the tunnel, Dad keeping the instructions simple: pass it, work harder than them, quieten the crowd. Standing just outside the centre circle waiting for the whistle to go, shaking my legs out. Looking up and seeing Martin Allen crouched on the halfway line opposite, like a sprinter in a 100 metres final, staring right at me, growling.

There is a reason Martin Allen has the nickname Mad Dog. It's not because he goes out in the midday sun. But the noises he's coming out with make me laugh rather than scare me. I've seen Billy Whitehurst. I survived that, albeit by not going anywhere near him. And Mad Dog might not even be the hardest man in his own team. Julian Dicks finds trouble so easily that when he has his testimonial years later, a friendly against Athletic Bilbao, it will climax in a 17-man brawl.

He probably shouldn't be playing tonight. He's just come back from injury. But he's known as the Terminator, so nothing is going to stop him. In the first minute, he goes flying into a challenge that a fully fit defender would consider chancy at best. As the roar goes up from the terraces behind each goal, I think he might be the only player in the world who would do that.

The West Ham fans are piling into me. There are shouts when I take throw-ins about what I look like and what Mad Dog's going to do to me. 'What you doing here, son? You should be at school!'

None of it feels like a shock. This is football. This is the language of football. The volume is up, but the song remains the same.

I get into the game early. Ian Bishop, hero of mine the year before at Bournemouth, takes a contrasting approach to Allen.

He's talking to me all the way through – 'Well played Jamie . . . ,' 'Ah, great touch kid, you did me there . . . ,' 'Loved that, lovely pass!' Even in the noise and the mayhem, I'll remember it. Twelve years on, I'll be playing for Spurs against Everton when a 16-year-old kid called Wayne Rooney comes off the bench for his own first-team debut, and I'll do the same. Talking him through it, never going easy on him, but letting him know he's doing okay, that he can handle this. 'Good luck today little man, enjoy it,' in the tunnel. Done by a little bit of skill from him on the pitch. 'Stop that!' I shout. You'd never waste breath on talk with an experienced player.

Today, there's no chat from Allen. He just wants to eat me. But Bish is cool. Bish has even longer hair than me. And he can chat because it's all a cruise for them. An own-goal from Paul Miller as he tries to head away a cross. I'm supposed to be tracking Bish, but Stuart Slater is making all sorts of runs down the left, and I'm shouted at to come over and double up on him. That's when the pass is slipped inside to Bish, and he has time to take two touches before smashing it past Gerry Payton and into the top corner.

It stuns me for a moment. I'm almost happy. It's Bish being beautiful. Then the player within me catches up with the kid. He's my man, that's not meant to happen.

Dicks hammers in a classic Dicks penalty. Allen heads in at the far post. They're too strong for us, and a special night for me slips away into another dark one in a bleak month for Bournemouth.

•

Ian Bishop: Martin Allen used to growl at us as well, don't worry about that. I knew what Upton Park was like as a West Ham player. It was intimidating when you were one of their own, let alone a 16-year-old kid playing for the opposition. Coming out the tunnel, there were the fans that close to you. It was fierce. I wasn't sure how Jamie would cope, but he was never out of his depth.

It was great just to see him out there at such a young age. I didn't want him to win, but I wanted him to do well. I knew I wasn't ready for that type of football until I was about 19. So I talked to him throughout the game. 'I'm going to go now, come with me.' 'Watch his run.' 'Nice touch, Jamie.' We chatted the whole time.

•

We lose to Plymouth, we lose to Leicester. We lose to Sheffield United, and so when the final game of the season comes, at home to Leeds, we need to win and we need Newcastle to thump Middlesbrough to have any chance of staying up.

Nothing about the weekend feels normal. Blazing August-like heat has come to the opening days of May, half a northern city decamped to the quiet south coast. The Leeds fans start arriving on the Thursday, and by Friday afternoon they've taken over the beaches and seafront. So many lads, all tops off, mullets and moustaches, cases of lager, flags, and Yorkshire cricket hats.

Theirs is a tough team, with Vinnie Jones and Chris Kamara, Mel Sterland and Lee Chapman. The support reflects that. Friday night is a lockdown in town. I'm out at Mum and Dad's, but I get the call from Deano in the Highlin. 'J, we ain't going out in that tonight . . .'

No-one's surprised. They're laying on big screens back in Leeds, hoping to stop fans travelling, but their 2,000-strong allocation went in hours, the queues outside the ticket office at Elland Road starting at five in the morning. They've been packing in more than 30,000 supporters for their home games. Dean Court holds just under 10,000. And it's a Bank Holiday, everyone off work, everyone ready to go on the lash.

So they do. By the time me and Dad get to the stadium, I'm already the most frightened I've ever been at a football ground. Thousands of fans charging across King's Park, lines of riot police with black crash helmets and round plastic shields. Dad's not picking me for this one. He didn't even want me to leave the house.

The gravel pitch by the car park is all Leeds. No kids, barely any women, just blokes knocking back cans and then lobbing them and anything else they can lay their hands on. We get inside and the first thing you notice is how quiet it seems compared to outside. The second thing you notice is what punctuates that peace. An irregular clanging sound, first intermittent, then more consistent. It's like a heavy rain on the corrugated roof, like hailstones coming down. It takes a while to realise that it's stones and rocks from the car park, cans and branches, thrown over the lines of police.

Bang. Bang. Bang. Hammering down now, everyone ducking even under the roof.

Everything about the place feels wrong. Bournemouth fans are not fighters. They're the wrong age, the wrong demographic. Not enough angry young lads, too many nice old boys. Maybe that's what's going to save it. This isn't a battle, it's a broken procession.

Out the back there are fans steaming across the car park, kicking up clouds of dust into the perfect blue sky. There's a roar rising up every time they charge, an answering one coming back from the cops as they go at them with truncheons and dogs. When the teams come out, Bournemouth in our red and black Milan stripes, Leeds in their pale yellow away kit, Top Man printed in blue on the chest, like they know it, like they believe it, the roar kicks up again and there's another assault on the turnstiles.

It's never a contest, not really. It's not pure muscle, this Leeds team. It's got Gordon Strachan on the right and Gary Speed on the left. But it's a lot of muscle. Their centre-backs clamber all over Luther Blissett. Chapman waits for the long balls from Sterland and Jim Beglin and chests and flicks them to Carl Shutt.

It's pure intimidation, out in the streets, on the pitch in front of me. And I think, this what I'm going to be up against soon. The fear sits like a sharp block in your chest, even watching, but this is the game I'm in. You have to fight. You have to earn the right to play.

In the first half hour, there's barely a single subtle pass in there. The ball doesn't see the ground. It's getting bashed everywhere – header up, flying kick, Kamara and Vinnie going into tackles, smashing people. So I try to place myself in the middle of it, even amid all the noise and distractions all around. What I'd do if I took the ball like Shaun Brooks there and had Kamara coming down my Achilles. How I'd find space with Chris Fairclough climbing all over me. Where the gaps are between him and Sterland, where Vinnie isn't tracking back, which side he doesn't want you running at, where you could do Strachan with pace and then get your arms out wide and your fingers up to keep his brutal enforcers at bay.

Chapman does it, in the end. Kamara down the right, swinging a cross in, Chapman up and banging a header in from the edge of the six-yard box like other players might bullet a volley. Moments later, way up there in the north-east, Middlesbrough start sticking goals past Newcastle. The fans know and the players do too, and so the game falls strangely flat, waiting for the final whistle and the pitch invasion that's coming. And as the Leeds fans pile on and the players and managers sprint for the tunnel, it barely feels like a home game anymore, and it barely feels like Bournemouth. There isn't even that much sadness now. People just want to get home safe, and forget about it. No-one's blaming Dad. Bournemouth fans don't expect to be playing teams like this. They understand we don't have the money and the players and the support of a team who were winning the league in the decade before. The sun shines and the fighting goes on in town and you hide away and wait for it all to pass.

Players will move on too. Bournemouth are back in Division Three. They need younger and they need cheaper and they need hungrier, and I know that's me. But there's still something surprising and wonderful about seeing the four carefully typed sheets of A4 of a pro contract in front of me on the morning of my birthday, a separate two pages of detail about bonuses next to them.

Right at the top, in capital letters, it says FOOTBALL LEAGUE CONTRACT. Football has always been about freedom for me, about avoiding the serious stuff, about fun and escape. Now, for the first time, it is work. It is a job.

And it reads like a legal document from the Shakespearean era.

AN AGREEMENT made the TWENTY FIFTH day of JUNE. Between James P Nolan, of AFC Bournemouth, Dean Court, Bournemouth. The chairman of and acting pursuant to Resolution and Authority for and on behalf of AFC Bournemouth Football Club Limited (hereinafter referred to as 'the Club') of the one part, and JAMIE FRANK REDKNAPP of 15 Whitfield Park, Ashley Heath, Ringwood, Hants, a Registered Association Football Player (hereinafter referred to as 'the Player').

The Player. That's what I am now. It's happened. It's real.

But it's still weird. The clauses range from the blindingly obvious to the baffling.

2: The Player agrees to play to the best of his ability in all football matches in which he is selected to play for the Club and to attend at any reasonable place for the purpose of training in accordance with instructions given by any duly authorised official of the Club.

Yep, I'd sort of assumed that.

6: The Club undertakes to provide The Player at the earliest opportunity with copies of all relevant Football Association Rules, Football League Regulations and the Club rules for players.

I'll be honest with you, I won't read those.

7: The Player shall not without the written consent of the Club participate professionally in any other sporting or athletic activity.

The snooker and table-tennis with Dad and Mark are intense, and money sometimes changes hands, but until my long safety work and backhand slice improve, we should be okay here. The badminton? Mr Jackson has seen the best of me. It wasn't quite enough.

11 (a): The Player shall not reside in any place which the Club deems unsuitable for the performance of his duties under this Agreement.

I'm living with the manager. My bedroom is about five paces across the landing from his. The manager's wife makes my breakfast and tea. I might have the most suitable residence of any player in English professional football.

12: The Player shall be given every opportunity compatible with his obligations under this Agreement to follow courses of further education or vocational training if he so desires.

He does not so desire.

The really startling stuff comes on the final page, under 28 (e): Basic Wage. It says that from 1 July 1990 to 30 June 1991 I'm going to be paid £130 a week. It says I'll receive an additional £100 for every appearance in the first team. And then a sentence somehow even more magical: *The Player to receive a once and only signing-on fee of £5,000.*

I can't quite believe it. They're paying me to do exactly what I've always wanted to do. I've understood that for a long time. But to mark the occasion of me agreeing to be paid to play football, they're giving me as much again on top as I should be getting across three-quarters of an entire year.

That's a lot of trips to John Anthony. That's a lot of CP Company and plenty of nights out for all us in the youth team. Even if I'm no longer in the youth team. At an age when I still should be.

Then I start going through the second section, the two sheets that set out the further bonus schedule. It's like walking into an enchanted kingdom, a Disneyland of lower league football.

Bonuses for Football League matches shall be paid as follows: £160 per win. £75 per away draw. £30 per draw.

Players appearing in the first team will receive £60 per week when AFC Bournemouth occupies a position in the top six of Division Two. This will increase to £120 a week when

AFC Bournemouth occupies a position in the top two of Division Two.

In the event of the Club achieving promotion to Division One, a sum of £200,000 will be divided among the players on an appearance basis.

It keeps going, in sensible, practical ways and in marvellous flights of fancy.

Bonuses for participation in the FA Cup will be as follows: 3rd Round – £150 per draw, £300 per win. 4th Round – £200 per draw, £400 per win. 5th Round – £250 per draw, £500 per win. 6th Round – £300 per draw, £600 per win.

Bournemouth have only ever reached the 6th Round of the FA Cup once in their history. That was 33 years ago. In the season just gone, we failed to win a single match in the competition, beaten up by Dave Bassett's Sheffield United in the third round. But this is a club looking forward, even as they sink lower.

Semi-final – £1,000 as losing semi-finalists, £4,000 per win. Final – £2,000 as losing finalists, £8,000 per win.

There is a convoluted equation somewhere where we sit in the top two in the table all season, and I play every game, and we win at home and at least draw away every match, and we get promoted and win the FA Cup, where I end the season with a final sum big enough to buy myself a yacht and retire.

But the morning of your 17th birthday, the ink still drying on your carefully drawn signature, with its loopy 'J' and proper circle of a dot above the 'i', seems a fraction early to be thinking about the end. Today is about starts. Today is walking out of the club secretary's office with a secret smile. Walking out feeling older, with a sense of belonging.

The little landmarks come fast in those early summer weeks. Contract tucked away in my bedroom drawer, I splash a little of that remarkable cash on driving lessons. Like all teenage boys, I consider them a quick formality to dash off before I crack on with my driving career. I've already got my eye on a cheeky second-hand Peugeot, not even a 205 but a spacious 309, hatchback, white paint-job with a black spoiler. It's going to cost me three grand, and I don't even like to think what the insurance is going to be, because all I'm seeing in my head is me cruising about Ringwood with a hip-hop mix tape banging out of the stereo, Dave Morris with window down in the passenger seat, Mark in the back arguing he should be in the front, Deano next to him so he can have a breather from getting his head down in the boot.

First thing the driving instructor asks me is who my Dad's going to sign over the summer to get us back up. Turns out he's a massive Cherries fan. So my first line back to him is a straightforward one. 'Would you like some free tickets?'

I pass first time. Seventeen years old, officially a professional footballer, officially allowed to drive. I'm a man, in a few ways at least.

11

THE CRASH

It's a warm summer, late June of 1990, the days golden and the nights all open windows and light skies.

Everything feels fresh and possible. A professional footballer's contract, a driving licence, money in my pocket. A season coming closer where I'll be a first-team player, maybe not every match, but on the bus each week, in the middle of it all. New music and new sounds to get into. Beaches and arms and legs going brown and sitting out late in the garden with the grass turning yellow and pale.

And football, everywhere. The World Cup in Italy, games at tea-time, games in the evening when you're done with the day and all you want to do is lie back on the sofa and soak it all in. The stadiums look enormous. The San Siro seems to stretch up forever.

If it's warm back here it looks scorching in Genoa and Naples, and everywhere the football is sensational. Cameroon beat Argentina in the opening game, and even when three defenders are trying to chop Claudio Caniggia in half there's something magic about it. Toto Schillaci comes on as sub for Italy in their first game against Austria, having done nothing before, and suddenly all you can see is him running away in celebration of a goal with his eyes popping out of his head. Lothar Matthaus is rampaging through midfields for Germany, Roger Milla shaking his hips by corner flags.

England no longer look like the old England. There's Mark Wright sweeping and wing-backs charging and Gazza clattering through with his arms up and a Gazza grin on his chops. When David Platt swivels onto Gazza's chipped free-kick and volleys in at the absolute death against Belgium, me and Mark are roaring in each other's faces and grabbing each other's ears and straight out in the garden trying to re-enact it as Pavarotti warbles away on the BBC highlights.

Dad knows how to get on to a good thing when he sees it. He's flown over to Italy on what has been described to wives and partners as a scouting trip but what everyone knows is a jolly boys' outing. There is a Bournemouth player in Italy, but unless Jack Charlton loses his marbles in the heat, Gerry Payton is not going to replace Pat Bonner in the Republic of Ireland's goal, and there's not a single other player out there that Bournemouth could afford to sign. So there's a minibus going from game to game, city to city, with the group: Dad and Bournemouth's managing director, Brian Tiler; Tony Deangelis, who's a mate through Lorenzo's Italian restaurant; Michael Sinclair, the chairman of York City; and Fred Whitehouse, Aston Villa's chairman.

Of course we're jealous. Dad phones three times a day to tell us what a great time he's having and to have his usual catch-ups with Mum, which neither of them can do without. He's got tickets for England's quarter-final against Cameroon on the Sunday night, but first there's Ireland against Italy in the Stadio Olimpico in Rome on the Saturday evening, and everyone wants to see it.

The heat has been building up all week, the day sticky and humid. Mum's doing a favour for Keith and Yvonne, one house down on Whitfield Park, babysitting their kids while they go out for a meal in town, so I go with her.

It's one of those tight, tense games when Italian players are throwing their hands up everywhere and Jack Charlton looks like he wants to march onto the pitch and bring a little 1970s Leeds commitment to proceedings. Giuseppe Giannini and Roberto Donadoni pulling strings, Roberto Baggio and Schillaci dancing to them. It's Donadoni's shot from outside the box that Bonner can only beat away and it's Schillaci who crashes the rebound home, and I think of Dad out there in those Roman celebrations and Irish commiserations, right in his sweet spot, football and former footballers everywhere he looks, good food and wine and his mates and semis still to come.

The weather breaks in the minutes after full-time. Flashes of lightning, thunder rumbling overhead. Heavy drops of rain on our shoulders as we walk up the gravel path and back to our house. Mum's a little preoccupied. No phone call from Dad this evening, even though he knows we were next-door and has the number. No message on the answerphone tape when we get in.

We sit up for a while listening to the storm clattering out-side, waiting for the phone to ring. Mum is quiet now. She's thinking and wondering. At midnight she sends me to bed. When morning comes, I go downstairs for breakfast and she's in the same place, looking at the phone, willing it to ring.

'Jamie, something's wrong.'

'Nah, Mum, he'll just be travelling. Or there's no phone at the hotel or something.'

'Jamie, I can feel it. I can.'

I'm upstairs getting dressed when the phone call comes. I'm grabbing the receiver from the bedside table in Mum and Dad's bedroom as Mum's picking up the one downstairs.

'Harry?'

'Dad?'

It's the wrong voice. It's Jim Nolan, the Bournemouth chairman. A heaviness to his voice, a catch.

'Sandra, listen. There's been an accident. A car crash.'

The world on pause.

'Harry . . . he's in hospital. But he's all okay, Harry's alright, Harry's okay. He'll be fine. Yeah?'

The world stopping.

'It was him and Brian and the boys. They got hit, their minibus. Harry's okay. But Brian . . . Brian's dead. Sandra?

'I've got to go and tell Hazel. Okay?'

And so summer comes to an end, in that frozen moment on an otherwise silent Sunday morning. Jim Nolan in his car driving to Brian's house to knock on the door and tell his wife Hazel. Me and Mark sitting with Mum as she breaks down. Feeling powerless, feeling cut adrift. Not feeling very much at all.

•

Harry: We'd been going to all the games. It was a trip of a lifetime, 43 years old, we had tickets to every game all the way through to the final. We were in Rome and Schillaci scored that goal, and we came out and spent some time talking to these Irish guys who were asking me about Gerry Peyton. We left there and it was late on, so we stopped to get a pizza on the drive back to the hotel. I remember being the last one out, still eating. All of them saying, 'Come on Harry, hurry up!'

I always sat next to the window in the minibus because it was really hot. I liked having the sliding window open. But this time, because I was so long, messing around getting my pizza and getting stuff put on and doing whatever, Brian had taken my seat. That was my last recollection, stopping for the pizza and Brian shouting at me, 'Come on, Harry!' and, 'Get out of my seat!'

•

This is what we are told has happened. On a three-carriageway road in Latina, just south of Rome, a car coming the other way driven by three celebrating Italian supporters has swung out to overtake. It has hit Dad's minibus head-on. The minibus has flipped over onto its roof and slid along the road. Brian has been killed instantly. The three Italians are dead.

Dad is a mess. He's been thrown clear of the wreckage by the force of the impact and then dragged away by Michael Sinclair, unconscious, soaked in petrol. He has a fractured skull, broken nose, smashed up ribs. There is a great gash on his leg.

When the ambulances arrive they think he's gone. They pull a blanket up over his head. Someone else makes off with his watch.

The minibus looks like a scrunched-up piece of paper. The other car could be anything. There is nothing recognisable about it. Just metal and strange twisted shapes.

It will be two days before Dad regains consciousness. Someone makes the decision – not me, not Mum – that it is Mark and me who will go out there. Mum can't see Dad like that. He has Michael and Tony with him, and they book the flights. Me and Mark in silence on the way to Heathrow, in silence on the plane.

Mark, three years older, takes charge. He steers me through arrivals, he takes me to the hotel that Tony has found. My head is just memories. Me and Dad when I was three, kicking a sponge ball around in the lounge on Palmerston Avenue. Taking his pitching wedge and putter down to the golf course by the river. Him lugging the Sunday papers into the boot of his car on Old Barn Road to help me earn my paper round money. Driving to the training ground, waiting for him in the car park, firing balls against the wall, queuing up in the Chinese takeaway with its steamed-up windows and telly on a bracket on the wall showing *Kenny Everett*. The little clenched fist on the touchline, the frames of snooker with the old soul tunes playing, the debut away at West Ham.

We get a taxi to the hospital in Latina and I've got myself ready to see him, and we can't get in. Something about opening hours, but because we can't speak Italian and no-one speaks English, we're in the reception area so close to him I could almost call out, but we can't get any further.

We stand there and ask and nothing happens, and we sit there and wait and every moment I'm picturing Dad all by himself, wanting his boys there, wondering where we are.

It feels like we are there for hours, stuck in time, when someone comes to take us through. Down a narrow corridor, the hospital small and its rooms dingy, until we are led into a long, white ward with high ceilings.

We can't see him. Where is he? I've got no idea what he's going to look like. Will I recognise him? Is he paralysed? Is he still alive?

I catch sight of the reddish hair first, over in the corner by a wall. 'There he is!' And we start walking over, like we're walking through glue, both whispering, not sure if we're allowed to wake him or if he'll even hear us.

He turns, and it's then I see the black eyes, the thick scabs. The bandages wrapped around his face, the dressing stretched down his bare leg. And it's like the world has dropped into slow motion, and the room spins and my stomach drops and I'm gone.

I wake up on a sofa in an office down the hall. There's a cold flannel on my head and a massive egg-shaped mess underneath, where I've fallen and hit my head on the floor. People are talking Italian to me. When Mark takes me back into the ward, Dad looks at me with a bemused expression under all the cuts and damage. Mark looks maybe the most anxious of all. Jamie, we've had enough Redknapps unconscious for now. Hang in there, little brother.

I'm not sure what I was expecting to see, or how I thought I would react. I have seen mates in hospital when they've been ill. I'm not usually squeamish. But seeing Dad and realising how he is, for the first time, and sensing how close death has come to him, has overwhelmed the hold I had on things. I lie there just looking at him, eyes moving round his injuries. My own head throbs and I feel sick.

I can't imagine the alternative ending to all this. I can't imagine living the rest of my life without my dad's help. So I try not to. I try to push all that away and give him a little smile back instead.

•

We visit every afternoon, even though the staff don't really seem to want us there, that every time it's a battle to get in and they want us out again far too soon. Dad wants to talk about the football. We tell him about Gazza's passes and Gary Lineker's penalties in the win over Cameroon. We leave the hospital and we try to find a bar near our hotel showing the Italy *v* Argentina semi-final, but I'm watching without watching. I've never taken in less about a game. I can't concentrate and I can't process it.

When England play West Germany in their epic in Turin, there is mayhem in the bar and all manner of antics going off back home. I'm a zombie. I don't shout when Andreas Brehme's free-kick loops off Paul Parker and up and over Peter Shilton, and I stay in my seat when Lineker hooks in the equaliser. I don't notice Chris Waddle hitting the post in extra-time. I don't keep score in the shootout or take in the reaction of Stuart Pearce or Gazza. I don't want to be in Italy and I don't care about the football. I just want to be at home with my mum and dad. The sadness of losing a semi-final cannot break through the darkness all around.

There are tickets for the final. Dad pulls his out of the drawer in his bedside table. There is another spare one that we don't like to think about. The ticket is colourful, yellow and green and blue. 'Coppa del Mondo FIFA 1990' at the top. Words in printed blocks that would usually have my heart thumping. 'Gara/Match 52: FINALE. Citta/City: ROMA. Data/Date: 8-7-1990. Ora/Hour: 20.00.'

It's in my hand as we go through the gate. I notice how high we are in the main stand. I remember the instructions: 'Fila/Row 75, Posto/Seat 003.'

And that's it. Nothing of the game touches me. I'm at the World Cup Final. I can see the golden trophy down there in front of me. All of it might as well be happening a thousand miles away. I don't stand, I don't cheer, I don't react. Nothing goes in and nothing goes out.

All I want is my dad, by my side.

Running with a ball. Stopping with his right foot on top

of it. Clipping it to my feet, me knocking it straight back, toe down, landing it in his stride.

Movement and togetherness. Connection without words. Security and safety and all of it instinctive and effortless.

I have to fly back alone. Mark stays to be with Dad on the journey back, 11 days on from the crash. They have to come back on a specially chartered medical plane that flies at low altitude to protect the swelling inside Dad's skull.

He's taken to the new Nuffield Hospital on Lansdowne Road in Bournemouth, and there it's better. The visiting hours are long and generous. Cards keep arriving from friends and supporters, and I take little balls of Blu-Tack and stick them up in neat rows on the wall behind his headboard. Dad starts looking more like Dad. He sits up and he looks around.

Mum stays with him all day long. She won't leave the room. Me and Mark go up to Lorenzo's, 10 minutes' walk round the corner up Charminster Road, and bring back his old favourites – Chicken Milanese, penne all'arrabbiata. He hates the fuss, Dad. He wants no-one around except us three and the newspapers and football magazines. He wants the *Racing Post*.

The question that no-one wants to ask is whether he can come back to football. For Dad this is the wrong phrasing. It's *when* he can come back, and the answer is straightforward: much earlier than the doctors are advising as a best-case scenario. Six months isn't just forever in his head. It's the Christmas run-in. It's games on Boxing Day and New Year's Day and one in between. It's all the transfer deals he wants to make. It's half a season.

It scares me. I listen to everything the doctors say. This is my project now, the recovery, getting my dad back. When he ignores what the specialists are saying, when he gets Tony Pulis and Terry Shanahan on the phone and starts talking contracts and possible signings, it's the old him but much too soon. But we never talk about it because that's not how a father and son does it. I don't lie next to him and let it all come out – the tears, the panic, the doubt. He never lets on about the headaches and the stuff that's left behind: a new twitch, in his eyes and the side of his face, the loss of his sense of smell. We both know it's there, but we both want to protect each other from it.

We will never talk about the crash. Not when he comes back to football and training, not when I leave home. Not when I'm injured myself, my career in doubt, not on my wedding day. It sits there between us, unspoken, untouched. And it escapes only in the most inconsequential way: that he won't ever eat pizza again, no matter where we are. An aroma that brings it all back, a memory he wants to leave buried. The last thing that passed his lips before the accident; the last thing he'll ever want again.

•

Harry: I didn't know what was going on really, to be honest. I can't remember anything about the accident or anything. I just end up in a bed, in a hospital, in Italy. I didn't know that Brian had died, I didn't know what had happened in the accident.

When Jamie and Mark came over it was great to see them, because I was so concerned about Sandra. I really didn't want her coming out because I was worried about her, as I've always been with her – where she'd stay, what she was going to do. The hospital wasn't particularly great. I'd rather have her at home. I do worry about her all the time.

I wanted to get out of there, more than anything. I didn't want Sandra to see me like that and I didn't want the boys seeing me in a bad state. And I kept thinking about Brian.

He was a diamond, Brian. He was chief executive, he ran the club, but he was an ex-player too, captain of Aston Villa. He played alongside the centre-half like Bobby Moore would have played. When Tommy Docherty went to Villa as manager, his first signing was Brian. He'd seen Brian at first hand at Rotherham and knew what kind of person he was.

Brian was a real great character. He was brilliant for me. He could read me like a book. He knew when I wasn't happy and he would get me out. He was a buffer between me and the board, for sure, but he also knew the game, having been a player for many years.

Listen. I was lucky, Brian was unlucky. It just shows, you never know what's around the corner in life. One minute we're making plans for a great day, we're going to watch England play Cameroon, World Cup quarterfinals, a great trip to Naples. Then suddenly, bang.

So when I think about it, it's this: maybe, if I hadn't hung back in the pizza place for so long, we wouldn't have been on the road when that car came the other way. That's what I think.

•

I know he talks to Tony Pulis about the crash, as the summer cools down and the season approaches. He talks to him about signing autographs for those Irish supporters, how time would have shifted if he hadn't stopped. How they'd have jumped in the minibus 10 seconds earlier and then none of it happens.

Tony is good with him. They listen to each other.

'H, part of life is fate. Don't kid yourself, mate. There's certain things meant to happen. They all come together and unfortunately these things come in. They're either good things or they're bad things, and they're all things you have to deal with.'

Tough men who close themselves off. Strong men who understand what goes on underneath. Kids who grow up open to it all.

Tony looks after me, too. Normality comes back through football, through all the little rows and battles as much as the thought of games themselves. Arguments that mean nothing in the big scheme but bring a smile on an otherwise quiet day when you might fall into thinking about other things. Paul Miller getting sick of Peter Guthrie and his endless chat and nonsense in training.

'Guthrie, you're the most unprofessional person I've ever seen in my life. How Harry signed a c*** like you, I don't know.'

'You know cos you are one, mate. You've done nothing.'

'Done nothing? Pete, seriously, I am so f***ing fed up with all this – you this, me this, you this.'

'Max, if you want a go, step outside mate, I'll knock your head off.'

'Yeah? Well listen, we got Wednesday off, it's coming. Why don't we get together Wednesday?'

'We will. We've got all day.'

'Yeah. We've got all day, and that's what you'll need to walk round my house, you idiot.'

Nonsense and silliness, and all of it helps. Footballers being footballers. Normal stuff on days without drama. Dad getting better, Tony keeping an eye out. Football starting to take me back once again.

12

THE NORTH

Harry: I first met Kenny Dalglish when he was a 15-year-old lad, down from Glasgow to train with West Ham for a couple of weeks. There was a couple of them from Scotland Schoolboys, a little midfielder called Jimmy Lindsay, who ended up signing with us, and a boy called George Andrews, plus a big Welsh boy, a left-winger, Davie De'Ath. All of us down at Chadwell Heath, not so much a trial as a chance for them to look at the club and the club to impress them.

I was 18, one of the younger ones, and our manager Ron Greenwood, said to me, 'Harry, can you pick up Kenny and the other little boys in the mornings and bring them.' So, I used to get Kenny up in the mornings and take him to training from his digs.

Now Kenny was already known about the game. Every club in England wanted him. He was just looking at everybody and taking his pick really. But we had a practice match one Saturday morning and he played in the first team, despite only being 15. Ball came into him, posted himself up on the edge, the angle of the box. He took it into his feet, held the centre-half off, dropped his shoulder, turned and bent it in the top corner.

Everyone started clapping him. Bobby Moore, everybody. I said to Ron Greenwood, 'Are we going to get him?' and he went, 'No chance Harry, going to Celtic.' And despite every other club in England wanting him, too. 'He'll got to Celtic,' and sure enough, he did.

And then it goes full circle. Kenny's done it all as a player, won everything, best player of his generation. He's taken over as Liverpool manager, won the Double. No surprises. I'm up in London at the Dorchester for the Footballer of the Year awards, Kenny's there too, John Barnes winning the main award, third Liverpool player in a row. I'm having a dance with Sandra, and Kenny is having a dance with Marina, and every time we pass each other like ships in the night there's a bit more chat.

'How you doing, Harry?'

'Yes, alright Kenny.'

Circling the dancefloor.

'Your boy plays, doesn't he?'

'Yes, he does Kenny.'

One-two-three, one-two-three.

'I've heard he's doing well.'

'Doing alright Kenny, yeah.'

Round and round.

'How old is he now?'

'He's 16, Kenny.'

'Is he?'

Couple of months on, Kenny's phoning me at the club, phoning me at home. He's saying, Harry, can we have him. I'm saying, Kenny, he won't come – he wants to play first-team, and he's not going to play at your club.

He keeps ringing me, ringing me. Let me have him. We've got to have him up here. Let him come for a week's training. I keep saying to him, Kenny, there's no point, he wants to play.

Kenny's rung us every single day. Every missed call is Kenny. He's ringing Sandra. Sandra's all polite, it's 'Hello Kenny, how are you?' He says something and Sandra says back, 'Oh sorry, Kenny, can you repeat that? I can't understand your Scouse accent.' And loud and clear he says, 'I am not a Scouser, I am Glaswegian.' Must be the only person in the world who didn't know Kenny was from Glasgow.

●

That was the start of it, Dad waltzing round the Dorchester in his black tie with Kenny dragging his wife Marina about in his wake. Then the World Cup happens and everything changes forever, and Dad's dancing days are on hold, for a while at least.

But I know what I want, and I know I'm not abandoning Dad and I'm not leaving Bournemouth, not yet. I've spent almost every day of my life with Dad. I've watched him look after Mum, protect her from everything he can, take me with him on so many of his trips and adventures. So if it's me and Mark holding tight the bonds for a while, that's fine. That's good.

I still have the same plan in my head that was there when I was 15 and having second thoughts about Tottenham. I want to play first-team football. There is glamour in being on Spurs' books and there is unbelievable allure in the best team of your generation wanting you, in a man who everyone you know talks of in the most glowing possible terms phoning your dad at home and telling him he wants you to sign for him. But it's experience that I need and it's real football. I didn't want to tread water at Spurs and I don't want to circle in Liverpool's reserves, great players though there may be in there. I want to be pushed and I want to be fighting to stay afloat. I want to play in front of a crowd. I want to see if I can cope with Billy Whitehurst and Martin Allen and going to Huddersfield on a wet Wednesday night.

So me and Dad come to an agreement. I'll go up to Liverpool for a couple of weeks in September, have a look around, just like Kenny did at West Ham a quarter of a century before. I'll go training, see what I think. Not a promise to join, because I want to play, and definitely not a trial, Dad keeps telling me, because they want you, Jamie, it's not about impressing them, you've done that already.

Dad convalesces in bed at home, with all the essentials within arm's reach: glass of Lucozade, copy of the *Racing Post*, phone with the long curly cable stretched out from the bedside table. He's tried sneaking into one of our pre-season friendlies, away at Reading, disguising himself in the stands with a woolly hat and duffle coat, but rather than watching the game incognito, all that happens is that he's spotted wearing a woolly hat and duffle coat. So he stays at home and puts bets on with the same rate of success as before, which is to say that the sooner he gets back to the training ground the better. The only success comes after him and Mark spot a horse running called Sweet Cherry and decide to lump on 40 quid at 14–1. Unlike most things connected to Bournemouth last season, it romps home and puts a grin on everyone's chops.

Meantime, it's Terry Shanahan in temporary charge and Tony Pulis helping him out. When we do the team photo in bright south coast sunshine in mid-August, they're the authority figures in white and blue tracksuit tops, stern bookends at the end of three lines of tanned, optimistic-looking players. I'm in the second row, between Efan Ekoku and goalkeeper Peter Guthrie, who's a converted outfield player and thus even more of a maverick than most players in his adopted position. Dad appears only when the line-up is printed in colour across two pages of the *Bournemouth Echo*, and then as a headshot from the year before, floating off to the side, watching on like some distant ghost.

Kevin Bond is captain again. We get on well. He knows what it's like to have a famous dad. His dad John, he played with mine at West Ham. And Kevin's a good player too, a proper striker of the ball. I hate a scruffy strike, and his is pure. I can tell he likes me too.

He does the honours with the team pen pics in the same edition of the paper. His comments are a mix of well-meaning criticism, heavy-handed gags and brutal honesty.

'PETER GUTHRIE, 28. Peter has not let us down. He has the ability, the only problem he might have is a psychologist.'

'SHAUN TEALE, 25. Shaun's not particularly big but doesn't lose much in the air. Has pace, but could be more composed when he has the ball.'

'DENNY MUNDEE, 21. It's a terrible situation for Denny just now, in and out of the team. Because he's a versatile player he will always suffer.'

'KEVIN BOND, 33. Will never make the grade! Seriously though, I've had my best pre-season for about four years. I've a slight calf strain but nothing to lose sleep over.'

I get away lightly, which obviously makes it that much worse when the profiles are being read out on the team coach.

'JAMIE REDKNAPP, 17. Will, not could, be a top-class footballer. Only a question of time before he plays at the highest level. Ready for the first team.'

The highest level for now is Bury at home in Division Three. Kevin lasts less than half an hour with the calf strain that no-one has to worry about before I have to go on in his place. We nick a draw, and then lose our next game, away at Wigan. We're sinking towards the bottom of a league we hoped we might run away with, our manager is stuck in bed going slightly mad and it's time for me to head north. The evening before I set off, bags packed, Kenny phones the house one last time. Dad is still pushing the agreed line. 'Kenny, he's not going to get in your team, he's not going to play, he wants to play first-team.' Kenny is a gentle man with a tough core. I can almost see that little crinkly-eyed grin of his. 'He will get in my team. I am going to build a team around him. He's going to play.'

•

On Monday morning, you meet at Anfield. You don't go to Melwood, the training ground in West Derby. You go to the stadium and jump on a bus: first team, reserves, apprentices, staff, everyone.

I know Melwood is special. Transformed by Bill Shankly, the place where league champions, European Cup winners, the country's finest players have run and passed and sprinted and scored. There's nothing flashy about it. A grey concrete wall with barbed wire on top, 1930s semis on the residential roads all around. Kids hanging around the gates, adults on stepladders trying to peer over the wall from the pavements outside.

The first team aren't doing much this morning either, just jogging out the game from the weekend, stretching and joshing. It's hard not to stare at John Barnes. I've got a photo of him cut out and stuck on the front of my scrapbook at home, alongside Glenn Hoddle playing for England at the 1988 European Championships, and Gazza with his arms up, brushing off Frank Rijkaard and Ruud Gullit for England against Holland, and Pele jumping up into Jairzinho's arms at Mexico '70. Here he is, in Adidas training top and shorts, breath condensing in front of his face in the cold air like smoke coming from the nose of a mythical creature, and I'm about 10 feet away, and it's all normal.

Ronnie Moran gives the youth team players a shout. Something about getting ready for a game at Wembley, which doesn't make sense when we're in England's north-west, at least until we all jog over to a cinder pitch in the corner, and I realise that's what they call this manky old patch that no-one really wants to use. It's supposed to be all-weather, although one of the other lads tells me it's almost the opposite. It's too hard to play on in sunshine, in rain and in any sort of wind. The only time it gets any use from the first team is when the grass pitches are frozen, in which case it's a very slight improvement.

It's an unusual sort of match. Apprentices on one side, coaching staff on the other. So that's Kenny, the manager, maybe the greatest player in the club's history. Ronnie Moran, former club skipper, now coach. Roy Evans, another part of the boot room at Anfield, another coach. An old boy called Tom Saunders, who must be 70 years old, who has scouted and coached the youth team and done almost everything over the past 30 years, but still has his boots on for a game. Phil Thompson, the man who had lifted the European Cup when Liverpool beat Real Madrid in Paris in 1981, currently reserve team coach. Ron Yeats, still the same size legs as when he was the club's centre-half in the 1960s, chief scout. Steve Heighway, legendary former Liverpool and Ireland winger, now in charge of the youth academy.

It's not a bad line-up. And then Kenny gives me a nod and tells me I'm in his team too.

It's flat out. There's no quarter given to the ones with older legs, not least because their older heads still mean they can play, and their older hearts are still as brutally competitive as ever. Tackles flying in, step-overs and shouts, the younger lads going full guns at men who had stopped playing professional football before they were born. Roy Evans has a lovely, cultured left foot. Ronnie Moran hits his passes hard with the side of his foot – bam, bam. He's also calling me Harry all the time, which I hope is a joke or a deliberate nod rather than a mistake. I know I've done nothing yet, not compared to these men, but I want to be known for who I am, not just for where I come from.

You soon work out how to play it. As soon as I get the ball, I give it to Kenny, who's still taking up the same positions as he had at Chadwell Heath with Dad outside him and Bobby Moore and Ron Greenwood watching on. Play it into his feet, watch him stick his backside out, roll the defender and bend it into the top corner. And when he does, he breaks out into that huge Dalglish grin, the same one as when he scored for Scotland against England at Hampden Park in 1976, or for Liverpool at Stamford Bridge on the final day of the 1986 season. Football makes him happy. Scoring goals, wherever they are, lights him up from inside.

It's tough. There's a shout from Ron Yeats, six-foot two and snarling, 'Oh, f***ing hell . . .' He's done Kenny, opened up his shin. Old habits for old centre-halves die hard. I'm not sure either that Steve Heighway likes me. He's obviously heard that I'd rather stay at Bournemouth than play in his youth team, and maybe he sees that as a dig against him and what he's built rather than me wanting to play. Maybe he thinks he's got better players in his youth team than me, which he might have, seeing that everyone's talking about this young winger they've got called Steve McManaman and a 15-year-old kid from Toxteth called Robbie Fowler who scores goals like other people breathe.

It's difficult not to be a football tourist. One morning I sneak into the club shop at Anfield and buy a glossy photo of John Barnes, taken as he sits on his haunches in his kit, the angle slightly from above, emphasising the size of his legs. I stick it in my kitbag and when no-one is looking take it over to him with a black marker and ask him to sign it. I don't want anyone else to see, but I want tangible proof that I've been here. I want something for the bedroom wall back on Whitfield Drive.

Barnes gives me a look. He takes the pen and writes, 'To Jamie, you're a good player. John Barnes.' Then he puts a big arm round my shoulder and gives me a quick squeeze. For the next few minutes, I can't speak.

It feels, too, like Kenny is keeping an eye on me. We play another game on the same pitch later that week. Kenny is leaning against the doors of the pavilion, watching on. Every time I glance over he seems to have his attention on me. Afterwards, he comes over and puts his arm around me and tells me I've done okay, and there's no way that can't make you feel special.

Every day I'm there strengthens the conviction within me. I could come back here. I could come back to play for this man.

•

Kenny Dalglish: Going to West Ham as a 15-year-old gave me an insight into what young players should expect, the friendliness of the club. And for what Harry had done for me then, I thought, the least I can do is look after his boy. You've got to realise how big a move that is for a laddie coming away from home at that age. It's a huge responsibility they're taking on and you're taking on. You've got to help them.

I saw Jamie at 16 and I watched him when he came up to us at 17, and he was so far advanced mentally in his understanding of the game. For a midfielder, for anybody. He was taking control of games, he wasn't shy, he wasn't going to cower. He knew how to play, and that's what we needed.

He understood too what a dressing room vibe could be. All dressing rooms seem different – different people, different ages, different personalities – but they're actually all still the same. There's always somebody getting teased, there's always an idiot, in the nicest possible way. There's always something going on, there's always a story to tell. I knew he would settle into ours, because he came from a pure football background. He knew what to expect and how to cope with it, because he'd been around it all his life.

I wasn't looking at his size. He could play, and that's the most important thing. How you play is more important than how you look. He wasn't one of those teenagers who you think, maybe in three or four years' time. But anyone could have seen that. I wasn't anything special in seeing what he had. You just need good eyesight. That's all.

•

The south coast feels soft and fuzzy when I get home. I feel strong. I'm six-foot tall now, legs filling out. Pre-season under Tony Pulis takes the puppy fat off you and puts fire in your lungs. Playing in the same team as Kenny Dalglish puts little layers of lacquer on your confidence.

I want to play all the time now. Coming on as a sub doesn't feel enough. Against Crewe, away at Preston, watched by Sir Tom Finney, home to Rotherham, I'm almost impatient to be playing.

Dad comes back, gets a standing ovation at Dean Court and struggles to hold back the tears. He sticks me on the right of a midfield with Matty Holmes, Shaun Brooks and Gavin Peacock, and we start to find our runs and angles and timings. When we put four past Rotherham I go looking for the ball all the time – no more waiting to be introduced, no looking over my shoulder. Get it, look forward, use it. Don't hope the game will involve you. Make it pivot around you.

I don't hear anything more about Liverpool and Kenny until we play Birmingham in late November, when someone spots Ron Yeats in the stands at St Andrews. So Kenny's being true to his word and keeping an eye on me. I can feel the pressure of being the centre of attention, but I don't over-think it. Play your game, Jamie, not someone else's. If they still want you, it's for what you are and what you do, naturally.

It's not the sort of game to get big, tall, strong former Liverpool skippers hot under the collar. It's 0–0 and there's only 7,000-odd fans in, and although our midfield is all creativity with Shaun and Gavin around me, it's our 'keeper Gerry Payton who is the man of the match. Afterwards too, the talk is all about Gav and a big move that's coming his way, but when a £275,000 bid comes in for him a week later, it's from Jim Smith at Newcastle, not Kenny in Liverpool.

Kenny's signed someone else, a kid called Don Hutchison from Hartlepool. He's an attacking midfielder. I read it on Ceefax and my heart sinks. Maybe I didn't do enough for Ron. They've gone for someone who bombs on more. I still haven't scored a senior goal in professional football. This lad Hutch has. He's also two years older.

Okay. It makes sense. But the newspapers are still talking me up for a move, and there are reporters everywhere when we play Hayes in the second round of the FA Cup. There are TV cameras round the house again, and that hasn't been happening in Division Three. Maybe the angle is that the manager's come back from the dead and he's got his kid son playing for him. I don't care. If I play well, they can't ignore me.

There is nothing that scares me now. Not Dad's scars. He is healing. He is better back in football. Not the players I'm up against, that they're trying to kick me out of games. Being chased is good. Not being chased means that you're not a threat.

Dad's the manager but he's also a 43-year-old father. I think he still wants to protect me. He knows I can play, but like all dads the memories of his son as a kid are lingering. He needs to hear the other players telling him I'm there now and he needs to see the enjoyment on my face to understand that I can handle it. He sees me roll over the top with Jimmy Gabriel's tackle and he takes comfort from that too. So my boy can look after himself. So my boy's maybe a boy no more.

Away at Grimsby on a frozen December afternoon we lose 5–0. 'A1 Windscreens' in large white letters on our chests where an F-minus should be. It's so bad that their fans spend the last quarter of the game chanting, 'Easy! Easy!' and singing, 'Harry, Harry, what's the score?' I come on and play okay amid the carnage, but everything else has gone wrong, and Dad goes ballistic in the dressing room afterwards.

'You've got no bottle! None a ya!'

Everyone heads down. Boots still on, claggy scraps of mud strewn across the floor.

'You don't care. You're a disgrace! A f***ing disgrace.'

Pulis by his side, nodding his head. Tony always cared as a player. You can have no natural talent and Tony won't be bothered, as long as you try. If you're one of six kids in a terraced house by the docks and the train tracks and you and your three brothers all share one bed, you never stop trying.

Dad is shaking his head, as if he's trying to hold on to a thought but can't stop it coming out.

'There's only one person that even cared or did anything in this game or tried to get on the ball. Right?'

Now I'm looking round. All the big names in there, all my mates. No, Dad. Please don't say me. Please don't say me.

All of a sudden he looks over and points. 'Him. A kid.'

We've already lost 5–0. This is bad enough. Let's just get some fish and chips and get on the coach home.

'He's 17, chrissakes! If half of you had his guts and determination we'd be alright. But you ain't, have ya?'

Then I understand. He's not thinking of me as his son anymore. He doesn't care. In this moment, I'm just a player. He's looking at me like he looks at Matty Holmes. His thinking has been stripped back to manager watching midfielder: he is good enough and he did play well and he did get his foot in and he did try.

I'm embarassed to death but it feels okay. I know what's coming from the senior players on the way home, but it's a good shame to go through. And so I'm ready to push on again when we travel to Macclesfield to play Chester in the third round of the FA Cup in early January, both teams away from home while Chester have their new stadium built.

It's a small ground, Moss Rose, not quite 2,000 fans squeezed in, and from the start it's obvious what Chester have decided to do: kick me up in the air. They've picked a big bloke in midfield, Graham Barrow, and he's got another unit alongside him called Barry Butler, and they're at me from the first whistle. Chat in my ear, studs wherever they can lay them. It's only 20-odd miles from Chester to Anfield, and they want to show me how far I've still got to go, how there are a lot of honest pros, and edgy ones too, between a 17-year-old kid and a move to the biggest club in the land.

The wind is battering down from the Peak District hills to the east and the pitch is more mud and puddles than grass. Getting the ball down to play is almost impossible.

I actually don't care. I know Barrow's got a job to do. Of course he's going to go over the top of the ball. That's what happens. I've got long hair, I'm a pretty boy. I'd want to kick lumps out of me too. If I can't handle this, how am I going to handle 40,000 at Anfield? How am I going to survive Vinnie Jones and Chris Kamara?

Look after yourself. Don't get hurt, but don't back down. Know when to go into tackles and when not to.

And I love it. Tony Pulis in there alongside me for a rare start, Paul Miller weighing in. Matty Holmes and George Lawrence going wide, Luther Blissett up front, someone else cleaning his Puma boots for him now.

I've got a good little understanding with Andy Jones. We're becoming mates, and we can read each other's games. If I get the ball, if I get my head up, I know he'll make the run long. If I'm under pressure, he'll come short. He's got a little look that tells me exactly where he wants it, just as Robbie Fowler will in a few years, just as Michael Owen will another five years on.

It's pure joy, knowing you know stuff that the opposition doesn't have a clue about. I make our first goal for Andy. Every time I get kicked I give one back, Jimmy Gabriel style, or hurdle it and leave them on their backside in the mud. When they tell me I'm shit and that they're going to break my legs, I just laugh and ask them what they're doing on the pitch then, and also make sure they can see me pointing to Tony. I run and I pass, collar of my shirt turned up, and I show for the ball and I dictate where it goes next.

We win 3–2, with a late winner from Efan Ekoku. On the five-hour coach ride home there are cases of lager to go with the teas and coffees and sandwiches. I find a space up front next to Dad and sit down to talk.

I'm still flush from the game, red-faced and glowing from the communal bath after the freezing afternoon, but I'm calm, too, the path ahead of me as clear as the late evening motorway south.

I know now. I can see Anfield ahead of me.

'Dad, I want to go there.'

'What's up, maestro?'

'Liverpool. I want to go. I'm ready. I know I am. Right now.'

•

I cut the match report from the Chester game out of the *Bournemouth Echo* to stick in my scrapbook. The paper's football reporter is Derek McGregor who goes to every match, home and away. The headline reads, 'FA Cup's Sweet For Cherries'. Five paras down he's piled in. 'On the record Harry

Redknapp, although bursting with pride, did not want to make too much of son Jamie's performance. I'll speak for him. The 17-year-old was magnificent. He showed remarkable maturity and courage under extreme pressure to emerge a real hero. Chester's hard men tried to psyche him out of the match. They failed. They tried physical intimidation. They failed. He ran his legs off for the cause and truly came of age.'

I don't save it to show to anyone else or to boast but as a memory, as a keepsake from a time that I can still reach out and touch but which is also already slipping into the past. I'm not the only player Kenny is bringing in to freshen up a squad that's got an average age of close to 30. On 10 January, he buys winger Jimmy Carter from Millwall for £800,000. There's a deal in the pipeline to bring Scotland striker David Speedie in from Coventry, and I'll be sandwiched in between those two. So my Bournemouth career is over, just like that. No send-off away at Bury, as the team win 4–2, because Dad leaves me out. There's too much attention, he says. And there are TV crews and reporters everywhere, it's true. For the first time I get a little idea of the hype that might follow when I get to Merseyside.

It's a cold night, 8 January, and it's a long drive to get to Anfield for the evening kick-off against Blackburn Rovers, an FA Cup third round replay. Tickets waiting for us on the door, lovely seats in the players' box. The photo on the cover of the programme is Ronnie Rosenthal, in the shiny red Adidas home kit with sponsors Candy in white italics across the front, standing near a confused looking David Burrows, the ball nowhere in sight. At the top, in massive typeface, the programme says

'LIVERPOOL' and then 'CHAMPIONS OF THE FOOTBALL LEAGUE'.

It's the classic Liverpool line-up of the era: Bruce Grobbelaar in goal, Steve McMahon in midfield with John Barnes and Ray Houghton and Jan Molby, and Ian Rush up front. Blackburn are lumpier, Kevin Moran marching around at the back, Frank Stapleton happy to dish it out up front. Houghton scores after 15 minutes, and the noise all around is so intense it hurts your ears. Rush adds another eight minutes later. McMahon gets sent off, and looks so angry as he strides off the pitch that he might march straight through the tunnel wall and out the other side. But it's the skinny substitute I can't take my eyes off, that kid McManaman who comes on for Rosenthal towards the end.

There's nothing of him. He's tall but gangly. His legs look the same girth from calf to upper thigh. But he starts running at the Kop End, dribbling and chasing. I think, this guy is amazing. And as the crowd responds to him, a kid from Bootle grabbing his chance, a thought settles with me: this is what I want to do. This is where I want to play.

I've never heard noise like it. Floodlights on, a bright green patch of grass under the dark winter sky. I watch McManaman and see the place seething and jumping, and I know. One day this could be you.

That night, Dad and I stay at the Moat House hotel on Paradise Street. We're told it's the best in town, where all the visiting celebs stay when they're up in Liverpool. It's a rectangular block of a place, grey concrete and metal, but the rooms are big, and there's a swimming pool, and we're knackered after leaving Ringwood before dawn, so we settle down in our twin room full of Chinese food and excitement.

Bang. Something has gone off outside the hotel, waking us up. It sounded like a firework, but no-one's letting fireworks off six weeks after Guy Fawkes' Night. It's only when we go outside in the morning, heading off to Dad's car, that we see it: a white outline of a body, chalked out in a taped-off section of the street. Coppers everywhere, people standing around in huddles. It's my first night in Liverpool, and someone has been shot dead right outside our hotel.

Dad looks at me and makes a face. 'Don't tell your mum, right?'

13

THE BOOT ROOM

The signing a couple of days later, for something that will change my life so permanently, is strangely informal. Kenny's smart, in a beige double-breasted suit with red tie, but initially I'm in a black Adidas sweatshirt with the white trefoil logo on the front, because Liverpool is an Adidas club. In my suitcase I've got something special I've brought for the occasion, a double-breasted burgundy jacket that hangs off me like it's two sizes too big but makes me feel grown-up enough to be here. I've picked it up from a place on Shamrock Quay in Southampton called Sakks Menswear, and it's a significant purchase. Definitely the most expensive item of clothing I've ever bought, and possibly a misjudged vibe. The shop is all Armani and Boss. It's not really aimed at 17-year-olds. But these are not normal times, and so I find myself having a discussion with the sales assistant about whether I'm more the Giorgio Armani range or the Emporio Armani.

Turns out I'm Giorgio. Turns out I also need a shirt with long, thin collars, a diamond-pattern tie that costs more than I previously believed a tie could and a pair of dark grey trousers. Luckily, you can get all of these from the Giorgio Armani range. They all go on for a photo with Kenny in front of the terraces on the Kop, where we stand with our hands stuffed in our trouser pockets like naughty schoolkids on the bus home, but the sweatshirt is back on when I'm asked to stand in front of the dugout on the right of the tunnel, the one that has 'HOME' painted in large white letters on the red wood. I can't stop smiling, and Kenny's beaming away like he's just notched another goal, and the only thing that looks remotely unhappy is the sad-looking pot plant in the corner of his office.

Kenny does the full tour without the photographers – trophy room, players' lounge, boot room. He waits until we're in that famous little room under the grandstand before his next revelation.

First he shakes his head. Then he grimaces. Dad's good at reading people. He can sense the change in mood.

'Kenny, what's up?'

Kenny shakes his head again. 'Ach, we've had a nightmare. It's John Barnes.'

No, not John Barnes. Anyone but John Barnes.

'Aye. Bad news. He's been in jail.'

Now Dad looks shocked.

'You're kidding me, Kenny.'

'No. Arrested for drink-driving. He's had to give a urine sample, all sorts.'

'Bloody hell, Kenny. Is he in trouble?'

'Aye, he is. We sent a lawyer down. He's taking care of it. He's got Barnesy out and home for now. Home with his coat and car keys and the little bottle of urine.'

225

Phew, this sounds better.

'Aye, but they're still charging him.'

Dad frowning. 'With what, Kenny?'

A sudden flash of a grin, a sparkle in the eyes.

'Wi' taking the piss, boys!'

That's Kenny. Serious but only on the surface. Understanding how nervous a 17-year-old kid in the boot room might be feeling, defusing those worries with a Kenny yarn.

The money, by the way, has done some weird exponential multiplying again. I'm being sold for an initial £350,000, with pretty much the same again on top if I make a certain amount of appearances. I've played a total of 13 league games for Bournemouth, more than half off the bench: three FA Cup games, three League Cup games, and two in the Leyland DAF Cup. And here I am, the most expensive 17-year-old in British football history.

I'm being paid a basic wage of £650 a week, but the basic bit makes no sense to me. I feel like a trillionaire. I haven't got an agent and we didn't even negotiate, because there's nothing to question. Dad has always told me down the years that if you work hard the money will come, that it's about making the right move, not chasing the percentage points.

Kenny introduces me to a man with the unusual name of Robin Money. He's the Adidas rep.

'Robin, this is Jamie. He's just signed. You get him what he needs, okay?'

What I need, it seems, is box after box of free stuff. Tracksuits. Sweatshirts. Trainers and trainers and trainers. No more getting two free pairs of rubbish boots and taking them back to the local sports shop to swap them for one decent pair. Suddenly, I can't move for boots. My bedroom will look like the store cupboard at that same sports shop.

I do interviews. Dad does interviews, slightly more used to them than I am. It's the most reserved part of the day.

'Jamie has the ability and the character to succeed here. He is joining a great club with an excellent manager in Kenny Dalglish. I'm glad the speculation and rumours are over and that Jamie can get back to playing football. He has been under a lot of pressure lately, but he has come through it very well, like I knew he would. Kenny anticipates great things from him and I'm confident Jamie won't let him down.'

It's one of the more prim and proper speeches I can remember my dad coming up with. This is a day when all I do is write my signature on a piece of paper a few times, and walk out onto the Anfield pitch with an Adidas Tango ball, and stand next to Kenny, and smile for some photos, and come out with a few clichés about how excited I am – a day when I don't run, or train, or kick a football about at all – but it turns out to be the most tiring one I can remember for months. When Kenny takes us out for a family dinner in Southport that night to celebrate, I want to talk about it all but I'm so whacked that I'm nodding off over my starter and falling asleep during my main. The emotion of it all has done me in.

Friday, my first day of full training. I know how dressing rooms work, so I know I'm getting no special treatment from the big boys. I also know that having the mickey taken out of you is a good thing. It's your acceptance. It's when every-one ignores you that you're in trouble. Mates take the piss. Strangers don't bother.

Into Anfield, up the stairs of the first-team bus. I walk down the aisle and look at the faces staring back at me: Steve McMahon, Alan Hansen, Bruce Grobbelaar. Ronnie Whelan, Gary Ablett, Glenn Hysen. There are spare seats next to each of them, but when I go to sit down, they all say the same thing: can't sit there son, that's someone else's.

One after another, all the way down the bus. Daggers from McMahon. Cold shoulder from Hansen. Whelan looking at me like I came in on the sole of his shoe.

There's this acidic sick feeling in my stomach. I try another seat. Not there, kid. Keep my head down, on to the next one along. There's a boot-bag on it. I don't even bother asking.

What do you do? I know I can't say anything. I can't com-plain. I've seen footballers, and I know when to talk and when not to. But I can't walk back off the bus or I'll never get back on, and I can't start crying, even if a part of me wants to.

John Barnes has been watching. There's a smile on his face. There's a smile on everyone's face, when I'm not looking. And it's John who stands up, a few rows from the back, and points at the seat next to him, and says, 'Hey Jamie, don't worry about them. Come in here.'

I'm in. I sit down. I stare at the floor because the acidic feeling is still in my throat. John's looking across at me.

'I remember you. You're a good player.'

I start to breathe again. This is going to be okay.

John looks at my hair flopping down over my eyes. 'Do you like girls?'

I know football. I know this is all part of the test. But I don't really know what to say to that.

'Yeah, I do actually.'

I tell myself that Hansen and Whelan would have done the same to him when he joined from Watford three and a half years before, that McMahon would have had it when he was Kenny's first signing in 1985. Maybe Kenny even had it when he arrived from Celtic. So I sit there and talk football generalities with Barnes, not pushing any opinions, not talking too much, nodding when he says anything. It's still weird to me that a man who has been a poster on my bedroom wall is now a living, breathing presence at my elbow. I can't tell him that because I know what the reaction will be from all around, and because I know from stepping up to the first team at Bournemouth that you have to act like you belong even when you don't. We'll be playing football in 20 minutes or so. When we're playing, I'll be okay.

It is a freezing morning at Melwood. There is ice on the puddles in the car park and frost in crisp white layers on the grass pitches and clubhouse roof. We are in our kit already, black Adidas sweatshirt from my signing, red shorts with my number on, black socks, and we are on Wembley, the horrible cinder pitch that no-one really wants to play on.

There is ice all over that too, glassy splashes of it over the pale brown surface, and so the groundsman has cut out a rectangle for us to train on. It's tight and bumpy and it's crowded too, and every time you look up you're face to face with another walking *Shoot!* poster. The reigning champions of the Football League, striding around, stretching and joshing and swearing at how hard and uneven the pitch feels under your boots.

We split into two teams. McMahon opposite me, maybe the hardest man in Division One after Vinnie Jones, hard enough to argue that point with Vinnie himself, definitely a superior player in every way. The ball coming in to my feet, McMahon thundering towards me out of the corner of my eye, moving my body to make a nice little pass out to the wing . . . and feeling the ground going from underneath me, and seeing cold blue sky up above, and landing flat on my backside.

The reaction is instantaneous.

'How much?' 'How f***ing much?'

They're laughing. I'm laughing too, although I'm dying on the inside. 'Get off your arse, Harry!' is the yell from Ronnie Moran. Good start, Jamie. Good work on the first impressions.

The first session of each week, I'll find out that the cones around the edge of the pitch are as wide as they can be. There is almost too much space. It's as if they want everyone to do more running than is strictly necessary, burn off some of the drink from the weekend. On Tuesday, the cones are slightly further in; by Thursday the pitch even smaller. You have no time and no space whatsoever.

Today is Friday. The ball gets played into me. I look up. Maybe I've got a second here. And even as I'm thinking it, Ian Rush's foot appears from nowhere and takes the ball away, and I'm standing there like an idiot. It's like one of those David

Attenborough documentaries when a tiger creeps up on a dozy goat and just munches it up. 'What the f*** happened there?'

Okay. That doesn't happen in Division Three. This is how good the level is. I'm going to have to be brave. I've got to get quicker here or I'm not going to be able to handle this.

Kenny has been here before. He signed his first professional contract with Jock Stein at Celtic aged 16. Maybe he can remember how that felt. But he knows I need a good night's kip, because back at Anfield he tells me I'm staying over at his that night, and he's taking me out for food in Southport, so I don't need to worry myself about anything. Great for me, not so lucky for his daughter Kelly, who gets kicked out of her bedroom so there's room for the guest.

You wake up at Kenny Dalglish's having spent most of your nights in the previous year at your parents' or in a spare single bed at the Highlin in Bournemouth, and it takes you a few minutes to remember quite where you are, especially when the bedroom belongs to a 15-year-old girl. You go down for breakfast and it's four kids sitting round the table and Marina doing tea and toast. Liverpool have got a home game against Wimbledon, and we talk about it a bit, what you do about John Fashanu up front, how Terry Gibson alongside him is maybe just as dangerous but a little more underrated.

We keep talking football in the car. Kenny drives the winding back roads to the city, through Downholland Cross and Lydiate, chatting about how good Gazza's been for Spurs, why Alan Smith works so well for Arsenal's style, what Joe Royle's doing at Oldham. We park up at Anfield, jump on the coach to the Holiday Inn for an early lunch with the players, get back in the ground for about 1.30 pm.

It's the first time I've been in the home dressing room. I just want to sit out of the way somewhere. It's quite enough that I'm breathing the same air as these legends, as Barnes and Rush and McMahon. Kenny reads out the team, and gets to the two subs, but I'm not really paying attention, nose in the programme, trying not to stare. Barnes is the cover star this week, flicking a header past Keith Curle in the game at Plough Lane back in September.

And then I stand up, and suddenly people are shaking my hand, including John Barnes. It's, 'Congratulations, Jamie,' and 'Nice one kid!', and the confusion must show on my face, because someone else says, 'You're on the bench, mate,' and I walk over to where the team sheet is pinned up on the wall, and sure enough it's there, in blue ballpoint pen, handwritten on the printed sheet: 14. Jamie Redknapp.

Not a word from Kenny to warn me. Which makes sense. I wouldn't have been able to eat any of that penne all'arrabbiata in Southport the night before, or got a wink of sleep in Kelly's abandoned bed. I wouldn't have spoken a word over breakfast or said anything in the car on the way down. No time to think about the jump in two weeks from Moss Rose in Macclesfield and 2,000 spectators to Anfield in front of 35,000; no time to worry about my boots being perfect or everything lined up just the way I like it in my bag and on my peg. I'm in the red Adidas kit for the first time and the game kicks off in an hour. Running out to warm up, getting a warm prickle down my back when the team is read out over the tannoy and I hear my name and hear the surprised cheer that follows.

Then the game begins, and it's just football. Quicker and more skilful than Divisions Two and Three have been, but still football, with the same angles, the same little gaps for passes, the same twists on the ball and turns. I'm on the bench but I'm in the match, plotting how I could find space, how I would use my arms to hold off Detzi Kruszyński, who doesn't look that physical for a member of the Crazy Gang, whether Rush would want the ball in behind John Scales or Keith Curle.

Barnes lights the place up. Steve Staunton takes a pass from Stevie Nicol and clips a beautiful long pass over their back four, and Barnes controls it with his right foot, flicks it up with his thigh and then crashes the sweetest volley over Hans Segers and into the top corner. At half-time I go out on the pitch, and there is no tension. I just want to get on. This is where I want to be.

The change doesn't come. Warren Barton smashes in a lovely right-footed free-kick from the left-hand angle of the penalty box, and when Kenny looks down at the subs' bench it's Rosenthal he sends on for Jan Molby to try to win it. I'm genuinely disappointed, not because I think I'm more danger-ous than a full international whose goals have helped Liverpool win the title less than a year ago, but because of McManaman, and what he did to the place against Blackburn, and because of Deano and Dave and my brother Mark back in Bournemouth, for the chance to phone the Highlin later and say, 'boys, did you see that?'

I settle for the team sheet off the wall, with its careful script and formal language. The Football League logo at the top, a black and white ball with a lion rampant on the top. 'To be handed to Opponents' in black ink, the date, the name of the referee as he might have been addressed in the Victorian era, Mr H W King. Our team written out two to 11, Grobbelaar getting a 'Goalkeeper' rather than a number one. And then what seems like the unnecessary stuff when you're Liverpool and you're at home: 'We are playing in the following colours. Shirts: RED. Shorts: Red. Stockings: Red.'

It goes in my scrapbook, carefully glued onto a thick grey page. The birth certificate for my Liverpool career, the official documentation that says I am here, that I belong.

•

Frank Lampard: When you're 12, Liverpool feels like a million miles away. Not just being the other end of the country, but because all of us had grown up with Liverpool being the team. To think that your cousin has made the jump from Bournemouth to there is a huge deal.

As you get older, you see it slightly differently. At the time, I was almost envious in a good way. 'Bloody hell, I wish I could make a move like that one day!' That was part of my obsessive nature. Jamie had the best clothes, looked the best and all that and now he's at the best club, Liverpool. I was still toiling my way through Under

12s football, not sure whether I was going to make it or not, and Jamie looked like he had. It was like, I want that, I really, really want that.

The good part was that we were close enough that he could make it look possible. He'd ring me up, tell me what it was like, tell me a story about John Barnes or Ian Rush. I remember taking in all those things and thinking: I need this.

There was a time, just before my 18th birthday, when England were preparing for Euro '96. Terry Venables invited me and Rio Ferdinand to train with the senior team. I was so in awe of them all. And there's Jamie with Gazza. Gazza's his mate, they're playing head tennis on the lawn and have their own little jokes and all that stuff. I couldn't believe it. But when he saw me it was just like a more mature version of all the years we'd had before. I looked up to him and tried to suck it all in. Three and a half years on, I was making my England debut and Jamie was in midfield with me. My first cap, his first England goal. Our dads sitting next to each other in the stands.

There are some negatives when you have a football family, how my dad was very driven. There were many more pros, having a lovely balance of not just my dad but also the Jamie side of it that I could really aspire to. It was no surprise to me when he started to come through at Liverpool.

Jamie was always about that quality and using the ball. That's not down to luck and God-given talent. Sometimes, it's about hitting a bird cage a thousand times.

•

There's another outsider around the place, the skinny 19-year-old kid from Gateshead, Don Hutchison. He's like a whippet going after a rabbit. Chasing on the heels of the strikers, lobbing in the occasional wild challenge.

I've already seen what he can do. The day before, standing by the door of the players' lounge at Anfield waiting for the cheese toasties they give out for lunch, I'd seen Phil Thompson limping around with a massive gash on his shin. Eight inches long, pouring blood. That was Don. Not much thought from him that the older men he's up against in the staff *v* reserves games might hold his future in his hands.

It's not just me on my own, then. Don's last game for Hartlepool before coming to Liverpool was against Scarborough; mine was Chester. He's miles from home in a city he doesn't yet understand. He's supposed to be the solution to a problem the current crop aren't even ready to admit to, because it involves them.

This is all newer to him than it is to me. His dad's a miner. When he needed a tie for his signing photos he had to ask his dad, and his dad had to ask the local pub. When he gets hungry after training he orders chips, because he's never had Tony

Pulis talking Martina Navratilova recipes in his ear. We're the same but we're different. And here we are together.

You try to gauge the moods and learn the routines. This is not a club or town for luxuries. When you get changed back at Anfield, you don't throw your dirty kit in the laundry skip. You stick it in the boiler room, muddy and wet. It dries overnight but it's never washed, not until the entire week's training is done. When you try to pull your socks on the next morning they're stiff as cardboard. You have to fold them and scrunch them to even get them on. The shorts and the t-shirt and the sweatshirt just smell. Sweat, dirt, blood. The greatest team in the land, the club that has won four European Cups in the past 15 years, that has won eight of the last 12 league titles, and you get one set of kit, and nobody complains.

You cannot escape the weight of history around the place because it is a living thing, a mix of people and stories and nights under the lights and a city that cares maybe more than any other. You walk through the corridors at Anfield, all red gloss paint over old wood, low ceilings and big dreams, and there are men who should be ghosts but walk and talk and growl.

Ron Yeats is in his office further along from Kenny, all his scouting reports piled up in front of him. Black hair going grey, not that you'd ever dare tell him, a man defined by his old manager Bill Shankly – 'The man is a mountain, walk around him!' A shout from Kenny – 'You in, Yatesie?' – and a reply like a rumble underground, 'Aye, that I am . . .' A man with the club in his heart, a servant and an institution and guard dog rolled into one.

The boot room down below, as modest as its reputation is vast. One small plastic table, a couple of chairs, Roy Evans and Ronnie Moran sitting on crates. Four shrink-wrapped slabs of lager cans stashed on top of each other in the corner. A metal-framed shelf on one side, a few random bits of kit, the wall at the back covered with boots on hooks, with hooks sticking out at the top like the branches of a stunted tree, so you can get more boots up and drying. John Bennison, another in his mid-sixties, grey but still lean from all the staff matches, once coach of the youth team, now helping Phil Thompson out with the reserves, opening a packet of custard creams. A saucy calendar on the wall, a china pot of tea on the table and an old Guinness ashtray between the cups.

There are the actual employees, and there are those who are just around, not paid members of staff but with roles that no-one can quite define, no official ID or tracksuits yet accepted by everyone, free to walk about and help out and share the gossip and camaraderie. There's Wee Richie, a little fella in an overcoat, almost Del Trotter, who comes in with CDs and films on VHS, tickets for gigs, a charmer who everyone seems to like and who can get you anything you ask for. Then there's a big old Scouse boy called H, Harold Hughes, who runs a pub in Croxteth and looks just as tough as a bloke who runs a pub in Croxteth should. It is clear that H loves Liverpool and that he loves Kenny. Kenny in turn sees a 17-year-old in his first week in a big northern port city and makes sure he makes the introduction.

'Any problems, speak to H, right?'

H looks happy with this. 'Whatever it is, la. This face has been punched a thousand times. One more won't hurt it.'

H is always around, all patter, throwing the one-liners and wisecracks about in that classic Scouse way. I get the feeling that he and Wee Richie can't always understand what I'm saying, but I'm comfortable in the middle of it all. There have been plenty of Liverpudlians who have come down to Bournemouth in the last decade, plumbers and sparkies looking for work, getting on their bikes, and the humour stays with you once you've seen it. If there are introverts from Liverpool I haven't yet met them, although maybe I wouldn't. The jokes aren't always kind but you have to roll with them, throw a little jab straight back, stay in the fight. And you realise that all this makes you part of something bigger than just a football team, maybe a stretched out family that's dysfunctional in places but special all the same; a tribe of ordinary people who are also extraordinarily passionate, who will test you before they let you in but will defend you until the end if they do.

•

John Barnes: I felt a bit sorry for him that first morning. Come and sit beside me lad, come and sit right there.

When I signed for Liverpool, I'd already been playing in the England team for four years, in Division One for six. Peter Beardsley was the same, John Aldridge and

Ray Houghton also experienced, proven internationals. Liverpool didn't sign young players to come straight through into the first team. And Liverpool was a very unforgiving dressing room, particularly for young boys from down south. It was a very northern dressing room. Straightaway Jamie would have seen and heard the way things were. He's a pretty boy from down south. They're going to take the piss out of him.

I know Harry and I knew the way Jamie had been brought up. The problem he had is that he was a young, good-looking boy whose dad is a well-known manager, coming to a club where they're notorious for taking the piss out of you. It was harder for Jamie than any other young boy coming to Liverpool because he had all that as well. So you could hear it on the coach and in training. 'What the hell are you doing here?' 'It'll be hard for you, it's got to be hard for you . . .'

Ultimately at Liverpool, it's whether you have the talent and if you've got a good mentality. They were always testing you out. The most important thing about football, particularly at a big club, is your character. We could see straightaway that Jamie could play. He was young but he was confident. He was good on the ball and he had ambition.

But that didn't matter. My favourite English player of all time, the most technically gifted one I've ever seen, was Glenn Hoddle. Glenn could never have played for Liverpool – not because he wasn't better than Sammy

Lee or Steve McMahon or anybody else, but because of his character. Not a better character or worse character, just not the right fit. Come to play for Liverpool in that era and it's unforgiving, it's cruel. Particularly for a young boy from down south.

The question when I saw Jamie on the bus that morning was whether he would have the mentality and the character. The players who can't put up with it will get lost or get kicked out of the club. They won't make it.

●

Mark has come to stay, help ease me in. Bringing the jokes, bringing the cartoon swagger. He wants to go to Wade Smith, the best clothes shop in Liverpool, four floors of football casual gear, of Adidas Trimm Trab trainers and Stan Smiths, of Kickers boots and Lacoste trackie bottoms, Armand Basi t-shirts and Fila sweatshirts. Over the next few years, I'll learn that people go to Wade Smith just to hang out, to pass through on a Saturday morning before a game if they're a casual, or after going to the record shops like Probe on Slater Street if it's tunes that rock their world. Picking up trainers, putting them back, fingering the material on the tops, listening to the chat and the tales of European trips and club nights that have brought this loose group of young lads together.

The Adidas Challenger trackie is the top of the pile for us. Mark has been happy enough to get the cross-Channel ferry to Cherbourg to pick them up, so when he sees how many they have in Wade Smith he can't believe his eyes. I've got the funds and almost nothing to spend it on, so I want to treat him. He's always been so generous with me. If he had £650 a week he'd be sending half of it straight to me. He's kinder and more generous. It's payback time.

You get noticed in Liverpool as a footballer and people talk to you like they've met you many times before. As we go round it's, 'Alright, Jamie lad?' and, 'Alright la?' and 'Boss gear, Jamo . . .' There's more but I can't always understand it. It's too quick or the accent fools me enough that I'm half a sentence behind before we've even got going and desperately trying to play catch-up, like a teenager on holiday with a bit of half-remembered GCSE French.

The Everton fans get a bit of a dig in. There's a queue behind us at the till as they ring up all our gear, heads turning to see what the new signing has bought, necks straining at what trainers he wears, and when I hand over my credit card the woman sticks it in the machine and frowns.

'Sir, it's not working. Do you have another card?'

No, I don't. I've just got a shop full of Scousers who are enjoying every minute of this.

'F***ing hell, wages not gone in yet, lad?'

'They not paying ya, Jamie?'

'Need us to lend ya some dough, kid?'

It's humiliation, in the funniest way possible, and I've got to laugh too. I start working it out. Right, my Barclaycard is set up on the basis of my Bournemouth £130 a week. I've not been at Liverpool long enough to get paid. Of course the card's going to start booting off.

The woman on the till is as understanding as she could possibly be. She tells me she'll put my stuff aside, that I can come back to collect it once my money goes through. So we have to turn and edge our way through the crowd, red faced, nodding at all the jokes, not even a single one of Wade Smith's trademark drawstring bags over our shoulders.

•

There's a fresh clipping in my scrapbook. For the first time, I'm the subject of a boxed-off fact file in one of the newspapers. When the reporter asked me, he must have got the answers faster than he could ever have imagined. I've been ready for this for years.

DATE OF BIRTH: 25 June 1973.

BIRTHPLACE: Barton-on-Sea.

HEIGHT: 6 ft 1 in.

WEIGHT: 12 st.

POSITION: Centre-midfield.

PRE-MATCH MEAL: Pasta.

PRE-MATCH DRINK: Water.

FAVOURITE TV PROGRAMMES: Only Fools and Horses, Cheers.

FAVOURITE MUSIC: Loose Ends, soul.

FAVOURITE OTHER TEAMS: AFC Bournemouth and West Ham United.

FAVOURITE ALL-TIME PLAYER: Trevor Brooking.

PRESENT PLAYER: Glenn Hoddle.

FAVOURITE GROUNDS: Upton Park, Wembley,
Anfield, Dean Court.

Kenny still lets me stay at his house on odd nights, still takes me out for tea. Kelly gets kicked out of her room again and then looks at me in the morning and asks me if I've nicked some of her make-up. I wind her up by asking if she realises it's unusual to have plastic sheets over your mattress when you're in your teens.

All of it is better than the digs that I've been placed in on Anfield Road, run by Mrs Sainsbury, an old dear with white hair and fearsome flatulence who sees no reason to put the heating on even on January evenings when ice is forming on the inside of your bedroom window.

The house was once a beauty. Three storeys high, Victorian villa, high ceilings and a tiled hall and architraves and stained glass still in the front door. But it's a long time since it was desirable and a long time that young lads from Liverpool have been billeted here. That first week it's so cold that I go to bed wearing my Adidas Challenger tracksuit. From the front steps you can see the back of the Anfield Road stand, with its red shuttered turnstiles and white cladding and sloping steel beams above the roof. Yet rather than feeling part of that vast open space, it feels claustrophobic and gloomy. Mrs Sainsbury makes your dinner in the morning and then leaves it under

Clingfilm in the kitchen for you to heat up in the evening, which is bad anyway and worse when it's ropey old grey sausages and mashed potato, and not even proper mashed potato but Smash, out of a packet and lumpy and tasteless.

There is a pay-phone in the hall. I stick my 10p in there, call home and get Mum to phone me back. Mum is still struggling with me having flown the nest after 17 years, and when she finds out what it's like for me she starts to panic. An electric blanket arrives in the post. She wants my brother to come up with tins of food, packets of bacon. There is talk of Pop jumping on the train with some of those cheese rolls he gets from the bakery in the East End.

It doesn't help that there is a sense of foreboding creeping over the club too. Kenny smiles when we're playing football and there's always a grin and a kind word when he sees me at Melwood or coming down for breakfast at his house in Southport. He hides it all. But you can feel the darkness of the Hillsborough Disaster sitting over the city, haunting ordinary conversations, creeping in when the rapid chat and jokes drop away. You can see it in all the players who were there that day, who went to so many funerals afterwards – in Hansen, in Whelan, in Grobbelaar.

So football matters but it doesn't, and the strains it naturally brings are amplified by everything around. The weekend after the Wimbledon game, we play away at Manchester United, yet to win the league under Alex Ferguson but with the FA Cup behind them and a Cup-Winners' Cup campaign working out well for them. It's a Sunday afternoon, live on ITV with Elton Welsby. I'm not on the bench but David Speedie gets the equaliser for 1–1, and he gets two more six days later when we beat Everton 3–1 at home. But that's as good as it gets for Speedie – he'll only score three more goals in his Liverpool career, none so important – and so for the team, and for Kenny, the season begins to slip away. In the fifth round of the FA Cup we draw 0–0 at Everton and then, in the replay on 20 February, just cannot escape.

I watch the mayhem from the stands. We go 1–0 up, but then back to 1–1. Beardsley with a beauty for 2–1, Graeme Sharp with the equaliser. Rush for 3–2, Cottee with an equaliser in the last minute. Extra-time and a Barnes special, Cottee squeezing in another for 4–4.

The defending is horrible. It's not the football that everyone will think back to in the future. It's the expression on Kenny's face as he stands by the home dugout with the goals flying in. He's a human statue, a man lost in a lonely nightmare. Bedlam all around, cavorting and hugging and hands on heads, and he doesn't move. A man for whom football has been everything, for whom football is no longer working.

I walk the couple of hundred yards into Anfield from Mrs Sainsbury's a few days later. It's a normal Friday morning, me in the squad for the Luton game at the weekend, kitbag on my shoulder. I walk in and there's a strange buzz about the place. Straightaway you can sense that something's not quite right.

Everyone is whispering, everyone is serious. The bloke on the door sees my face and looks away. I ask him what's up.

And it comes blurting out, first from him, then from everyone within earshot.

'It's Kenny. He's leaving.'

'What do you mean?'

'He's gone.'

'He's packing it in.'

'He's doing a press conference right now.'

I've seen what he was like the other night, but I still can't process it. Kenny can't have left. He's everything to Liverpool. He's told me I'm in the squad for the Luton game at the weekend.

He signed me. Kenny is my only connection to this place. He can't have gone. Not now.

I rush into the home dressing room. The players are there, sitting round in little huddles. Staring into space. Ronnie Moran is taking the team list for Luton off the wall and sticking a new one up. I look for my name. It's no longer there.

He sees my expression. Ronnie's a good man. 'Jamie, we need experience around us right now. Don't worry. Your chance will come.'

My bag for the trip to Kenilworth Road is at my feet. Now I'm thinking that I may need to pack a bigger one, ready for a longer journey south. No-one rates me here except a man who is already saying his goodbyes. I know I'm being selfish, but that's how my brain is trying to cope with it: a crisis for a man after a disaster for the city, and me just a little piece of flotsam bobbing about on the ripples far away.

We sit there in the dressing room. No-one is quite sure

what to do, or who is in charge. Then Alan Hansen stands up, and as the club captain, at Liverpool for the past thirteen and a half years, he silences the room. He's not always a serious man, Hansen, but he can be, and his face is a mask now.

'Right. So we all know now. Kenny's gone.'

He looks around the room. No-one speaks.

'Kenny's gone, and you're probably wondering what happens now. Who's taking over. Well, it's for these four walls for now. But I know I can trust everyone here, so you's may as well know. I'm taking over. I'm the new Liverpool manager.'

Whoah. That sort of makes sense. He hasn't played much over the past few years. His knee's been bad. Of course, he'd be looking forward. Kenny loves him. They play golf together on the links at Hillside. They live within a mile or so of each other. They signed the same summer, one from Celtic, one from four miles across Glasgow at Partick Thistle. This is natural. This was always going to happen.

Hansen's still looking awfully solemn. 'There's going to be a lot of changes around here. Starting now.

'John Barnes?'

Barnes nods.

'Barnesy, I know you like your Kentucky Fried Chicken. Well, there'll be no more of that. You need to get fit.

'Steve Nicol? I know you like going to that pub on the Wirral during the week. Don't argue, I know you do. There'll be no more of that either.'

I risk a quick glance around. Nicol's gone even whiter than usual, which is quite something for a Scotsman living in a rainy coastal town. Barnes looks like he wants to slap someone. But Hansen's just getting warmed up.

'Grobbelaar, I know where you've been going lately. Don't give me that face. That's over, got it?'

He keeps going. Round the room, revealing the secrets, cutting them dead. He doesn't bother with me and Don, but he doesn't have to. We don't matter. Not anymore.

When he's finally done and he turns on his heel and stalks out of the room, there are two reactions. One is outrage.

'F***ing hell, who does he think he is?'

'He's one of us! He's done the same.'

'I know what Jockey's been up to. He's hardly the Queen Mum, is he now?'

There's outrage, and there's pragmatism. Two of the young lads are straight out the door to the pay-phone in the players' lounge down the corridor. You can hear them yelling down the line, one to his mate in Ireland, another to his brother. The gist is the same: get an absolute pile on Alan Hansen as the next Liverpool manager. And do it now, before anyone finds out and the odds fall through the floor.

It's mayhem, at least for the full two minutes until Hansen walks back in, this time with a massive grin all over his kipper.

'Boys, you're all idiots, and I'm only joking. I just wanted to say that I'm retiring too. I'm finished. It's been an absolute pleasure. I love you all.'

Now there's laughter, belly laughter from everyone. Everyone except the two lads who have been on the phone, who now look like they're going to chuck their breakfasts up all over the dressing room floor. And I'm good too, at least until I go back over the road to Mrs Sainsbury's, and an empty house with a cold bedroom and a bag that no longer needs my boots in.

I sit on the edge of my single bed in the little room under the eaves at the top of the house, three in the afternoon, light going from the northern sky, yellow streetlights starting up. I try not to think about it all, and it crowds in all the same.

I could have stayed at home. I could have grown up in a town that I knew and loved. I could be out now with Deano and Dave Morris, playing snooker at Mum and Dad's, driving over to the Highlin for a messabout and some tunes.

I still want to be here. I'm not throwing toys. But I know what this means. I know what some will be saying: 'He should never have gone there in the first place . . .'

I hear the door slamming downstairs and Mrs Sainsbury shuffling around. She'll be getting the sausages and Smash off the sideboard in a minute and putting it on top of the micro-wave for me. And it's that thought, the lumpy Smash and the gristly sausages, that finally releases the tears. Sitting on my bed crying, wanting to be here but not like this, wanting some-one to just give me a chance.

I can hear the phone ringing in the hall and Mrs Sainsbury clattering after it. There's a pause, because she's half-deaf in one ear and it takes a while for anything to work its way through. Then she shouts up. 'Jamie? Jamie? Someone on the phone for you!'

I wipe my cheeks and trudge down the stairs. Maybe it's Mum. I can't tell her how it really is, she'll have Dad in the car in seconds. No-one else has got this number. It can't be Mark or Deano, although I wish it was.

I take the receiver off Mrs Sainsbury, mouthpiece covered.

'Who is it?'

She shrugs no idea.

'Hello?'

It takes me a moment to understand the Scottish voice coming back at me, to work it out, to realise that it's Kenny. I'm in a sort of shock still from the morning's news, and I have no idea how he knows I'm here or what the number is at Mrs Sainsbury's. So I don't say much, standing there red-eyed, and I just listen to a man who's going through a private hell himself taking time in the middle of all that to speak to a kid who's been in the city only a month.

He's calm and he talks and I listen. Jamie, you're going to be alright. Don't worry about anything, you've got such a bright future. The club are going to look after you and you'll be fine. I believe in you. You can play.

I listen and the tears are rolling down my face again. Jamie, you've got so much potential. You've just got to keep believing in yourself. I've seen it. I'm sorry this has happened, but it changes nothing for you.

He tells me to come up to Southport after training tomorrow. We can have a round of golf at Hillside. It will all be okay.

And that's exactly what happens, in the middle of this storm about the sudden departure of Liverpool's greatest player and a manager no-one could ever imagine walking away. I drive up to Hillside and Kenny and I walk the links and hit shots. The sun shines and the wind blows and everything feels like it will be okay, and we talk football and he teases me about my putting and you can almost forget everything that is falling apart around us.

When people are kind to you and go above and beyond what others do, you never forget it. That's how I will be with Kenny. For the rest of my Liverpool career he will invite me to his house again and again, call me up for golf, find out what I'm doing, even come to watch a reserve team game I'm playing. And so my only regret is that I will never a play a game for him. I'll wish I had won one game for him at least. Just one.

•

Kenny Dalglish: You don't want to let these young players down. You want to encourage them to be themselves, and so you make it as homely as it possibly can be for them. I remember the same with Robbie Fowler when he was 15 or so. I was leaving Anfield one night and he was stood at the bus stop, him and his da.

I said, 'Where are you going?'

He said, 'Just waiting for the bus.'

'Well, jump in.'

'But you stay in Southport.'

'No matter, it will be faster than the bus.'

So he jumped in the car with his da and I gave him a lift into Dingle. He came in the next morning and I said, 'You alright?'

'No, my da was gutted.'

'Gutted? I gave you a lift to the door!'

'Ah, but none of his mates saw him coming out of your car!'

There are certain attributes you need for football to be successful, and the first thing is that you have to understand the game. The second thing is to play it so there's no fear. That's the most important thing to me. And the fear thing, because of all the things that Jamie had seen with his dad, and all the times he'd spent around football – it wasn't there with Jamie like it might have been in another 17-year-old who hadn't had that football education.

I don't think it's right to pigeonhole people. You are your own self. You can't be anyone else, you can't replicate anybody. So as a manager you have a look, you have to see what the young players have about them. These kids have got to be comfortable when they come in.

You need character to be a player. You cannae be afraid. The fear might have been with Jamie two years before or a year before. When he started playing for Bournemouth, he went through that initiation. He came to us and he was ready to do it.

There are just some things when you go to a club the size of Liverpool that can make you think, 'What am I doing here?' He never had that, not deep down. He was more like us.

It's up to you as a manager. You would do different things for different people, but you can't let them down.

And you know. Those two, Jamie and wee Robbie, the staff knew it.

Come training, those two were straight in the staff side. Straight in.

14

THE OUTSIDER

With Kenny gone the city of Liverpool and the club feel as if they have been placed on pause. Ronnie Moran takes over as caretaker manager – he makes it clear he doesn't want the job permanently – and he tries to deal with an uncertain present by going back to the past.

It's the older players who are back in the starting XI, the traditional Liverpool way he tries to rediscover. But when you're on pause you can't move forward, and the team seems paralysed – losing away at Luton that first weekend after Kenny is gone, going one up but folding to Kingsley Black and an Iain Dowie double; losing the second FA Cup replay to Everton and a Dave Watson goal, losing again at home to Arsenal to let George Graham's lot take over at the top of Division One.

The *Sun's* chief sportswriter John Sadler thinks he knows what the problem is. He says Kenny was finished when he signed those three duds. He spells it out: David Speedie, Jimmy Carter and me. The physical evidence that the King had lost his mind.

It feels like a horrible thing to say about a 17-year-old, about a kid yet to make his first-team debut, and it stays with me. I want to prove the journalist wrong, but I also wonder if I am actually to blame in some way. Maybe signing me did make things worse for Kenny. What if he'd spent the money somewhere else, on a striker who started scoring goals right away, on a new central defender to take the place of Alan Hansen?

I realise the guilt doesn't make logical sense, but I also know that I've lost my safety net. When a club buys you, you're elevated above the other players around your age and position, simply because they've spent hard cash on you. I've seen it at Bournemouth with Luther Blissett and Ian Bishop, and Gavin Peacock when Dad splashed out £250,000 on him. It's the new car on the drive rather than the old one. It's the jumper you chose rather than the hand-me-down.

Now I'm just another kid, except I'm not. I'm the one from out of town. I haven't been around the club for a year or so, like Nicky Tanner and Mike Marsh, and I'm not a local boy like Alec Watson, Dave's little brother. Phil Thompson likes Scouse lads in his reserve team. Of course he does. He's from Kirkby. He was Liverpool skipper. He feels it in his blood. This is our club, not yours.

What do I do? I can let the scared feeling build up in my chest. It wants to, I just have to allow it in. I could go back to Mrs Sainsbury's and lie face down on the pillow so no-one in the house can hear my crying.

All that is easy. But I can't do that, because that's giving in. I know there are people within the club who think I can't hack it. If I fold, if I leave now, I'll be happier for a day, maybe a week. And then I'll be haunted by something else: by the thought that

I didn't give it everything, that I let someone else dictate what I should be doing.

I understand I'm lucky, too, even in that freezing room at the top of the house, even at training where a few of the reserve-team players still won't speak to me. There are lads from the youth team in Bournemouth who have been let go, who are now hunting round smaller clubs and lower leagues looking for another chance. Fighting that horrible realisation that despite all their obsessions with the game and how much they know about it and how hard they've worked, maybe they're not getting anything back from that investment, and they're going to have to find something poorer and duller and lonelier to do. Deano's still training with the youth team, but there's been no mention of a pro contract. Dave Morris is having talks with Hereford. My brother Mark has missed almost a year with that ankle problem that no-one could diagnose, and now Dad might have to let him go, end his own son's professional career. The game waits for no-one and looks after even fewer.

I'm still playing for Liverpool, even if I'm yet to play truly for Liverpool. And so I just get on with it. When I'm low, when I'm ignored at training or homesick or shovelling lukewarm Smash around my plate, I tell myself that it's a small price to be paying. I'm in the game. I'm at the biggest club in the country. I could go down south to Tottenham or Arsenal, but I don't want to. I can't stand the idea of people thinking I couldn't hack it. I am not going to be a failure. I am not going to be a footnote.

I am not on my own. A dark-haired 16-year-old kid from Dublin is also staying at Mrs Sainsbury's. He's called Marc Kenny, although Phil Thompson has given him the nickname Hollywood, on account of his show-stopping 50-yard passes, passes he can clip or chip or cut. He's got fantastic ability. He's the youngest of eight kids and he has a lot of chat on him, and I like all of it.

There's cheek and then there's Marc Kenny. We're sitting on the sofa in the living room, watching *Coronation Street* because that's what Mrs Sainsbury likes. She's in her armchair, all four-foot tall of her.

'Jamie, will you look at the state of her!', Marc whispers with a wink. 'What an effort. She's as wide as she is tall, Jamie. What's happening with her hair? She looks like a kid dressed up like ET at Halloween. Doesn't she now?'

That's only the start of it. Mrs Sainsbury's hearing may be even worse than her cooking. So Marc tests her out by letting off little farts. First a tiny one, audible only if you know it's there, then an increasing range. It's easy finding the ammunition with all the boiled cabbage and starch she sticks on our plates each day. The genius of Marc is the way he can vary the volume at will. Each one he lets off is slightly louder. They sound like ducks quacking where I am, next to him, but Mrs Sainsbury doesn't twitch. Marc's having to force them to even get a puzzled glance over from her, and even then he just shifts in his seat as if it's the springs in the old sofa just flexing and groaning.

It's extraordinarily hard not to burst out laughing. I'm

having to clench my teeth together and stare at Curly Watts on *Corrie* as if I'm in love with him. I can't look right at Marc and I can't look left at Mrs Sainsbury. I'm squeezing my fists tight. I'm holding my breath.

But, of course, Marc can't leave it there. Marc can never leave anything anywhere. He has to push the boundaries. So he goes quiet for about two minutes, building up the pressure, summoning up his Hollywood game. And just as the volume on the TV drops down at the end of the adverts, he lets rip with everything he's got.

Windows rattle. Ornaments wobble. Mrs Sainsbury's head flicks round like a shocked owl's. And as the laughter explodes out of me, Marc leans away and looks at me with exaggerated horror.

'Jamie! You bloody dirty animal!'

Everything is more fun with Hollywood. There is a statue of the Virgin Mary on the first-floor landing. She has her own table and a view up and down the stairs. Every time Marc walks past he crosses himself and asks for salvation from our evening meal. At night, he kneels down in front of it and asks the Blessed Virgin for protection from the mice that are everywhere in that big, old draughty house.

One of his brothers comes over on the ferry from Ireland to visit. We meet him outside and he's all praise about how amazing it is living so close to the ground, and couldn't the house fit in a treat with all those Georgian ones on Grafton Street back home. Then he comes in and sees the 50-year-old carpet and the damp patches on the ceiling and the two mice having a full-on scrap in the middle of Marc's bedroom floor, and he's off back towards town and the pubs before you can even show him the cold dinners in the kitchen.

Marc is often up before it's light. He's out of there before any of the mice can get to him. He goes across the road to the club and gets tea and toast, anything to escape the house. There is a phone box at the end of the road that we can use to call home, because the one downstairs is for incoming calls only. Phoning Dublin is not cheap. It becomes cheaper when Marc works out that if you cover a 20p in silver foil and do it the right way, the phone thinks it's a pound coin. The magic coin, we call it, and it saves us both.

We survive together. Neither of us feels much obvious warmth from Phil Thompson. He wants us to play one touch, two touch. That's fine in training. It forces me to get my pass away earlier. It also starts to wear away on my ability to beat a man, to dribble round an opponent and get away, like Dad used to, like Gazza does. And it's how training is done and how you're treated as a kid on the outside. You walk into the dressing room at Anfield to get changed and you're already as nervous as you've ever been in your life. You take a big deep breath, sit down and hope that no-one notices you. Knowing that someone's going to say something – where are you going, what have you done, what's your haircut like, what are you wearing, what's different about you.

You don't want to be different. You don't want to stand out. But the way you speak, the way you look, sets you apart. The way you want to behave is not the accepted way. I want to stay on at Melwood after training to do my extras. I want to work on my free-kicks and ball-striking like I did with the goal painted on the wall at Bournemouth. I have to, so I can keep improving, but I also need to because it's good for my head. When it's me and a bag of balls and a goal, I'm in control. No-one can touch me. Everything around me falls away and fades. No smell of cabbage, no cold single bed, no doubts.

But no-one here stays behind after training. I ask to stay and I'm told to get back on the bus. I wait until we get to Anfield, stick a load of balls in the boot of my car and drive back.

That's when you hear the whispers. Arse-licker. Billy no-mates. Pretty boy.

Phil Thompson does it old-school. As the weeks go past, we're given a rare weekend off, so I ask if I can go home to see Mum and Dad, come back for training Monday. He says no. We play a reserve-team game against West Brom. I don't play well. I'm struggling with my game, I'm homesick. We lose.

Afterwards he singles me and Don out in front of the other lads. He tells us our parents would have been embarrassed by that display. As he's telling me and I'm staring back at him, I can feel my eyes starting to go. My form is not good, I know that. I'm doubting myself more than I ever have. But they would not be embarrassed, not my mum and dad. So I say to myself, don't you dare cry. I know I have to win some people over. I will prove everyone wrong. I will.

Nicky Tanner is the leader of a little gang. They have a catchphrase that they shout when your back is turned, or when there's enough of them around. 'Crap!' Said in a pretend

Scouse accent, too high, too squeaky. Like it's a joke, except we all know it's not one. It's power. It's making yourself feel better and running others down. I get it. Don Hutchison gets it.

I try to pretend I haven't heard. I want to turn round and knock him out. Instead, I try to stay rational. I'm not playing well. I haven't given them a reason not to call me crap. Him and his mates, they don't like us new kids coming in, threatening their places. That's how football works.

I'm tougher than they think. I've seen all this at Bournemouth. This atmosphere, the you-or-me thing, the fight to get through. It's nothing that I haven't witnessed before.

I don't want anyone feeling sorry for me. I'm lucky. I'm at Liverpool. And I know what I have to do.

The harder the times, the more you practise. Take my bag of balls, go out in the rain, hit them, hit them, hit them.

•

Phil Thompson: I remember when Jamie came on the trial. I was expecting a little teenager, five-foot five. Then he turns up six-foot-one already, big floppy hairstyle, physique of a 20-year-old. I thought, oh my God . . .

Even in those two weeks, you could see he was blessed with ability. You could see a little kid playing in the back garden doing his keepy-uppies, getting his touches in, playing the ball against the wall. All these things came very natural to him.

When he arrived for good it was straight in with me in the reserves, and it was a little bit of tough love. You could see he'd come from a really good family, that he'd had a good upbringing. And I'm thinking, this lad has got ability, but is he going to be able to hack it here, at a club with all these unwritten rules about how you go about things and how you do your job?

I'm putting these questions to myself about him. Okay, his ability is unquestioned, his technique is nigh-on perfect, he can control it in any circumstance. He can turn, he has great mobility. The only person I'd seen caress the ball with his instep like he did was Glenn Hoddle. Those were the things he had in his locker.

My worry was with his personality and the long hair, and the clothes. The young apprentices were mainly Scousers, and they're looking at him going, 'F***ing hell, who's this flash bastard?' It was different, where he'd come from. So that's the burning question for me: can he actually handle this? Have you got that little bit extra to make it?

Ronnie Moran had been my mentor when I came through as a kid in the early 70s. There was no tougher man, and I used to think he hated me. He picked on me when we had our five-a-side against the staff. I'd be thinking, 'The bastard, he's just picking me to make me run for him.' I can hear Ronnie screaming at me now. 'Pass it early!'

It wasn't until I was about 26 that I asked him about it.

'What did you see in this skinny lad?'

'Thommo, we could see a lad who could play. We were trying to give you our experience. Yes, you could run, you could run all day, but we were trying to teach you when and how to close down, when to pass, when to play it simple. All those things we were trying to give you because we knew you could play.'

That was the thing that Jamie came through. That was the tough love a lot of the players had to come through.

Steve Heighway, youth team coach, used to always have a go at me: 'You're too hard on the players.' I thought, they've got to take it from me in the reserves, because they're going to get it another 50 per cent more off Ronnie Moran in the first team. You've got Roy Evans giving it both barrels. You're going to get it from 40,000 fans each week. If you can't hack it just from me as one person, you won't make it through the rest.

Liverpool is a tough area and you get pulled in different ways. The nightclub scene, the pub scene. Everybody wants a bit of you, and you have to suss them out. Are you good enough, are you clever enough? Can you look after yourself?

It was about what was right for the club and what you were looking for in players. To succeed at Liverpool you needed that inner belief. You had to have that drive in you.

•

Marc Kenny gets tested too. Both of us at the biggest club in the world, both a long, long way from home. Tight families but hours away. Quiet thoughts inside when nobody else is around: how are we going to get through this?

Together. We'll do anything rather than waste the afternoons and evenings away with Mrs Sainsbury, so we head into town – to the snooker hall, to a restaurant on Stanley Street called Casa Italia. It's warm, cosy, reminds me of Lorenzo's back on the south coast. It's opposite the bronze Eleanor Rigby statue, and when we're done we sit out next to her, and the inscription on the plaque on the wall – 'Dedicated to all the lonely people' – works for all of us. One night, Marc says we're going to a nightclub on Belmont Road called the Wookey. It's down a back lane, half a mile or so from the house, half-timbered front like a country pub but nothing at all like a country pub inside.

It's mayhem. Everyone off their faces, properly mangled. Marc's a good-looking boy so he doesn't need an angle, but he comes up with one anyway: we're brothers, me the elder one, him the talented, misunderstood one. No-one seems to worry that one of us has a Dublin accent and that the other one could be from Essex. In the Wookey they don't care. If it adds to the good times, it's fine. There's no hip-hop being played. There's no house music. You don't go to the Wookey for the tunes. You go for the abandonment of all the usual rules.

Deano comes up to stay for a weekend. It's magic to see him. We know each other well enough that I can't pretend everything is okay. He understands how football works and he sees when I'm happy and when I'm struggling. Just before he leaves, he tells me they're all proud of me, him and Dave and the other lads in the youth team. It helps and it makes me more homesick, both at the same time.

It's different, Liverpool. Everyone is a comedian. Everyone has a line to throw at you. It's Liverpool against the world, but it's also tribal within. When I was a kid and Bournemouth were away, I'd often get the train over to The Dell and watch Southampton instead. Good football, Division One, not even a thought that I didn't support them. So with Liverpool away one weekend and me not anywhere near Ronnie Moran's squad, I suggest to Marc that we go over to Goodison Park. It's only half a mile across Stanley Park. We can see the crowds streaming towards the ground through the condensation of the window in my attic room.

There are some stiff looks as we go through the turnstiles. Okay, it's Everton, I'm Liverpool, there might be a few wrong 'uns who want to make a point, but it's fine – we're in good seats on the Top Balcony of the Goodison Road stand. I've got a baseball cap pulled low over my face. I'm Liverpool, but I'm invisible.

It takes 10 minutes. One minute I'm watching Pat Nevin beat his full-back and lay the ball off for Robert Warzycha, the next something solid is cracking me on the back of the head.

It's a meat pie, thrown with pace and superb accuracy, served up with a side dish of partisan abuse.

'F*** off, Redknapp! What you doing here, you red-nosed p****?'

I can feel a chunk of steak or chicken or whatever it is stuck behind my right ear. I turn round, and the pie sniper stands up to take the acclaim of those around him.

'Eh, f*** off!'

There is laughter all around. Everyone in on the joke except me and Marc, and he's shrinking down into his seat, edging away from me as if he's nothing to do with the target, as if we're back on the sofa at Mrs Sainsbury's with him shifting the blame for his stink bombs.

I try to focus on the pitch. Jimmy Gabriel's down there, my old mate, back on the Everton bench alongside Howard Kendall. Jimmy always looks after me. If he was here . . .

CRACK.

Another pie, slightly different angle, this time landing smack between the shoulder blades, sliding down my back in a mess of gravy and bits of meat and broken pastry.

No laughs from Marc now. He's gone as white as Everton's shorts. 'J, we're going to get bashed up here. We gotta go . . .'

Go? But then everyone will see us. It will actually make it worse. We'll be running away.

I've had some lonely times in the past two months. This might be the worst, sitting there, covered in gravy, a sitting duck, ignoring the football now, just staring at my watch and willing it to get to 3.45 pm.

Actually, I think, let's make it 3.43 pm. We don't want to be going up those stairs when thousands of others are off to get their half-time cups of tea. When the stalls are open so everyone can fully reload on fresh pies.

Sorry, John Ebbrell. Sorry, Ray Atteveld. We can't stay a moment longer. And the shouts follow us up the stairs as we sprint like lunatics for the exit and the streets beyond. 'Red-nose p****s!'

So Liverpool is not Southampton. I can't get near the first team, but rival fans still hate me as if I can. It's the last time I ever go to Goodison to watch a game.

There are rules I have to learn, currents to plug into. It's a different sort of love in this city.

In training, it's Ronnie Moran on my case all the time. He's still calling me Harry. Every time I get the ball to feet it's, 'Pass! Pass!' I want him to leave me alone. I suck it up because I've seen this at Bournemouth. I've seen how adults behave towards young lads in a way they couldn't in any other line of work or situation. But I can't work out why he's having a go at me all the time. What have I done wrong that the other young lads haven't?

So I ask John Barnes about it on the coach to Melwood one morning, and he nods his head.

'Jamie, it was exactly the same when I joined from Watford. He's shouting at you because he likes you. He rates you. The kids he's not shouting at? He doesn't think they're worth bothering with. He doesn't think they'll make it.'

'But why's he not shouting at Steve McManaman?'

'Because the day Ronnie stops shouting at you is the day you've made it. Macca's made it. He's first team. And he thinks you will be too.'

•

Marc Kenny: He was always different, Jamie. First time he arrives at Mrs Sainsbury's, he's being dropped off by Kenny Dalglish. The only lift I ever had was from Mrs Sainsbury's son Tommy. I watched Jamie get out of this huge car and I thought, who's this f***ing Charlie?

The two of them would go off for golf and I'd be stuck in my room covering coins in foil for the pay-phone. Hiding under the duvet trying to get warm. Mainly getting fat, because of the food. I arrived in that house weighing eight stone wet through and I left weighing about 18.

I'm a year younger than Jamie, but I was maybe more grown up in the ways of the world, coming from a city like Dublin. We were both petrified little boys, don't get me wrong, but a lot of lads from where I was from were over in England trying the same thing. Gary Kelly had come from my club Home Farm and was at Leeds, Graham Kavanagh was at Middlesbrough. Before us there had been Liam Brady and Ronnie Whelan and so many others.

It was still such a shock to us all. One minute you're kicking a ball around twice a week with your mates and the next you're training every day and having a coach tear into you all the time. I got subbed on by Phil Thompson in one game and then subbed off in the same match. That nearly broke me. I'd go back to the digs and get into bed and cry my eyes out. You were meant to survive that.

Me and Jamie, we helped each other through. With my seven brothers I was always looked after at home, so Jamie and I needed to bounce off each other. We kept each other afloat.

He always had that little bit extra about him. You could tell he'd been playing proper games in the Bournemouth first team. He'd been playing with men and I was still a boy. I watched him and it was only a matter of time before he took the next step up, because his passing ability was always way ahead of everyone else's. At times he was almost too clever or maybe too quick for some of the other players. He was on a different wavelength to most of the boys. They had to move him up. He needed better, stronger players alongside him.

15

THE DON

Mrs Sainsbury's nest is growing. Another Dublin lad arrives, a little striker called Tony Cousins. Don Hutchison moves in, gets his head round what it's like and then moves out again almost as quickly. He's rented himself a flat, which makes a lot of sense, but being Don he gets one in Speke, out by the airport, which makes almost none.

We end up in a nightclub in Speke one night, where a girl lets us go back to her house on the proviso that we give her a piggyback ride all the way. The combination of the club, the two-mile piggyback and the sights we see on the way are enough to convince me that Speke will not be high on my list of preferred neighbourhoods. For Don, it's just a name that lodges in his head. He knows Anfield and nowhere else. So when he sees a flat and sees it's in Speke, a light goes on.

He hates it. It's miles from us, miles from anywhere except the airport and the towers of the chemical works at Ellesmere Port across the Mersey. Meanwhile, I know I have to escape too. The food, the carpets, the smells. There's a local comedian called Willie Miller who does lots of the clubs in town, hosts events in the players' lounge at Anfield before matches.

Willie knows everyone. He's everything about Scouse humour condensed into one man – always a grin, quick one-liners, piss-taking, working his angles.

He tells me about his mum Marie and stepdad Bob, and how they've put up young footballers before. They live just south of Croxteth Hall Park, up Deysbrook Lane from the training ground at Melwood. The red-brick close where *Brookside* is filmed is just round the corner, Jimmy Corkhill and Sinbad and all the rest. I jump in the white Peugeot and drive over for a look. Compared to Mrs Sainsbury's it is a palace – detached, bay windows, a double garage to the side. I get offered the bedroom at the top of the stairs, the biggest one after Bob and Marie's, for £130 a week including breakfast, tea and all my washing done.

I think about it for around five seconds. I feel bad about abandoning Marc Kenny at Mrs Sainsbury's, but he's got Tony, and I'll still see him at training every day. I can get away from football now, rather than living in the shadow of Anfield. I can look forward to dinner without mice for company.

Don is immediately interested. The two of us are rapidly becoming allies, both late Kenny signings who no-one seems bothered about anymore. He doesn't know when to stop. I've always enjoyed hanging out with these sorts of mavericks. It brings me out of myself. I see Don crashing about, completely unaware of the carnage he's leaving in his wake, and I think, he's my man.

I've been with Bob and Marie about a week when Don comes over and we both sort of ask: could he move in too?

Bob has no interest in football, Marie is out of the house each morning for work. But they both like the sound of £260 a week compared to £130. And so we're in, and the good times begin.

I do better with the rooms. Mine has the en suite. Don's is ten feet by three feet, has a single bed and a basin and his little silver portable CD player on a shelf, so half the time he's down the corridor and in mine, asking to borrow clothes, eyeing up a Stone Island jacket I've got that changes colour with the temperature.

On the tarmac drive outside he parks his red Scirocco, with its spoiler and three doors and black hub caps. He calls it the Beast, which worries Marie, a quiet woman who frets about a lot of things. She has a bad ankle which she tells us about on one of our first nights and continues to tell us about at every opportunity. Her story is that she went abroad on holiday one year and was bitten by a spider. The bite swelled up when she got home, so she went to see a doctor, who had a look and then reeled away in horror because the spider had laid its eggs in there and her whole ankle was a moving, twitching nest of hundreds of baby spiders.

To be fair to Marie, it's a great story, even if it's hard to secure definitive proof. The lads in the reserve team are huge fans, and the story spreads across Liverpool, with fresh layers added each time it's passed on.

The two of them have one main rule for us: no girls overnight in our rooms. The rest is straightforward. Dirty washing in the basket on the landing. Dinner made in the morning and left out under Clingfilm, an uncomfortable reminder of my last lodgings. They have a nightcap each evening while Don and I play on our new Game Boys. It's a charming domestic scene: stocky Bob and Marie a martyr to her ankle, sitting there with their whiskies, Don and me bleeping away on *Tetris* and *Super Mario Land*.

Maybe the end of this winter is particularly cold. Don wanders round with his thin little duvet each evening, wafting it hopefully over radiators that are seldom turned on. When we don't fancy what's being served up, we slip it back into the pot, jump in the Beast and drive to the Pizza Hut round the corner, or if we're feeling flash the branch of Est Est Est in the Albert Dock. We sit there dutifully eating pasta, because everyone knows footballers should eat pasta, and we talk about training, about players we love, about what it would be like if we ever got in the first team. Then there's Lucy In The Sky, a little café on Cavern Walks run by a lovely woman called Margie who does us cheese toasties for lunch and chocolate fudge cake for afters. This is fine for Don, who has the same body fat as the jockeys up the road at Aintree, but for me, it starts to notice. In photos, my face appears chubby. I'm a 17-year-old who spends two hours a day chasing footballs. I should not be chubby.

It's always Don's car we go out in, whether it's for tea or to go to the snooker hall or cinema. He thinks of the Scirocco as others think of a Ferrari. When he decides the spoiler isn't quite enough, he comes back from Halfords one afternoon with a bright red steering wheel.

He drives, I do the tunes. Slick R&B, hip-hop, anything produced by Teddy Riley. New Jack Swing, New Jill Swing.

Tony! Toni! Toné!, the soundtrack from *Boyz n the Hood*. Maybe some Loose Ends for more of a British feel. All of it bought from a record shop up in Wigan that John Barnes has been talking about. When the weather warms up a little and DJ Jazzy Jeff & the Fresh Prince get busy, we'll hammer 'Summertime' on the way to training and all the way back – miming the scratching at the start, one of us doing the chorus, then taking alternate lines. Guys out hunting and girls doing likewise.

The money is enough for what we're interested in. Buying a house is not among those things. I'm 17, I don't want to be living on my own. I want to be looked after. And so it's all disposable, and that makes every day fun. Into Wade Smith for a new shirt for the weekend, a pair of boxfresh trainers that aren't smart enough to get us into anywhere the first team are going. You can experiment on looks when you've got £400 in your pocket after outgoings, when you've been used to £27.50 a week at Hartlepool, like Don.

Perhaps influenced by the Fresh Prince's promises of what summer afternoons might bring, perhaps subconsciously channelling the Man from Del Monte, I get fitted out for a linen suit. It works, cooler than my burgundy Giorgio Armani sports jacket, just old enough to make me look cleverer than 17 but not like I work in the local branch of the Midland bank.

Don decides he'll do the same, except he spills lager down the lapels on its first outing and has to stick it in the washing basket on the landing. When the suit comes back from Marie, something significant has changed: the length of the arms and legs. The shoulders still fit and the buttons still fasten, but the cuffs sit halfway up his forearm and the ankles have shifted to just below his knees.

He looks like a big man in a small potato sack. Because he's Don, he wears it to the reserve-team game we're playing at Notts County anyway. There's something beautiful in his brazenness, in his determination to eke some value out of his investment. I've paid for it, I'm wearing it, is his attitude.

When you take gambles they don't always come off. In May, we travel to Singapore to play Arsenal in an end-of-season jolly called the Caltex Cup. It's like a four-day stag-do. No-one cares about the football. There are some great lads in the Arsenal team – Paul Merson, Tony Adams, Ray Parlour, who I've met before – and everyone gets stuck in.

John Barnes has another idea. He talks to the concierge, gets a steer and takes us to apparently the best tailor in town. When we arrive, he opts for an incredible silk suit. It's hand-made, a thing of absolute beauty. As they measure him up for it, the material sits on him but also appears to float on his frame. Because I still want to be John Barnes, I ask for the same thing. Two-tone purple silk, a shimmer to it, a shiny bagginess.

Only when I get it home, when I leave the comforting flattery of the tailor's assistant, do I realise the disaster I've stumbled into. I look like MC Hammer. I wear it one night out, endure strangers doing the Running Man dance in front of me and shouting, 'Can't touch this!', and never dare bring it out of the wardrobe again.

•

Free and easy away from football, still second-class citizens within it. The split within the club between Ronnie Moran's first-teamers and us lot, the kids and reserves, could not be wider. They get changed in the home dressing room at Anfield before training; we trudge into the away one. They trot off the coach at Melwood to the good pitches; we turn right to the ones that are a mud heap.

Some of us are starting to crack. Marc Kenny gets it. Hutch gets it, I get it. None of us feel as if we're getting any closer to the first team.

There are strange code words and signals that we have to learn. Ronnie Moran shouts, 'Harry Lime!' and it's the signal for the third man to make a run. If you don't know enough about Graham Greene and Orson Welles to make the connection, you can work it out – one man plays it to the second, the second plays it back to the first, the third man makes a run for the next pass. It gives a surreal feel to a muddy patch of grass in West Derby – Ronnie bellowing, 'Harry Lime, Harry f***in' Lime!', and then someone else yelling, 'Dotch!' at Hutch, because it's a mixture of Don and Hutchison, and then another shout from Ronnie, 'Away the noo!' in a Scottish accent, when it's time to sack it off and get back on the bus. Maybe it comes from the Bill Shankly days. No-one seems to remember, but I always listen to what Ronnie says. I'm gradually realising what a special man he is, just as I'm seeing that Roy Evans is a gent, a real diamond.

Results are continuing to stall, though. There's a crazy 7–1 win over Derby at the Baseball Ground, but they're bottom of the table and Peter Shilton is in his dotage. QPR come to Anfield and win 3–1. We go to Southampton and lose 1–0. Coventry nick another draw. And then someone gets off the coach one day and hears chief executive Peter Robinson on the phone to someone he keeps referring to as 'Graeme', and we all guess what's coming next.

Ronnie doesn't want to turn the caretaker's job into the permanent one. There's John Toshack impressing everyone over in Spain, winning La Liga with Real Madrid and then going back to Real Sociedad.

Neither of them has done as much as Graeme Souness. Five League titles, three European Cups and four League Cups in seven years as a player at Liverpool. Three Scottish Division One titles and four League Cups as manager of Rangers. He'd been the obvious name talked up when Kenny had gone, but he's invested at Ibrox, the second biggest shareholder, blank contract in front of him from new chairman David Murray, and it had all gone quiet again.

Now he's back. And when he arrives at Anfield in mid-April, it's with a cloud of respect and hope and open fear. He's an alpha male, Souness. You get that as soon as he stands at the front of the coach. You can't argue with his reputation or his track record. He has charisma and he holds your gaze.

It's inevitable, then, that Don will get stuck into him. Souness joins in the training games, just as Kenny had, just as all the staff still do. There'll come a session where Don will take a pass, lay it off and go for the return, just as Souness is reaching peak speed, coming in at the ball horizontally with his studs up. This is the signal for any sensible young player to hold back a fraction, let the new manager win the ball. Only a madman would see Souness coming in high and late and decide that the only option is to come in higher and later.

It's like watching a crash in a cartoon. Limbs everywhere, dust flying up, a noise like an axe chopping wood. You almost expect to see giant words appearing in capital letters – BAM and WALLOP and YOUCH!

Because Don is my mate I'll laugh as much as I've laughed for months. Don will only just be getting started. They'll be up and snarling, both of them, hands on each other's throats and faces. A heavyweight versus a flyweight, but the skinny one will have no idea.

Don doesn't know. He doesn't know anything. He doesn't know how you speak to managers, he doesn't know what the etiquette is.

I've grown up in football and I know when you speak and when you don't. Don is like the anti-me. He just reacts as he would with his mates back home. When a coach tells him to do something and he disagrees, he tells them. He's quite happy to have an argument. He'll stand his ground and fight.

You can feel invincible at our age. The 22-year-olds seem ancient to us. The 27-year-olds go to different places wearing different clothes and listening to different music. The ones in their early thirties seem so far away that they may as well be teachers or policemen. And then John Barnes sits down next to us one morning on the bench at Melwood where everyone stops to tie up their laces.

I've been watching John in training. He's even better than I realised. Both feet perfect, always the right touch. Never ever hurried, even with David Burrows and Gary Ablett at his ankles. It's easy not to do enough when you're training with the reserves like I am. No-one's watching you. No-one cares. But I know I have to because I'm so far off Barnes' level. I know that he's done the same at Watford, staying behind, turning himself from a Middlesex League player at Sudbury Court into an England regular. I'm doing this for me, because I want to play like John Barnes one day.

The first team are all jogging off to the nice pitches. John stops and sits. Still young, still nervy in his presence, we listen while he tells us. Jamie, Don. You're here for a reason. You're good enough. But this will go fast. You won't be the kids forever. Make the most of it. Give it everything.

No other senior player does that for us. We're outsiders still, the forgotten boys of a previous manager. But someone is watching. Someone cares.

•

John Barnes: Liverpool wasn't set up to help you. Ronnie Moran would just say, 'Work it out yourself. If you have any problems, either you work it out yourself or you're not going to make it.'

If you were injured they wouldn't speak to you because you couldn't help them football-wise. You could be Pele, they wouldn't want to know you. It was all about winning, all about football. You couldn't go to them with problems you were having because some fans in town or somebody didn't like you or something like that. Because they'd just say, 'Hang on a second, grow a pair of balls, get on with it.'

That was the Liverpool way, and I knew that was the Liverpool way. When Jamie was having problems and went looking for help, it went against the philosophy of the club. But I also knew that a player who wanted to be a good professional might have needed some advice and assistance, so I would try to do what I could.

A lot of people want to come to you with their problems when things aren't going well, but when things are going well, they're not interested. There was another player who would come to me when things weren't going his way, but when they were, he was supercilious, he was flash. I had no time for him. Whereas Jamie wasn't like that.

The advice I always gave Jamie was to believe in yourself. You know you're a good player, don't worry about what other people think. If you've got the right integrity and you're authentically a decent person, a good professional, want to do well, there are going to be some people who like you and some people who don't. But you can sleep well at night because you know you're doing the right thing.

And Jamie, for a young player, usually did the right thing. Even the times when he did stupid things, as we all do when we're young, he realised and he took himself out of that situation. He would hold his hand up and admit his mistake, rather than making excuses. Every young player does daft things. I did. I'm still doing them now. As long as you know in your head what you've done wrong, and you tell yourself that you're not going to do it again, that's the best way to be.

At Liverpool we used to go straight to the pub after training. We didn't train in the afternoon, we didn't do any set pieces. Jamie did a lot of that himself. That wasn't the Liverpool way, but I think he had that in him. He had that determination, that drive.

I knew after two or three weeks that he was going to be okay. Not from his football ability but from his mentality. Even when they were taking the piss out of him, he never showed it. He had the right spirit, the right attitude, for people to see that he wanted to be a footballer. Try hard and train well. A lot of the senior players wouldn't let him see it. They'd still try and take the piss out of him, but they were accepting him because of that. He was earning their respect.

It would have been easy for Jamie not to be humble. You're 17 years old, you come to Liverpool, the girls are going to like you, your dad is Harry Redknapp, people are going to be jealous of you. When you get older you realise how insignificant it all is, but for a young player to have the head on his shoulders as he did, looking the way he did, the way he was, that's not normal.

He wanted to be a footballer, he wanted to play football, he wanted his football to do the talking. Don't get me wrong, David Beckham was a good player, but he wasn't better than Jamie. Jamie wanted to be a footballer before he wanted any of the other stuff. That's why I have so much respect for him. That's why I really took to him.

●

Don is laid-back. He's quite happy going to the snooker hall in the afternoon. He's also never known anything different, so when we start going back to Melwood each afternoon in the Beast, he gets into it. Everywhere in Liverpool you see the work ethic of the people in cafés and shops.

The city is starting to grow again, come alive, new venues opening, new buildings going up. It feels like we have to reflect that with what we do – the extra hours in training, working on our games, finishing late, the going out afterwards, sharing that buzz, the little ripples of excitement that are coming through with the new music and clothes, with the optimism of house music and kids going to Ibiza and bringing it all back with them.

I want to be normal. I want to go to the local pub with my mates. But you can't, not as a footballer in Liverpool. You can't be one of the lads, because the whisper soon goes out that there's a couple of players in, and everyone is staring, wanting to get involved in seconds. There are certain places you have to go, clubs where you'll be safe, if you behave yourself.

I don't really want to drink. I want to be an athlete. I never drank in Bournemouth except for maybe a sip of Dave Morris's vodka orange, just to get that taste of it. Try that in Liverpool and the senior players don't like it. You stand out, so you get stick. This is all part of it. You have a drink and you play the game. That's the culture.

There are certain places the big players go to. The favourite, maybe, is the Conti, Club Continental, on Wolstenholme Square. Neon sign high on the wall outside, private car park for the big names, soul and R&B inside.

On a Saturday night, it's like *Scarface* in there. Dancefloor at the bottom, balcony up above with private tables for drinking and dining. The senior players are up there, looking down, the best-looking girls in the place all around them.

Me and Don are downstairs looking up, in there with the girls dancing round their handbags and the lads in their best suits leaning on the bar. I'm not ready to take the stairs. I'm not big enough. Maybe when I've played a few games I'll be ready to go up there and be comfortable. John Barnes tells me I can come up with him and Ian Rush. I can't, not yet. I'd feel embarrassed, looking over that balcony while people point up at you.

You have to be careful. Go to the wrong place or the right place in the wrong part of town and the trouble swamps you before you realise. There's a place in West Derby that we end up in one night, where a pint glass comes sailing over the crowd and bounces off the side of my head. Luckily, it doesn't break, but it's a warning.

I'm shy, I'm not flash. I'm doing nothing at Liverpool. Somehow I'm still known, in this city, with its obsessions and fierce loyalties.

Don is sometimes oblivious to it all because he's charmingly naïve about everything. He just enjoys making people laugh, even if he's the butt of the joke. He can get himself in trouble because he always wants to take things further, see if he can squeeze some more laughs out of it.

We're a good combo, on the dancefloor at the Conti or in Kirklands wine bar on Hardman Street, with its lovely old wrought-iron front and its angles inside. Don will chat to anyone. You can send him into a situation with a couple of girls, bottle of Budweiser in hand, and then stroll in to rescue them. But we're both tall, and so we stand out when we don't want to. Girls like footballers, so boys who like those girls don't like footballers.

It's a tough town and you have to get a feel for when it's right and when there's trouble. When Liverpool get a result on the weekend you can feel like you're in the safest environment you've ever known. Everyone's your mate. Other times you just sense someone's going to light the touch paper and you've got to get out. You have a few drinks, because everyone else is and you're a bit looser, and then all of a sudden it's fists everywhere and elbows and shouting and ripped shirts. If the first team lose, I don't want to be seen out. You can't be in a bar with your clothes and your money. You have to understand the culture that surrounds you.

So we keep our heads down and we follow the music. John Barnes gets us into a local DJ called Charlie C, who plays the Conti and bangs out the best hip-hop and R&B. Charlie does us mix tapes – some Keith Sweat, Wreckx-n-Effect's 'Rump Shaker', Joe Public with those Teddy Riley beats and the JB's samples, Johnny Kemp and 'Just Got Paid'.

What we're not meant to do is bring any girls back to Bob and Marie's overnight. It's their number one rule. It gets broken, they kick us out, we have to beg them to let us stay.

When Don and I have steady girlfriends, it's weird for both of us. We're both really nice to the other one's girl, siding with her in arguments, chatting too much. Not trying to pull her, but getting on the other one's nerves, almost trying to drive a wedge between them.

We're jealous of them, basically. We don't want to share each other with anyone. We go everywhere together now. When it gets serious with a girl, we both panic: someone's going to ruin this.

Don needs looking after. When we go on holiday that summer to Ayia Napa, he's bowling about in the midday sun on the first day without any sun cream on.

'Don, listen, it's hot here, mate.'

'What you talking about?'

'Don, you need sun cream.'

'Jamie, it's the same f***ing sun as we get in Newcastle. It's not a different sun, is it?'

Like he's straight out of *Viz*. I leave him an hour. Then it's, 'Don, you're getting red, you got to put some cream on . . .'

He's stubborn now. Won't listen. Acts like he can't feel it. Then we get back to our apartment, and all of a sudden he faints. Absolutely gone, horrible case of sun stroke, so red you can feel the heat coming off him from two yards away.

He's in bed for two days. Someone calls his mum, who suggests we cover him in yoghurt to try to cool his skin down a little. Even through the pain, unable to move, his skin blistering and cracking, Don looks for the laughs. One of the other lads comes back from the shop with two more pots of plain natural yoghurt. Don is face-down on his single bed, naked, the outline of his Speedos the only white thing on his body. Yoghurt is being rubbed into his raw back when he lifts his head from the pillow and grimaces.

'F***ing hell, lads, you could at least have got me a fruity one.'

Whatever we get up to, wherever Don's maverick tendencies take us, we always come back to football. Every night there is a game on and we watch it, whatever the league or Cup competition. We analyse matches and chew over players and tactics. We will talk about football all the time, every day.

Kenny is still keeping an eye. One Thursday he calls me at Bob and Marie's. There's a French game on here, Jamie, come on over. So Don and I fire up the Beast and roar on up to sleepy Southport, and we're on the sofa with Kenny, with Kelly and Paul, with Lynsey, who's only nine, and Lauren, who's still a toddler. Kenny's got Canal+ Sport on cable, so we watch a random Ligue 1 match and break it down as if it's the most important game in the world.

It's not even Marseille, with Basile Boli and Abedi Pele,

Chris Waddle and Jean-Pierre Papin. It doesn't matter. It's Don, and Kenny, and football. And that's just fine.

•

Don Hutchison: I wasn't even meant to be at Liverpool. Hartlepool told me after my last home game for them that I was going to sign for Aston Villa on the Monday.

Sunday afternoon the phone rang at my mum's. When she answered it the man on the other end of the line told her he was Kenny Dalglish. She put the phone straight back down because it was clearly a wind-up.

Kenny phoned back. This time she put me on, and Kenny told me, I understand you've given your word to Aston Villa, will you do us a favour, come down here on Monday, have a look at the place, let me have an opportunity to talk to you. We'll put a car on, take you to Villa in the afternoon. Okay?

It's Kenny Dalglish. I'm not going to say no. I go to Anfield, get the full tour – the dressing rooms, the pitch, standing in front of the Kop, touching the 'This is Anfield' sign, ending up in the trophy room. At the end is an open door, the chief executive and a contract.

What can you do? Kenny's like, we'll sort it out with Villa. Okay. Where do I live? Across there. Mrs Sainsbury's. There's a couple of other young lads in there. It'll be a home from home.

I was two years older than Jamie, but I was much less mature than him, much more emotional. I didn't know the world he'd come from, the knowledge he'd got from his dad and all those football people all around him all of his life. I was a miner's son with no football in my family. I had literally played for Hartlepool, and then only for half a season.

It was totally different at home. Players there were just all cracking on with their careers, men like Joe Allon, good pros. It was an easy transition from being a kid into the first team. It was quite rapid. Then you got to Liverpool, and it was brutal. All of a sudden, I'm not even sure I want to be a footballer.

Even the nights out at tenpin bowling used to end in upset. It would be me and Jamie against Marc Kenny and Steve Harkness. If we were winning, Harkness would start a fight, just so it couldn't finish properly. The atmosphere around the reserve team was so horrible, so ruthless, that I got to the point of thinking, I'm not cut out for this. I can't go back to digs every night crying.

So Jamie and I were good for each other. I had an amazing ability to get into trouble. He had an amazing ability to get out of it. You know the kid at school when it all goes off behind the teacher's back and you're the one that has the blackboard rubber bouncing off the top of the head when they turn round? That was the scenario. And Jamie would always have his head down, all inno-cence, never to blame.

He was like the culture person, compared to me. He knew about fashion. He and his dad would routinely eat in Italian restaurants. I'd never in my life had an Italian. He did things that made no sense to me, like phoning his dad three times a day.

'What you phoning your dad again for?'

'To talk. When was the last time you spoke to your dad?'

'I dunno, two months ago?'

My old man's method was, if I don't call him, I'm alright, if I call him, what's the trouble? Jamie had a completely different relationship with his mum and dad. I'm not saying mine weren't loving, but my old dad went down the mines. We didn't feel the need to speak, ever.

We had our fallings out, us two, but we had special moments too. Jamie was Liverpool captain and I was Everton captain in the Merseyside derby at Anfield in 1998, the last time Everton won there, when Kevin Campbell scored the winner and three men got sent off. We got a great photo of the two of us that day. Then we were in the tunnel alongside each other when Scotland and England met for the European Championship play-offs in 1999. Up against each other in midfield, me scoring at Wembley in the second leg, them winning 2–1 on aggregate.

Two kids all grown up by then. Still tight, still smiling.

16

THE BREAKTHROUGH

He's a hard man, Graeme Souness. He cares about this club and he cares about this city. I'm not certain what he thinks of me – I'm not important enough for a one-on-one yet, an arm round the shoulder, a quiet word – but I know you don't mess. Everyone learns that. I've got to work. I've got to make myself important enough.

•

Graeme Souness: It was easy to see what Jamie had. Really good technique, which is what you get by playing games and training every day with good players. He was always a good size, like my shape when I played. And he could move the ball, one and two-touch, and if you've got that as a midfield player and you've got the desire, you will be successful.

He had an understanding of how football works, a football maturity at a younger age. The realisation better than anyone else at his age about what you have to do to reach the top level. Equally important, I saw a willingness to learn. He wanted to improve. He would always stay behind, always spend time with the ball, maybe more than anybody else. That's what I remember.

There was Jamie, Robbie Fowler, Steve McManaman. You walk into a job as a manager and you hope you've got that. I just wondered if they were all just a little bit too young that first year. Ideally you want to be introducing young guys into a team that's going forward, that's settled and strong, but they were coming into a team of serial winners who hadn't won anything for a couple of years. And teenagers, you don't know if they're going to be able to handle 40,000 people in the stands watching them, how they'll handle it when every single game is important. You can't pick and choose when you're on it, as a senior player. It's all the time, every week.

The only doubt I had about him was whether he was too nice. Playing in midfield means you have to cross that line occasionally. It's a physical thing with a young lad. As you get older you don't even think about it, you become battle-hardened.

But you can develop that part of your character if you're surrounded by the right people. Your background doesn't matter. I think it's in you. You see it in military men, public school boys who come from wealth and yet are warriors. It's in you and it's just a case of how it's pulled out of you, the environment you find yourself in.

•

That summer of 1991, I turn 18 and the manager starts to make the team his own. Out go some of the older players: Peter Beardsley, David Speedie and Gary Gillespie. Steve Staunton leaves because there's a UEFA Cup campaign coming up, and you're only allowed a certain number of non-British players in your team, so an Irish left-back up against Englishmen like David Burrows and Gary Ablett is always going to be vulnerable. Dean Saunders arrives from Derby for a record-breaking £2.9 million. Mark Wright comes in at the back from the same club for not much less. Mark Walters comes down from Rangers, where he's proved himself to the manager again and again.

So my football is played almost exclusively in the reserves, in the Central League, and every day is a scrap. Liverpool have two sides, the A team and the B team, and they're both feral. It's a fight with the opposition and it's a battle with my own team-mates.

Everyone loves a tackle. Never have I been as glad of Jimmy Gabriel's technique. Then there was Dad getting in my ear on the pitches down by the river at Mudeford: 'Jamie, you gotta get after people! You gotta let people know you're there.'

Maybe the other lads don't think I've got that edge. The local lads are born to tackle. Even the young kids in the youth team are at it. They'll go to ground with studs up at any point. Doesn't matter how hard the pitch, how bumpy or cut up. It's street football come to grass, as if they're still playing on a patch of concrete with someone lobbing the ball up in the air and 16 of them all charging for it at the same time.

I love it. There are some nasty players out there, people who don't just want to hurt you but to finish your career. The protection is limited from the referees at this level, where it's desperation to get out and to get up to the good stuff. It's dog-eat-dog and dog kick the other dog up in the air.

These are the lessons from playing first-team football at Bournemouth. I'm glad I've lived in that place and come through it. I'm glad I've had Billy Whitehurst whistling like a boiling kettle and Martin Allen growling like a dog. I've seen Tony Pulis open up another man's shins and jog away. I've had Graham Barrow trying to launch me into the Peak District. If you could pay for a formal football education, then I've just been through the working player's Eton.

So now, when Liverpool reserves play Everton reserves, it goes off. They know I'm the kid who got signed for a lot of money. They assume I'm a flash southerner. They don't know me. So they try to do me, and I try to do them.

It's Everton but it's all the clubs across the north. We run out onto the pitch and I can see them thinking it. He's tall. Long hair. No way this kid's tackling.

And so the spite follows.

'Shithouse.'

'Tart.'

'Gay boy.'

I come back at them. There is an edge to me now that is sharper than even a year before. I've got a nasty tongue, when I need it. I can be horrible when I want to be. All those bus journeys from Anfield to Melwood, being moved from seat to seat. The piss-taking about my hair or clothes.

I'm not a kid anymore. I know what gets said, but I'm ready to respond to that now.

'Who the f*** are you? What's your name? Nah, never heard of you, never will do.'

I don't shy away now. Channelling my dad when he loses his temper, giving it a little Pulis. I'm not starting fights. But if they say something to me, they're getting it back tenfold.

Sometimes, you say things on the pitch that you're not proud of. That's how it is. It's the night out in the Wookey, it's the dancefloor at the Conti. Read the mood, know when to move on and when to stand up. You have to look after yourself because everyone is busy fighting their own battles.

'Redknapp, you're f***ing shit. You're in the ressies. Waste of f***ing money.'

'What about you, mate? You're doing the same thing as me. And you ain't getting out of it.'

I like laughing at people. That works for me. It takes their anger and ridicules them with it. Watch them mis-control the ball on the bobbly pitch.

'You're good, aren't you?'

Skip over a tackle.

'Kiss my arse, son.'

When you drop down to the B team, it's youngsters trying to prove themselves and local semi-pro teams from Merseyside like Marine and Southport. The opposition are big, tough boys. They have skill, and they all want what you have. When I was down south, none of the other teams wanted to play for Bournemouth. What I soon find out is that everyone wants to play for Liverpool. You are the one standing in their way. You will be the one they want to remove.

We have an Irish lad called Davey Collins who'll play centre-mid or defence. He doesn't quite have the ability to escape this level, but he's exactly what you want at your side when the sly digs begin and the obvious violence erupts. He's big and he's hairy and that's ideal. When opposition players try to take liberties with the young ones who want to be Steve McManaman, he's straight in there. When I get involved, there's often initial confusion. The soft lad, has he really just done that? Sometimes, I get the benefit of the doubt when I've gone in late or over the ball. He's got a baby face, he can't have meant that, right?

You pull on the red shirt with the three white stripes over the right shoulder and each team raises their game. It's a heavy pressure, but it's also a special thing. There is a Liverpool way of playing – pass, pass, pass – but even when you outplay teams they'll still pile into you with anything they have. When we play Southport, there is a midfielder opposite me called John Bishop. He's got a lot of chat on him, genuinely funny. We pass it round him while he's still cracking jokes. When I run past him too, he says something about me running with my toes pointed in like a duck. He's funnier than he is good at football, which will help him in the future.

When you're in the A team, the mix is angrier. There's me and Don and Macca, but there are also older pros who don't want to be there, who've been pushed out of the first team having got used to its comforts and profile. You're a team, but you're not a collective. Thrown together by circumstance, competing against each other to get out and away as much as taking on the opposition.

When you play away from home, you often draw a decent crowd. Supporters of other clubs get a buzz off seeing superstars reduced to this, of being able to tell their mates that they spotted a future star when no-one else had.

When you play at home, it's just weird. Anfield, when I first saw it under the lights against Blackburn, was nothing like this. It was all noise and colour and fierce support. Now it's echoes. It's wayward shots bouncing around the empty terraces. It's Phil Thompson's shouts bouncing off the upturned wooden seats.

There is one supporter I always look for. Pop used to come down to as many of my Bournemouth games as he could. He's in his late sixties now, but he's still thin and sharp and full of life, and if I'm playing at the weekend he's up at the first crack to get the Tube from Mile End over to Euston and the train up to Lime Street. I pick him up from the station and he'll always pull a cheese and mustard pickle roll out of the pocket of his overcoat and hand it over. That's until I have Macca in the car with me one Saturday and Pop looks upset, although I'll only find out why when I speak to Dad on the phone from Bob and Marie's on Sunday night.

'Jamie, it's Pop. He's just called me, he feels terrible.

'He says to me, "Harry, Jamie gives me a lift with Steve McManaman, I gave Jamie a cheese and mustard pickle roll, but I didn't have one for Steve McManaman."

'I've said to him, "Dad, don't worry, he's probably earning ten grand a week, I think he can afford a cheese and mustard pickle roll."'

But Pop is a kind man and he's got Nan in his ear about it too.

'I've seen Macca on the telly, he looks like he needs fattening up.'

So the following week, when I swing by Lime Street, he pulls out two cheese and mustard pickle rolls.

'One for you, Jamie, one for Steve McManaman.'

And every time he comes up, over that year and beyond, when we're both in the first team together, when we're in the England team together, he always brings extra rolls. One for me, one for Macca, and later on, one for Robbie Fowler.

Robbie's a ham man. But the three of us will sit there at Anfield after matches, win, lose, or draw, eating rolls from east London that Nan has gone and got and Pop brought up.

•

There's a lot of Pop that I see in Macca's dad. Everyone seems to know him round Kirkdale, where Macca's grown up. He's been a decent footballer, his reputation gained from playing in the local leagues and on the streets. Macca's mum is sweet and kind. Macca's dad looks out for you. You know that he knows the game. If you get a, 'Well done, kid!' from him after a reserve game, it means a lot.

Macca is only 16 months older than me but he seems much more, a Bootle boy that the local lads at the club have taken to heart. He never seems to get any stick from Ronnie Moran, maybe because they think he's already there. I thought I could make it look easy. Macca makes it look easier. He's already beating Division One full-backs for fun. The coaches just let him get on with it, knowing he doesn't get fazed, that he'll stand up for himself, that he'll fight anyone he has to.

He is a freak in training. When we've done our long runs in pre-season, he's been like a thoroughbred racehorse in the Derby. He starts at the back of the group with the goalkeepers and the older and slower ones who can't run. He'll ease into the middle of the pack, where I am, and have some chat there. And then without any obvious effort he'll move to the front, stay there for a couple of laps and then stretch away to win it by miles.

The fact he carries no weight obviously helps. So too does his childhood running cross-country races. But he's so good with the ball too that he's one of the few you desperately hope is on your side in training matches, because he can make you look like an idiot. He can move his eyes and you go the wrong way. When he's galloping down the wing at Anfield he does a step-over and half the Kop buys it and shifts right. He never looks like he's going fast, but he can run faster with the ball than without it, which is maybe the rarest trick in the game.

He's a good man, too. He's cool. He knows how the world works, the street knowledge, the chat and the edge, but he's kind as well. He has empathy when some of the other young-sters around don't.

I want to be like him. I want to be able to play like that. If I can carry on doing what he's doing, I've got a chance of being a player.

●

Steve McManaman: I'd turn up sometimes as a school-boy during the holidays and train with the apprentices. As a 14 and 15-year-old, I went through all that rigma-role of getting on the bus from Anfield to Melwood and all the players going, 'Have you got a girlfriend? Have you touched her yet?' These players we knew were winning league title after league title after FA Cup, so you were sort of in awe of them. You were absolutely shit-scared to do anything. You had to evolve really quickly into the Liverpool way.

By the time I was training with them every day, they never said a word to me because I'd got a bit older. When Jamie arrived, everyone knew his dad. You saw he was a nice-looking lad. So you knew straightaway that the first team would be ready to have a little pop, because that's what they tried to do to make you feel at home. You sat on the bus, got picked on a little bit and got off the other end.

It was very hard, if you were a 16, 17, 18-year-old playing in the reserves trying to make it into Liverpool's first team. Phil Thompson would literally go round the dressing room saying you're shit, you're a disgrace, your mother and father would be appalled at you. He would shout and scream like you've never, ever heard in your entire life. The next day he would see you and go, 'Morning boys!' He was fine. It was like it hadn't happened.

I think it was always the way with Liverpool in that era. You win the league, that means nothing now, let's go again. You have to wear the same training kit all the time because it makes you hard. I think Phil had gone through that and he was trying to instil it in the young players because that was all he knew. He was a Scouser, he probably got brought up the hard way, and he's just thinking, right, this is good for them, rather than pussyfoot around them, say well done or hide his feelings. It was just how they were, I think. They just made sure they hammered you until you learnt the hard way.

For the local lads, because we all went home to our parents, it was easier for us to take. I was never that bothered about that type of criticism, because I always knew the next day he'd be fine. For the lads who were going back to digs, it was really difficult to take.

You come to Liverpool, which is a hard enough set-up as a football team itself, to try and replicate what the past players have done. You go into every room and there's a picture on the wall of how much they've achieved. Ronnie Moran and Roy Evans talking the same mantra as if they're still going to win every single year, and then you go home to digs where you're effectively on your own in a bedroom. If I'd had a bad day at training I'd just go home to my parents who made it all better again. Those boys couldn't. And it was bloody hard.

There's no way on earth that I could have done what Jamie did. I remember going down to Lilleshall to try to get into the England Under-18s. You would only have a couple of nights there, but I'd get so homesick. I'd always cry off and want to come home. I completely understand how seismic it is to move away from your parents at that age. There's no way I could have moved away from my parents when Jamie had to.

•

August begins okay for the first team. Three wins out of five, even if a couple of them had been shaky. But September slows up, draws at home to Villa and Stoke and Sheffield Wednesday, losing away to a Leeds team that's added some flair in Gary McAllister and Steve Hodge to the blunt force that did for Bournemouth just over a year before. John Barnes does his Achilles and looks like being out until the New Year. By early October we're 13th in the table. Manchester United are top, Everton above us. Coventry and Crystal Palace are above us, Wimbledon well clear.

This is not meant to happen to the most dominant team in English football. You can sense the discontent in the stands and on the streets. Going out in town means keeping a cap on and your head down.

Souness keeps reshaping, sending Jimmy Carter to Arsenal and getting Rob Jones in from Crewe. So that's two of the last three Kenny signings gone, the ones that the *Sun*'s chief sportswriter says were proof he had lost his mind. Just me left standing. Nicky Tanner and Mike Marsh getting their chances in the first team, that little clique starting to work out.

I'm not entirely sure the manager even knows my name. I hope he does, but Souness is a man who keeps his cards close to his chest. I look across at Melwood from the pigsty reserve pitches to the smooth grass where the first team train and I wonder if he ever looks back. I watch Steve McManaman, now completely part of that scene, and I hope his success in stepping up is making the coaches think more of us young ones can do it too.

Maybe it's Macca's example. Maybe it's all the injuries, or the slide down the table. But Souness starts bringing me into first-team training. My heart almost stops with excitement on the Monday, but the learning begins straightaway.

They're still running the old shrinking pitch thing that did for me on my first session with Kenny way back in January. Now I've learned. You get nicked a couple of times and you understand you can't do it again. If you give a goal away for your team in the practice games, you're not doing it again. The message is stark: if you do it and you don't learn, you're out.

You're on the other pitch again with the reserves, and someone else has taken your opportunity. The sooner you learn, the sooner you are quick with the ball, the sooner you have fewer touches, the quicker you'll progress.

So now Ian Rush doesn't nick the ball off me. There is no David Attenborough nature doc moment. I know where the tigers are and how quick they're coming in.

We only just sneak past Stoke in the League Cup and have to come from behind to get a draw at Chelsea. And in that selfish way that football works, every underwhelming performance and result makes me think: I've got a chance here. The manager is looking for lifelines. He's having to gamble. There aren't many alternatives left in the queue ahead.

It's a brisk Tuesday morning when he tells me. A light training session at Melwood before the first team fly down to Paris and then on to Auxerre for the first leg of their UEFA Cup tie. We're jogging round the perimeter wall, dead leaves piling up in drifts against the pale concrete, when he's there alongside and stopping me with a hand on the shoulder.

'Tell your dad you're playing tomorrow. You've been doing well. I know you're ready.'

And that's it. All the doubts, and the waiting, and the loneliness, and it's here. It's on.

You don't show anything when you get news like that. You play it cool in training, make sure you're standing in the right places as they go through the set pieces. You keep it all in, until you get back to your digs and the phone in the hall.

I call Dad, before I've put my kitbag upstairs, before I've

thought about food, before I even think about what it really means.

It's how unsurprised he is that stands out. Always the same belief from Dad, not tub-thumping, just his football logic.

'Course you are, maestro, they need you. You're good enough, you know what you're doing. Yeah, it'll be good, that, proper club, Auxerre. Good manager they got there, Guy Roux, nice fella I'm told.'

He says he'd love to come but he can't. They've got a game this evening, Bournemouth. So the Autoglass Trophy preliminary round tie, southern section, group 2, takes precedence over his son's Liverpool debut, and that's fine. A crowd of 1,800 people will watch the 3–0 win over Swansea. You're either in football, or you're not. You don't dip your toes.

The night before is the hardest. It's not the strange hotel room in a foreign town. It's the nerves. I try the old tricks from back home – laying my clothes out for the morning, putting everything in the right place on the bedside table. I can't polish my boots like I used to in my room on Old Barn Road, or check the laces. I can't fold and re-fold my kit, because that's all taken care of by someone else now.

No-one to talk to about it. I know Macca through football but not yet so much outside it. He's got his mates from home, and when you're from the city you never abandon the old connections. You have to show you're still one of the boys, that you don't fancy yourself as something more. My nights out are with Don and Marc Kenny. Macca always looks out for you and includes you in his plans – 'Listen Redders, we'll be in here later' – but in the same way as if he'd moved to Bournemouth and I was still with Deano and Dave Morris, he has his long-termers.

I know I've been making progress. I thought I might get on the bench. Starting the game, anchoring the midfield behind Steve McMahon and Ray Houghton – now I can't sleep.

Someone has mentioned that I'm the youngest player ever to play for Liverpool in Europe. It's not that that's keeping me awake. I'm trying to see the passes. I'm trying to picture the runs of Macca and Mark Walters out wide.

Staring up at the off-white ceiling above my bed, listening to a hotel's 3 am bumps and creaks. Going to the bathroom for a pee and to refill the toothmug from the tap. Trying to bring myself back to the good stuff.

I am ready. I am old enough. This is what I wanted: to have at least one first-team appearance on my record. Whatever happens now, I've played for Liverpool. I haven't wasted the last eight months. I made the right choice coming here.

It's a long drag, the day before an evening kick-off. You don't come to Auxerre to see the sights. It's tea and toast in the morning, a walk around the hotel car park. It's putting on your tracksuit and staring at yourself in the mirror hoping the bags under your eyes don't mean there's nothing in your legs.

It's an old, compact ground, the Stade de l'Abbé-Deschamps. A single-tier terrace behind both goals, thin white metal poles holding up the roof, a yellow electronic scoreboard. Big blue letters on the white paint: Tribune E. Leclerc. Tall trees behind, home-made banners hung over the metal fences.

In the tight dressing room, my nerves are stretched out tight. I look around at these players who I have always held in awe: McMahon, Nicol, Rush, Grobbelaar. My heart is jittery in my chest. Others are sitting there reading through the programme, as animated as commuters on the train to work. I'm running my own repeated journeys from my peg to the toilets and back. You go and you come back and you immediately need to go again. Nothing is solid for long before and after a game.

Everything is constricted – my chest, my calves, my head. The stress and the expectation conducted through my body.

You're on your own, now. It's self-preservation with footballers. You're a team, but you are also ships in the night. Together only at the whim of a manager who himself is being squeezed from all sides. You're there looking after yourself, your chances, your livelihood. I've seen it at Bournemouth, on those nights where we were sinking, when players are looking around after a poor game, looking at the kid who's come on for them as a sub and made it look easier again. The doubt and the apprehension and the sweat and mud and fear.

I know Auxerre will be a good team. Guy Roux has been there for what seems like a thousand years, and he's always brought through proper players playing proper football: Basile Boli, Eric Cantona, Laurent Blanc. Cantona's moved on, not least for punching their 'keeper Bruno Martini, but the menace remains.

I can guess that the football will be fast and skilful. What shocks me is the noise coming down from those low stands. You can only get 20,000 people into the ground. But there are only 35,000 inhabitants of the town, so pretty much every male between the age of 13 and 70 has made it in, and every one of them is jumping.

Scarves waving above heads, hands banging advertising hoardings, chants and horns. It's a different sort of noise to anything I've heard before. I'm used to 3,500 polite Bournemouth supporters spread around Dean Court. I've played away at West Ham and that was loud, but it wasn't like this. It is a wall of aggression, a physical thing that you can feel in your chest. It almost pushes you around.

When you're on the ball, you can't hear your team-mates shouting for it. When they have it, you can't direct them or call for the pass. Whistles screaming in your ears, boos vibrating in your chest.

Your brain can only process so much information under the relentless pressure. It's like playing with one eye shut. All your calibrations are off. Your touch is heavy and your time squashed. Plans given to you in the dressing room are ripped up and forgotten.

We are struggling. Players are trying to help themselves rather than those alongside them. You need steering through it as a young player, but when the experienced players are stumbling too you are also suddenly feeling their tension. You're not getting the ball in space and time. You're getting the ball when they're panicking – hit at you too firmly, too high, with their winger coming in at you hard.

I'm at the back of a midfield three, number seven on my back. McMahon and Ray Houghton are ahead. Deep-lying works fine when you have time, but we're being swamped. And you need to be negative in that role. You need to be pessimistic. When you're 18, you're fearless. You feel immortal. You are young and fit and getting better every day, so you don't see danger coming.

They score their first just before half-time. Neat angled passes through midfield, me nearly getting a right foot in to stop the final pass but Jean-Marc Ferreri running away to clip it past Grobbelaar. Ticker-tape cascading down from the stands, white and blue balloons going up, flags snapping left and right.

I get cramp early. It's the nerves, all the relentless emotion of the past 24 hours. Every time I try to run, it grabs my right calf and stops me dead.

I try to run it off. The same thing happens on the left. Rhythmic clapping from the stands, the blast of air-horns, songs that I don't understand. Angry gestures from the senior players, arms waved, passes going long.

The second goal comes with brutal inevitability. The ball loops up in midfield, back over my head, and I stretch and try to direct it to McMahon, but it's ahead of him and they're away again. A ball out wide, a cross bent in behind Nicky Tanner, time to control it and bang it home.

I walk back slowly towards the centre-circle and beat myself up about it. My legs have never felt this heavy, but you never give the ball away. That's your job. A big huddle of white-shirted players cavorting in the far corner, all mullets and moustaches. Us in red like strangers.

Souness, emotionless in his black suit by the dugout, takes me off with 11 minutes to go. Mike Marsh runs on as I jog off. I pull on my red and green Adidas trackie top and sit there next to Nicol holding his hamstring, and I go invisible.

•

Steve McManaman: Once you got called into the first team, they just left you alone to make your own way. It was, right, we've chosen you, just get on with it. And if you didn't get on with it and you started to struggle or you weren't good enough, they would soon kick you out.

There was no-one I can remember that ever put their arm around me and tried to tell me what I was doing wrong or what I should be doing and this would be better. You just trained, and if it wasn't good enough they would shout at you while training. You just had to learn, and if you didn't learn you'd be left by the wayside.

At Liverpool as a 17 or 18-year-old, you have to be very good even to be there. We were training every single day with eight or nine players who had won the league multiple times. You had to be very good to be on the same pitch as Jan Molby, Ronnie Whelan, John Barnes, Steve McMahon, Steve Nicol, Bruce Grobbelaar. If you weren't very good, you weren't there.

We were all close at that age, us youngsters, even early on. You could see that half of the first team were looking to get out. They would take their eye off the ball a lot, which would not help me and Jamie, who were trying to learn as much as we possibly could from them.

When you've got somebody of that age with you in the team, knowing what it's like, you don't forget it. Our camaraderie was always very strong, because we needed to stick together to survive.

•

I don't expect to get picked that weekend against Coventry. Jan Molby is fit again. Given the choice between an 18-year-old and a 28-year-old who has played at World Cups and won three titles, the manager is only going to go one way. But I'm not involved again in a League Cup match against Port Vale, or as we lose at home to Crystal Palace and draw 0–0 at West Ham. Mike Marsh is the cover on the bench. When there's only two subs there's no room for those out on the fringes, and Marsh is decent – good technically, never gives it away, runs all day.

On a night when Anfield comes alive again, Macca inspires a remarkable second-leg comeback against Auxerre. Molby buries a penalty like he always buries penalties. Marsh heads in. Mark Walters wins it late on.

And this is the selfishness of the footballer. It's professional jealousy. When you're not being picked, when the team is moving on without you, you almost want them to lose. It's horrible admitting it to myself, but I don't want to see Marsh scoring goals from midfield. It's not just me. He would be the same if I was in ahead of him. So would McMahon, and Molby, and Ronnie Whelan if he was fit. You get a taste and you want more.

On the bench for a horrible defeat at Peterborough in the League Cup. On the bench again, this time with Don, as we win 2–0 against Swarovski Tirol in the next round of the UEFA Cup. Not playing either time, waiting and working in training, hoping the manager drops in alongside me again on another run.

It happens in early December. An away game at Southampton coming up, a nod from Souness on the Thursday. On the bench for a Division One game for the first time, a coach journey back down south, familiar motorways and A-roads, back the way I've come all those months ago.

The Dell feels creaking and unchanged from all my trips there as a kid. Two tiers on the stands along the touchline, that strange wedge-shaped open terrace at the Milton Road end.

There are hard men in this Southampton team, Neil Ruddock and Barry Horne, and there's a 21-year-old up front called Alan Shearer who everyone has been talking about. Shearer's on the front of the programme, arm up after scoring a goal against Chelsea, Dennis Wise lurking in the background with the sort of look on his chops that says he wants revenge.

Bournemouth are at home to Brentford in the second round of the FA Cup, so Dad is at Dean Court. Here instead is Mum, and Mark. Pop is here too, cap on, down on the early train, giving me a wave from his spot in the main stand.

It's a cold, dark afternoon, the floodlights on the roof of the two grandstands burning bright from early on. And it just feels good, the familiar and the family together, a game that I fancy I can get into if I get on, a team that need something to fire them up once more.

It is scrappy. Southampton are down the bottom of the table so they fight for everything. Shearer is a strong boy, Iain Dowie alongside him an even blunter instrument. Bruce Grobbelaar is having one of his ranting days, for good reason. Shearer bashes into David Burrows and runs onto the loose ball and lobs him from 25 yards, and it's suddenly very quiet among the red scarves and beanies in the away end.

There are 27 minutes to go when Roy Evans taps me on the leg. Souness is looking down at us on the bench. He nods.

Unzipping my thick coat, green shirt underneath. Showing my studs to the linesman. A hand through my hair. A handshake with Jan Molby as he rolls off like a sailor coming off a ship. Across the white touchline and on.

It's different, this time. I'm not looking around, I'm not listening to the noise. I'm just playing football, taking the ball, moving it on. Head up, quick shouts, seeing the runs.

Making my own runs, too. Macca having a little shuffle and dribble. Houghton on the right side of the box, looking up to see David Burrows charging in at the back post.

I don't even think about it. I'm running into the box while watching the ball, round the back of Micky Adams.

Burrows diving in. Tim Flowers down. The ball bouncing across the six-yard box.

I slam it home from about three inches out.

Macca nearly beats me to it. He almost tackles me over the line. And then I'm in the net, clinging on with my hands, half falling backwards. Staring straight into the eyes of a great wave of Liverpool fans just beyond the fence, screaming at them screaming back at me, the noise and the joy and the mad disbelief breaking over us all.

Me and them and us, lost in the same beautiful bedlam. The intense intimacy of a goal, feeling exactly the same way in exactly the same moment as thousands of total strangers.

It's Macca who fishes me out. An arm round the shoulder. And I float through the rest, wanting every pass, chasing every loose ball. Looking up at Mum and Mark and Pop when the final whistle goes, clenching my fist. Standing in the tunnel, rushing out words to the reporters who stick microphones and tape recorders under my nose.

'I can't put into words the feeling.'

Except I can, straightaway. 'It's unbelievable, incredible. I really enjoyed it.'

Pouring out of me now.

'It was the easiest goal ever, but you have to make sure, you have to put them away. I think I'll always remember it.'

Someone sticks me on the radio with Dad, who's won 2–1. The happiness ricochets around between us. Later, there will be the biggest Chinese takeaway of the year. Mark calls the night out. We end up in Madisons with Deano and Dave and everyone else who's come to town. Pop raising his glass as he sends us on our way, Mum with the secret smile and the warm embrace.

I am 18 years old. I have so much ahead of me, victories and cruel disappointments, battles and defeats, things I can't possibly imagine. Games in places I've never heard of, mistakes and injuries, regrets and days of pride so intense I could burst.

I know none of that and none of it matters, that night in my home town. Everyone there I want to share it with. So many who helped me along the way. Tunes playing and Mark dancing and everywhere you look a massive grin.

I've not made it, not yet. I've played twice and scored once. But I'm on my way. I'm not a failure now, not a total one. If this all ends here, I've played first-team football for the biggest team in the country. I've scored. I'm in the official records.

I hope Kenny's noticed, up there in Southport. I hope he's smiling on the golf course. I hope Graeme Souness knows I'm ready for more. This can't all end here. This is a beginning. This is the start.

Tomorrow is another day. Tonight we have all this together. Moving on, looking forward but remembering what came before. Ready for it. Ready for what may yet come.

•

Harry: I knew, from the age of five years old, that he was going to be a footballer. It wasn't a case of me going out and spending hours and hours practising with him. That was all he wanted to do, play football. Coming training every day with Bobby Moore and Geoff Hurst and all the boys. He was playing Under-10s when he was six. Always around footballers, playing football.

The stuff around him was one thing. But he had to have the ability. That was in him. There's a photo Sandra had where he's volleying a ball at five years of age with perfect technique, dropping his shoulder, head down, toes pointed. He had it and he worked at it.

I was so proud when he went to a great club like Liverpool. Their traditions, their style. Without the injuries he would have achieved so much more, no doubt about that. People don't realise what he went through. All the rehab, having treatment from the physio at three in the morning after a midweek game, trying to get fit for the Saturday. The operations and the hard work. The injuries stopped him getting anywhere near what he could have been.

I remember reading a big article with Gordon Strachan. He said, when you play Liverpool, Jamie controls the tempo of the game, everything comes from Jamie. Terry Venables said to me after Euro '96, 'Harry, we would have won it if Jamie hadn't got injured.' I've never told Jamie how that made me feel.

But what's always been important to me is that he's a great lad. That's what you want from your boy. He has time for everybody, he talks to everybody, gives his time. He is very much like his mum, in that she is very disciplined. He's always looked after himself. He's had a drink, but in the main he eats the right food, he keeps himself in great shape. That's come from Sandra.

Me, I think it's a very important thing to be nice to people. It don't cost you nothing to give people your time.

Maybe that's my most valuable influence. When I see that in him, I think, that's Jamie.

That's my boy.

•

King's Park, training with the Bournemouth first team long ago. I'm 13, bunking off school. Dad's brought me along. 'Jamie, don't tell your mum.'

The grass is too long and the ground uneven. You can hear the seagulls swooping overhead. It's raining. I don't mind.

Gerry Payton is in goal. The rest of the first-team squad are doing shooting drills, running on to crosses from Dad and trying to score from the edge of the box.

'Jamie, stand by the goal. That's it, about two yards from the post. Yeah.

'When they shoot, you gotta control it, right? First time.'

Shots hammering in, deflections off the post, balls tipped round by Gerry. I'm moving from left to right, forward and back. Left foot, right foot. Killing it on my chest, on my thigh, on the outside of my foot.

Grown men hitting it as hard as they can. Me controlling it and bringing it down as if it was coming to me softly, as if it was rolled to my feet.

Looking up at Dad between shots, searching for his reaction.

Thinking about when he'll glance across in the car afterwards on the way home. The nod, the quick smile.

'Nice touch, maestro. Nice touch today.'

The little tap on my knee.

'Yeah. That's my boy. You done well.'

ACKNOWLEDGEMENTS

A huge thank you to all the people who have helped in the making of this book, including Dean Giddings, Dave Morris, Simon Jackson, Mr Broadwell, Alan Bungay, Tony Pulis, Graeme Souness, Kenny Dalglish, Ian Bishop, Don Hutchison, Steve McManaman, Phil Thompson, Frank Lampard and John Barnes. And to Neil Vacher at AFC Bournemouth, for your fantastic archive.

Thanks to Jonathan Taylor, Tom Whiting and the great team at Headline for making it all happen. It's been brilliant working with you.

To all the team-mates, coaches and managers I've been fortunate enough to spend time with – each and every one of you made a difference to me.

To Richard, Sara and Katie at M&C Saatchi Merlin – I wish you'd been my agents from the very start. Thanks for everything you do.

To my brother Mark – I could never have wished for a better brother. You've always been so understanding.

To my cousin Frank – I'm so proud of what you achieved. Thanks for letting a few of your goals rub off on me.

To Nan and Pop, for being the most fantastic grandparents. I will never stop thinking about you. And Billy boy, my mum's dad, for your physique and for building that all-important bird cage.

To Mum, for being the most gentle, loving mum any boy could ever have. When I needed someone you were always there, the light when it was dark. I'm still convinced I got my skills from you. And for Dad, for all the love, the help, the guidance, the stories. I love you both so much.

And to Tom Fordyce, who wrote this book with me. I'm so glad you came into my life, and so glad you pushed us to this point. You've been unbelievable – thank you for your incredible effort and dedication.

INDEX

INDEX